STUDIES

IN THE

LIFE OF CHRIST.

BY THE
REV. A M. FAIRBAIRN, D D.,
PRINCIPAL OF AIREDALE COLLEGE, BRADFORD,
AND AUTHOR OF
"STUDIES IN THE PHILOSOPHY OF RELIGION AND HISTORY."

WIPF & STOCK · Eugene, Oregon

Wipf and Stock Publishers
199 W 8th Ave, Suite 3
Eugene, OR 97401

Studies in the Life of Christ
By Fairbairn, A. M.
Softcover ISBN-13: 978-1-6667-3439-3
Hardcover ISBN-13: 978-1-6667-9019-1
eBook ISBN-13: 978-1-6667-9020-7
Publication date 8/23/2021
Previously published by D. Appleton & Company, 1902

This edition is a scanned facsimile of
the original edition published in 1902.

THIS BOOK

IS DEDICATED,

IN

LOVING GRATITUDE AND FILIAL REVERENCE,

TO

𝔐𝔶 𝔐𝔬𝔱𝔥𝔢𝔯.

PREFACE.

THESE "Studies in the Life of Christ" were originally prepared as a series of Sunday evening discourses, while the author was a minister in Aberdeen. This is stated, partly, that he may connect them with a city and people he will always love, and, partly, that he may thus most simply define their real character and limits. They are not exhaustive and critical discussions on the Gospel History, but, at most, attempts at orientation—at reaching points of view from which the life of Christ may be understood and construed.

The author hopes, should life and health be granted to him, to return to this greatest of all Histories, and deal with it in a more critical and comprehensive spirit; especially in its relations to contemporary history, and in its action, through the Apostles and the Church, on the creation of Christianity. Meanwhile he sends this volume forth in the hope that it may help to make the Person it seeks to interpret more real, living, and loveable to the men of to-day.

AIREDALE COLLEGE, BRADFORD,
November, 1880.

CONTENTS.

		PAGE
I. THE HISTORICAL CONDITIONS		1
II. THE NARRATIVES OF THE BIRTH AND INFANCY		30
III. THE GROWTH AND EDUCATION OF JESUS: HIS PERSONALITY		46
IV. THE BAPTIST AND THE CHRIST		64
V. THE TEMPTATION OF CHRIST		80
VI. THE NEW TEACHER; THE KINGDOM OF HEAVEN		99
VII. GALILEE, JUDÆA, SAMARIA		113
VIII. THE MASTER AND THE DISCIPLES		130

CONTENTS.

IX.
THE EARLIER MIRACLES 149

X.
JESUS AND THE JEWS 165

XI.
THE LATER TEACHING 182

XII.
THE LATER MIRACLES 197

XIII.
JERICHO AND JERUSALEM 219

XIV.
GETHSEMANE 239

XV.
THE BETRAYER 258

XVI.
THE CHIEF PRIESTS—THE TRIAL 280

XVII.
THE CRUCIFIXION 308

XVIII.
THE RESURRECTION 331

I.

THE HISTORICAL CONDITIONS.

THE greatest problems in the field of history centre in the Person and Life of Christ. Who He was, what He was, how and why He came to be it, are questions that have not lost and will not lose their interest for us and for mankind. For the problems that centre in Jesus have this peculiarity: they are not individual, but general—concern not a person, but the world. How we are to judge Him is not simply a curious point for historical criticism, but a vital matter for religion. Jesus Christ is the most powerful spiritual force that ever operated for good on and in humanity. He is to-day what He has been for centuries—an object of reverence and love to the good, the cause of remorse and change, penitence and hope to the bad; of moral strength to the morally weak, of inspiration to the despondent, consolation to the desolate, and cheer to the dying. He has created the typical virtues and moral ambitions of civilized man; has been to the benevolent a motive to beneficence, to the selfish a persuasion to self-forgetful obedience; and has become the living ideal that has steadied and raised, awed and guided youth, braced and ennobled manhood, mellowed and beautified age. In Him the Christian ages have seen the manifested God, the Eternal living in time, the Infinite within the limits of humanity; and their faith has glorified

His sufferings into a sacrifice by the Creator for the creature, His death into an atonement for human sin. No other life has done such work, no other person been made to bear such transcendent and mysterious meanings. It is impossible to touch Jesus without touching millions of hearts now living or yet to live. He is, whatever else He may be, as a world's imperishable wonder, a world's everlasting problem, as a pre-eminent object of human faith, a pre-eminent subject of human thought.

For the very greatness of the work makes it the more necessary that we see the Worker, not as He lives in our faith and reverence, but as He lived on our common earth; a man looking before and after, speaking as a man, and spoken to by men. But this is no easy matter. Hardly any man can come to the problems that centre in Jesus as to the problems of the purer sciences, those that can be solved by the passionless processes of mathematics. The name of Christ is a representative name. It means Christianity. Men who are convinced that the religion is false, assail it through its Founder; men who believe that it is true, defend it through His Person. They too much interdespise each other to be altogether fair to history. The former reproach the latter with being apologists—men whose primary aim is not to find the truth, but to defend what has been, with or without sufficient reason, believed; the latter seek to silence the former by censure, charging them with rationalism or unbelief, with being men who love what is negative, and hate what is positive. Yet it were well if both classes could unite to help each other. The one interest that is common to both is the truth. To find it is here, as elsewhere, the grand necessity; yet without the clear eye and open mind it cannot be found. By all means let us get near enough to Jesus to see Him as He really was. The river is inexplicable without its source; Christianity a mystery, an unread riddle, without Christ. If the stream does not disgrace the fountain, the fountain will not disgrace the stream. If Christianity does not make Christ ashamed, Christ will not shame Christianity. The Founder is greater than the faith He founded, as mind is nobler than all its works. However highly the Christian religion may be rated, the religion of Christ, revealed in His words, articulated in His person, ought to be more highly rated still. The ideal is ever above the real. The picture painted on the canvas is poor compared with its image in the painter's mind. The palace or temple built in stone but feebly realizes the ideal of the great architect. The universe is but a poor and inadequate expression of the Divine thought. God is greater than the universe, and His thought than all things. So we may be certain that, whatever our faith or our fancy may imagine Jesus to have been, the reality was greater than our dream. True faith proves its truth by its willingness to use all the lights of modern science and all the eyes of modern criticism, that it may get the nearer to the historical Christ, convinced that it can look in His face without fear and without dismay. The men that best knew Him most loved Him, and to stand in His immediate presence is to be touched with a deeper reverence than can be awakened by the broken image reflected in the traditions or phantasies of men.

Strauss, in one of his most satirical moods, said, "The critical study of the life of Jesus is the pit into which the theology of our age necessarily fell, and was destroyed."[1] But the precise opposite is the truth. There is no study that has so renovated and vivified theology, that has so tended to translate it from an arid scholasticism into a humane and fruitful science of religion. The historical Christ is the eternal rock down to which Christian science

[1] *Das Leben Jesu fur das deutsche Volk*, p. 5.

must dig, and on which it must build, if our religion is to live; He is the everlasting and sunlit mountain up which our thought must climb, if we are ever to stand where Moses stood, and, like him, see God face to face. And this necessity reposes on a twofold reason. (1) The historical person of Christ is at once the basis and source of the Christian religion. He made it, He is it. Its distinctive and essential elements are elements that can be found in Him. Whatever cannot be found there belongs to its accidents, not to its essence. And so the better we know Him, the better we know our faith; the more He is made a reality to heart and mind, the more will it be the same. He who best knows Christ is the best Christian. (2) Knowledge of the historical and personal Christ is necessary to the knowledge and realization of the Christian religion. An abstract theology is but a speculative system, necessary, perhaps, to satisfy the intellect, and be to it, from the standpoint of the religious consciousness, an explication of the universe of nature and man. But religion is concrete and complex, must stand before us articulated in a person, that persons may know what it is, and how it is to be realized. There may be a science of religion, but religion is not a science, is rather the richest reality science can investigate. But to be a reality it must be embodied in thought and feeling, in action and conduct—*i.e.*, in a person or persons. It has no being till it is so embodied, but is the moment it is personalized. And he who first embodies it is its creative personality, the one in whom it lives, moves, and has its being. And Christ is here our creative personality. Christianity must be studied as it was realized in Him, and only as men embody His ideal do they remain Christians, or does the Christian religion continue to live. The one thing that can lift the churches of to-day above the sectional in character and aim, above the mean jealousies and ungenerous rivalries of a miserable ecclesiasticism, is a loving and sympathetic study of the Christianity of Christ. Here, indeed, the first is the best, and the divinest ambition is to be religious not after the manner of the churches, but after the manner and in the Spirit of Jesus the Christ.

We start, then, from this position. The person of Christ is the explanation of Christianity, its first cause, its perennial inspiration, its imperishable ideal. In Him our religion was first realized, and by Him created. But have we any right so to regard Him? He lived like all of us under and within the conditions of space and time, was an Heir to the past before He was a Creator of the future. Was He not, then, made by His historical conditions? Were not they the forces that formed Christ, rather than the Spirit that lived within Him?' These questions suggest some of our gravest problems:—

What does our religion owe to Jesus, and what to Judæa and the Jews? Is it the ripe fruit of His Spirit, or the fair and final blossom of dying Judaism? Was He its legitimate, though outcast and hated, Son? Was He created by His circumstances, the child of a land and people prodigal of choicest gifts and propitious opportunities? Was He but a Voice, throwing into memorable and immortal speech the truths given Him by the fathers of His people and the schools of His faith? These are questions history and historical criticism alone can exhaustively discuss, but at the first blush only one answer seems possible. Circumstances may be plausibly thought to make a man where they are equal to his making, where he does not conspicuously transcend all they are and contain. But where he does, it were as absurd to make the circumstances create the man as to make the night create the day, because after and out of the dark comes the light. Jesus was born in Judæa and nursed in Judaism, but He rose out of them as the sun rises out of the grey dawn to pour his beams over heaven and earth, and flood them with the glories of light and colour. Jesus was the antithesis and contradiction of the conditions amid which He grew. By His coming they were changed, and in all their distinctive features annihilated. What He brought with Him was so much more than they contained, that passing from Judaism to Jesus is like passing from the hill top tipped with the cold but beautiful dawn to a plain lying warm and radiant under the unveiling and revealing light of the summer noonday.

But while the historical conditions do not explain Jesus, without them He cannot be either explained or understood. The mysterious force we call His person was clothed in natural forms. The conditions under which He lived were human conditions. He was open and sensitive to every influence, inherited, traditional, social, physical, intellectual, moral, religious, that can affect man. He was a son, a brother, and a friend. He was a Jew by birth, speech, and education, and the Spirit, the *Geist*, of His land and people and time worked on and in Him with its plastic hands. Where He was divinely set there He must be humbly studied, and only as He is so studied can it be seen how He resembles "the bright consummate flower" which crowns the months of culture and of growth, and yet, when it bursts into blossom, beauty, and fragrance, is so unlike the dark earth, hard seed, and green stem out of which it has grown.

The question as to the causes and conditions which contributed to form its founder, is one of the deepest moment to every religion. It helps to determine its claims, the degree in which it has been a discoverer or revealer of new truths, a creator of fresh moral forces for humanity, a minister to the happiness and progress of man. It helps, too, to determine our estimate of its creative personality, to show him as a maker or an adapter, as one who depraved by his touch or transfigured by his spirit what he found before and around him, becoming to after ages the embodiment of the most deteriorative or the most regenerative influences. Thus the question as to the century in which Buddha was born, and the circumstances amid which he lived, powerfully affect our criticism both of the man and his religion. It affects our interpretation of its most characteristic doctrines, our judgment as to its relation on the one hand to the Sankhya philosophy, and on the other to Brahmanism and to the political movements of India; and these, again, influence our estimate of a religion that is at once so rich in ethical spirit and so poor in intellectual content. Buddha, regarded as a man who simply translates metaphysical into religious doctrines, and precipitates a political by converting it into a religious revolution, is a less original and beautiful character than the Buddha who so pities man and so hates his sorrow as to find for him by suffering and sacrifice the way to everlasting rest, the path to the blessed *Nirvana*. And so, too, with Islam and its founder. If Mohammed be compared with his heathen contemporaries and their ancestors, and his system with theirs, he can only profit by the comparison, stand out as a pre-eminent religious genius and benefactor of his country and kind. But if his doctrines be traced to their sources, Judaic, Magian, Christian, if it be found that he depraved what he appropriated, that he practised what his own precepts forbade, turned his sublimest doctrine into a battle-cry, building on it both a military system that lived by the lust of conquest and a civil code that showed little mercy to the vanquished, then we find that he is a political much more than a religious genius, with an ultimate personal influence that works more mightly for evil than his law works for good. Knowledge of the historical conditions may thus so modify as to change from favourable to adverse our judgment of the historical person.

Now what were the historical conditions under which Jesus was formed? Are they in themselves sufficient to explain Him. Did they embody intellectual and spiritual forces potent enough to form Him, and, through Him, His religion? Was He, as we have been assured, a pupil of the rabbis and a child of the native Judaic culture?[1] Was He indeed "called out of Egypt," a Son of its later wisdom, educated in Alexandrian philosophy illumined by the light that lived in Aristobulus and Philo?[2] Or was He by the accident of birth a Jew, by the essential qualities as by the nurture of His spirit a Greek, gifted with the serene soul and open sense of ancient Hellas,[3] softening by His Hellenic nature and culture the stern and exalted truths of Hebraism? It is impossible to discuss here and now the many points involved in these questions: all that is possible is to indicate the historical conditions amid which He lived, His relation to them, and theirs to Him.

1. THE LAND. Modern historical thought sufficiently recognizes the influence of a country and climate upon a people, upon the collective nation and its constituent units. Physical conditions have both a moral and an intellectual worth. The great people and the great man are held to owe much to nature without, as well as to the

---

[1] Salvator, *Jésus Christ et sa Doctrine.* Paris, 1838. Renan, *Vie de Jésus*, chap III.

[2] So Gfrorer in his work, *Ueber Philo und die Alexandrinische Philosophie.* In his preface he declares Christianity to be a mere confused compound of Alexandrian wisdom without any originality. In his later work, *Geschichte des Urchristenthums*, he seeks to trace the most distinctive doctrines of the New Testament and the oldest Fathers t · rabbinical sources, and the New Testament history, so far as it has any affinity with Talmudical legends, to rabbinical traditions.

[3] Strauss, *Das Leben Jesus für das deutsche Volk*, § 34.

THE HISTORICAL CONDITIONS. 9

nature within. And the land is here of singular significance, both in its physical and historical aspects and influences. It was small but goodly, in many places rich in the fruits of the earth, fair, fragrant, and fertile as the garden of the Lord. It was a land of hills and valleys, lakes and water-courses, mountains that guarded, streams that made glad its cities, especially queenly Zion, beautiful for situation, the joy of the whole earth. Shut in before by the sea, behind by the desert, girt and guarded to the north by the royal ranges of Lebanon and the lofty heights of Hermon, to the south by waste lands, its fruitful plains, full of corn and wine, seemed to the wandering sons of the desert to flow with milk and honey. To tribes weary of change and migration in the wilderness, Canaan was by pre-eminence the land of rest. And so many distinct yet related families had striven for a foothold and a home in it, for room on its plains and a right to its cities. The sons of fathers who had parted as kinsmen in the desert met as foemen on the plains, as invaders and invaded, as Hebrews and Phœnicians. On the coast once famous cities stood, the cities of the men who made the commerce of the ancient, and, through it, of the modern world—men full of resource and invention: builders, dyers, carvers of ivory, weavers of rich stuffs, discoverers of the secrets the stars can whisper to the seafaring, bearers of manifold impulses for good and ill to the cities and isles of Greece. On the one side lay Egypt, on the other Assyria; over and through the land that intervened they had fought out their rivalries, and made their names, their armies, their civilizations both familiar and fearful to the sons of Israel.

But though they and the later and mightier empires of Greece and Rome might conquer, they could never absorb Israel. The more his land was invaded the more sacred it became to him, and the oftener he lost his freedom to the foreigner the more hostile and inaccessible did he grow to the influences by which the victorious alien can assimilate and extinguish the vanquished.

In the time of Jesus, Palestine existed in four great divisions—a northern, central, eastern, and southern: Galilee, Samaria, Perea, and Judæa. Of these, only the first and last concern us. Galilee was the richest and most varied province, Judæa the most secluded and barren. In the north Galilee was guarded by the snowy crown of Hermon and the wooded slopes of Lebanon, and was graced in the south by Carmel and Tabor; while in the south-east it embosomed the lake of Gennesareth, out from which opened those glorious plains that were to the fond imagination of the people as the garden of God. On the west its table-land overlooked the blue sea, where went the stately "ships of Tarshish," and by the side of which stood ancient Tyre, the home of men with other aims and ambitions than had been known to Israel. And the land was rich in men, the fields in husbandmen, the towns and villages in merchants, the lake in fishermen. One who knew and loved it said, "It is a fertile land and full of meadows, where trees of every kind grow, and promises through its luxuriant fruitfulness a rich reward, even to the most miserable husbandry."[1] And the life the people lived is sketched for us by many a quiet touch in the Gospels. In the market-place labourers wait to be hired,[2] and children dance and sing, sport and quarrel.[3] In the highways and by the gates the lame and the blind sit asking alms.[4] In the synagogues the people meet and the rabbis read and expound the Scriptures.[5] On the lake the fishermen ply their craft, and by its margin, in field or on the rocks, dry their nets.[6] The shepherd on the hillside or plain tends his sheep, seeks in the desert or on the mountain the lost lamb, tenderly bearing it home.[7] The

[1] Jos., *Bell. Jud.*, iii 3 2.
[2] Matt xx 3, 4.
[3] Matt xi. 16.
[4] Ibid xx 30.
[5] Luke iv 16.
[6] Ibid v. 1–3.
[7] Luke xv 3–6.

careful woman searches for the piece she has lost;[1] and the woman who is a sinner wakes to penitence and shame, and the love that is born of holy gratitude.[2] Men build barns and store grain, and die in the moment of proudest prosperity.[3] The diseased seek the physician, the widow loses her only son, and the father, fearing he may be left childless, inquires for one who may heal his daughter.[4] The rich man leaves the steward to manage his estate, and he abuses the brief authority in which he is dressed, beats the maid-servants, and is the more a tyrant that he is a tyrant's slave.[5] Men are so deep in business and pleasure, with lands, or oxen, or newly-wedded wife that they cannot mind the things of the kingdom of God.[6] In the many towns, and populous villages, and thriving districts of Galilee " they ate, they drank, they bought, they sold, they planted, they builded, they married, and were given in marriage."[7]

The people that so lived were mainly, but not entirely, of Jewish descent. Their land was too open and busy to be exclusive—the people too remote from Jerusalem, and too jealous of its priesthood to be dominated by the narrower Judæan ideal. The men of Jerusalem used to say, "there was no priest among the Galileans;" and the Galileans were the happier in life and freer in faith for wanting the priest. And the scribes who there flourished were more varied and less rigid in opinion than those of Judæa, and so the stricter southern said of the looser northern province, "The men there do not learn the law from one master." And they could learn of foreign as well as of native masters. In Galilee there were Gentile cities like Scythopolis, and cities like Tiberias, where Greeks dwelt, and where Greek culture and art were not unknown.[8] Through it, too, there was

[1] Luke xv 8, 9.   [3] Ibid. xii. 17, 18.   [5] Ibid. xii. 45.
[2] Ibid. vii 37, 38.   [4] Ibid. viii. 49–56.   [6] Ibid. xiv. 17–20.
[7] Ibid xvii 28.   [8] Jos., *Vita*, 12.

continually flowing a stream of commerce, and Syrians and Arabians, Phœnicians and Greeks often made their homes in a land which was a highway of the nations. These elements and influences were strong enough to modify and enrich, but not to change the native faith. In Galilee there was less aversion to Gentile culture than in Judæa. Aristobulus, the first of the Jews to discover Moses in Plato, and the law of Jahveh in the philosophy of Greece, was a Galilean. So were Alexander Jannæus, the Asmonæan most skilled in the wisdom of the Gentiles; and Justus of Tiberias, who, though a Jew, was possessed of the best Hellenic culture. There, too, coins with Greek inscriptions circulated, amphitheatres and palaces ornamented in the Greek and Roman styles were tolerated, and even the Roman eagles, which could not be introduced into Jerusalem without danger of insurrection, were allowed to pass unchallenged through Galilee.[1] But while this contact with a wider world made the men of Galilee more open in mind and heart than the men of Judæa, it did not make them less devoted to the faith and hope of Israel. Sacred history and song had consecrated their land. The victory that Barak had achieved and Deborah had sung was won by Galileans on Galilean soil.[2] A later poet, who rejoiced to see God arise to scatter His enemies, praised the heroic feats of " the princes of Zebulon and the princes of Naphtali."[3] Cowardice was never a vice of the Galileans;[4] and in the darkest period of Judaism names like those of Ezekias, Judas Galilæus, and John of Giscala justify the saying. To the religion of Israel it had given prophets like Hosea and Nahum, and to its literature poets like the singer of the Song of Songs. They loved the city and and service of their faith, and to the last " they went up

[1] *Antt.*, xviii. 5. 3.   [2] Judges iv.–v.   [3] Psa. lxviii. 27.
[4] Jos., *Bell. Jud*, iii 3 2.

to Jerusalem, as was the custom of the feast."[1] But the grand religious agency in Galilee was the synagogue, not the temple; its ideal was that of the scribe rather than that of the priest. As a necessary consequence, they were more concerned with the ethical than with the ritual in Judaism, with the interpretation of the written and oral law than with the observance of the instituted and hierarchic worship. Their Judaism was one of the letter, but even as such it was nobler and purer than the Judaism of the temple and the priesthood.

Judæa was in its physical aspect a less favoured land than Galilee. It, too, had its fair and fertile districts, like the plain of Shephela, so rich in glorious historical memories; and the country around Bethlehem, so suggestive of heroic names and inextinguishable Messianic hopes, and the graves where grew " the palm trees by the water, the rose plants which are in Jericho.[2] But if it could not as regards its physical features rival the grandeur of upper or the lovely luxuriance of lower Galilee, in what pertained to historical and political interest it stood preeminent. The people were of purest Jewish blood. The men of Judah and Benjamin who had returned from the captivity, settled in Judæa, and there proceeded to realize their hierocratic state. They built their temple and their holy city, and fenced themselves round with laws and customs which should at once prevent imitation of the heathen, and maintain in purity the worship of Jahveh. Their success was in many respects wonderful, perhaps more wonderful than any achievement on record in the domain of national polity and life. Their ideal was to be a people apart, the elect of Jahveh, the only people that knew Him, the only people He knew. In order to realize this ideal, their polity was so framed as to blend and identify the religious and civil, the worship of God with

[1] Luke ii. 42. [2] Ecclus. xxiv. 14.

the being and conduct of the state. The one God had His one temple ; the capital was the holy city, the seat of civil authority, the scene of national worship. The act of collective reverence was an act of loyal obeisance ; the service performed in the temple was rendered to the great King. The action of this ideal on the land and state was to penetrate both with a deep religious meaning—to associate both with the will of God and tl e ultimate destinies of His people. The city and temple made Israel a unity in his very dispersion. Though Jews might be counted by millions in Alexandria or Rome, yet the home of their spirits was Jerusalem ; to it their hearts turned as not only the city of their fathers, but as the one place where the God whose chosen they were could be worshipped by His collective and united people. And this belief was expressed, maintained, and strengthened by loved institutions. There were great festivals that drew the scattered tribes to the city of their faith, the home of their hopes ; and they came there, as many often as three millions of men[1]—" Parthians, and Medes, and Elamites, and the dwellers in Mesopotamia, and in Judæa, and Cappadocia, in Pontus, and Asia, Phrygia, and Pamphylia, in Egypt, and in the parts of Libya about Cyrene, and the Romans sojourning in Jerusalem, Jews and proselytes, Cretes and Arabians."[2]

And the city that was the scene of so immense assemblies had necessarily a peculiar character of its own. It existed for them, it lived by them. There were priests needed for the conduct of the worship, twenty-four courses of them and 20,000 men.[3] There were Levites, their servants, in immense numbers, needed to watch, maintain, clean the temple—to do the menial and ministering work necessary to its elaborate service and stupendous acts of worship.

[1] Jos., *Bell Jud*, vi. 9. 3.   [2] Acts ii. 9-11.
[3] Jos, *Vita*, i., *Contra Apion*, ii. 8.

There were scribes needed for the interpretation of the law, men skilled in the Scriptures and tradition, with names like Gamaliel, so famed for wisdom as to draw young men like Saul from distant Tarsus, or Apollos from rich Alexandria. There were synagogues, 480 of them at least, where the rabbis read and the people heard the word which God had in past times spoken unto the fathers by the prophets. The city was indeed in a sense the religion of Israel, incorporated and localized, and the man who loved the one turned daily his face toward the other, saying, " My soul longeth, yea, even fainteth, for the courts of Jahveh." " I was glad when they said unto me, Let us go into the house of Jahveh. Our feet shall stand within thy gates, O Jerusalem." [1]

But the land and city had meanings no political or sacerdotal institutions could express. It had been the arena of a great history, which was less the history of a nation than a religion. Jahveh had given the land to the people; within it His kingdom was to come, His society and state to be realized. On its plains, even where most arid, Abraham had lived, and had sanctified them by his presence and his intercourse with God. Into it the people Moses had led out of Egypt had passed with Joshua, and there in the valley of Ajalon was the place where he commanded the sun to stand still, that he might the more utterly smite the Amorite. On these fields the people of God had done battle with the Philistines, Samson had descended from the hill country to woo their daughters, to suffer his terrible punishment, and work his splendid revenge, and the ruddy-faced David in his humble yet glorious youth had met and vanquished the proud Goliath. On the hills above, the Maccabees had defied the tyrant, raised the standard of freedom and faith, and saved Israel. Northward is Bethlehem, the birthplace of David, sur-

[1] Pss. lxxxiv. 2 ; cxxii. 1, 2.

rounded by the hills on which he had watched his flocks; while beyond is Jerusalem, the city where he reigned and Solomon judged. On all there lies a light that fades not, but grows richer and more radiant with the ages. Zion has heard the sublimest of the prophets say unto her, "Thy God reigneth." The mountains of Judah have been touched by the beautiful feet of Him who brought good tidings and published peace. The ways that converge upon the city have been consecrated by pilgrims' songs, that are songs of cheer and hope for pilgrims of all lands and times. The city is embalmed in the most glorious sacred poetry of the world, so humanly universal, so divinely immortal, that once man has learned to use it he can never cease to sing. And the land transfigured by these meanings and memories is mightier in spiritual than physical influences; the hands by which it shapes men are moral and religious rather than material and fateful. Its plastic energies are born not of nature but of spirit, and are to the susceptible soul as the inspiration of God, but to the insusceptible soul they are not, or are hardened into institutions and traditions that can neither maintain nor communicate life.

Jesus thus lived in a land full of many influences, historical and physical, small in size, but mighty in power. Greece is great for ever as the home of the Hellenes, the men so gifted with "the vision and the faculty divine" as to discover and reveal to the world the beautiful in nature and man. The city that rose beside the Tiber, and swayed for centuries the sceptre of the world, has made the hills on which she sat throned famous for evermore. The queenly Nile and the rivers of Mesopotamia have been immortalized by the ancient empires of Egypt, Assyria, and Babylon. But to only one land was it given to bear and nurse two peoples, most dissimilar while akin, small in numbers but most potent in influence—the Phœnicians, who made for us the art of commerce and found for us the pathway of the sea, and the Hebrews, the people of the Book, "to whom pertaineth the adoption, and the shechinah, and the covenants, and the giving of the law, and the service of God, and the promises; whose are the fathers, and of whom as concerning the flesh Christ came, who is over all, God blessed for ever. Amen."[1]

The land, then, was an appropriate home for Jesus. With its ideal significance, the purposes to which it had been, as it were, dedicated of God, He stood in essential sympathy. In and through Him, indeed, the ideal was destined to be realized. And as in Him its history culminated, He could not have been apart from it. Nowhere else could He have found the conditions necessary to His becoming what He became, doing what He did, fulfilling the mission He fulfilled. In Galilee He found the political and social conditions that allowed Him to reach His end, to realize His ideal; in Judæa He found the historical conditions which made His ideal possible, intelligible, real. But in both cases it was simply *conditions* He found; in neither did there exist the creative *causes* that found and made Him. Judaism was a condition, but not the cause, of Christ's being; and while the condition may be necessary to the operation of the cause, it is insufficient to the production of the effect. Without Judaism, Jesus had been without an arena on which to live and develop and act; but without Jesus, Judaism had been without the Christ that created Christianity. Galilee was, by the very circumstances which qualified it to be a condition of his growth or becoming, disqualified to be a cause; Judæa, by the very conditions which qualified it to be an arena for the evolution of the ideal He was to realize, was disqualified for effecting its realization. And the evidence lies in their respective characters and histories, and in their respective relations to

[1] Romans ix. 4, 5.

Him. Galilee never struggled towards the production of a being like Christ, and so has no one that can be compared with Him. He stands alone in its history. Though it furnished Him with a soil on which to grow, yet so soon as He had grown into the Christ He was to be, it knew Him not, wondered at and followed Him for a few days, then despised and forsook Him. Judæa, though it longed for a Messiah, never dreamed of a religion without a temple and with only a single and invisible Priest. Out of the institutions it favoured and maintained no one who so held and taught could ever have issued. When, without a priesthood and opposed to the priestly spirit, its Messiah came, Judæa had nothing more or better for Him than the cross. The land supplied the conditions necessary to the forms of His being, character, and action; but in Himself alone lived the cause of what He was and became and did, of all He said and has achieved.

2. THE PEOPLE. Descent is a potent factor of character. The past can never disinherit the present; the present can never dispossess itself of qualities transmitted from the past. The great man cannot be understood apart from his people—must be approached through his country and kin. Jesus was a Jew, a son of Israel. Israel had not been a royal or imperial people, had no claim to stand among the empires of the world. Once, for a brief season, they had become a great power. Their history boasted but two splendid reigns, one famed for conquest, the other for wisdom; yet in each case the splendour was dashed with darkness. The great kings died, and the great kingdom perished, fell into two miserable monarchies, always rivals, often at war, threatened or held in fee by the great empires on either side. And the people were as destitute of literary genius as of political importance. They were not gifted with the faculty of making a language beautiful and musical for ever, of

creating a literature that could command the world by its rich and exact science, sublime and profound philosophy, pure and exalted poetry. They were, too, not only without the genius for art, but possessed the spirit to which art is alien, an unholy and hateful thing. They had had as a people nothing cosmopolitan in their past, had never, like the Phœnicians, penetrated the world with their inventions and commerce, like the Greeks, with their literature, like the Assyrians or Romans, with their arms; but they had lived a life that grew narrower and more exclusive every day, and had become among the nations not so much a nation as a sect.

Yet this people had had a glorious and singular past. If ever a people had been created and destined for a great work in the sphere of religion, it was the people of Israel. They accomplished in obscurity and amid contempt and against difficulties that seemed inconquerable, a work that is in its own order the foremost work ever done in the world. They created not simply a new religion—that was in primitive times an almost daily feat—but an idea and embodiment of religion so absolutely new, yet of such transcendent truth and potence as to have made religion a new force for man, sweeter, truer, and more ethical than it had ever been conceived to be. It is not possible to tell here and now how they did it. Enough to say, they had been creators of a new and peculiar conception of God and man, of society and the state. Two thousand years before our date they had fled as a band of slaves from Egypt and found freedom in the desert. There their leader had given them laws which were his, yet God's. They were organized into a nation, with God as their King, and settled in Canaan to realize a Divine kingdom, an ideal state, instituted and ruled of God. In it everything was sacred, nothing profane. The common duties of life were subjects of Divine commandment. The nation in its collective being was meant to be the vehicle and minister of the Divine Will. Worship was, while individual, national, the homage of the people to their invisible King. While the nation by its worship and through its priests spoke to God, God by His prophets spoke to the nation. They were, indeed, the voices of God, speakers for Him, revealing His truths, enforcing His will. But a recognized is not always an obeyed authority. The notion of religion was sublimer than the people had mind to appreciate or will to incorporate and adequately actualize. Worship is easier than obedience. Men are ever readier to serve the priest than to obey the prophet, and sacerdotalism flourished in Israel while prophecy decayed and died. And so, while the prophets created a literature embodying an unrealized religion, the priests created a nation, a people devoted to the worship they administered, the symbols and ceremonies they had instituted.

There were thus two ideals in Israel, each the express antithesis of the other. The one was prophetic, the other priestly. The prophetic was an exalted ethical faith, possessed of an intense and lofty consciousness of the absolute holiness of God, and of the need of holiness in man, or the perfect conformity of the human to the Divine will, to the obedience He required and approved. The priestly was an elaborate, sensuous, and sacerdotal system, which aspired to regulate the relations between God and man by sacrifices and symbols and ceremonial observances. The prophetic we name Hebraism, the priestly Judaism. The grand aim of the first was to create alike in the man and the people moral obedience, and so it was ever preaching "the righteous God loveth righteousness;" "He is of purer eyes than to behold iniquity;" "Justice and judgment are the habitation of His throne;" He cannot allow the ill-doer to go unpunished or the well-doer to live unrewarded. The grand aim of the second was to create a people devoted to sacerdotal customs, a state so constituted and conducted that men should regard the laws of the priest as the laws of God, and performance of his rites as supreme conformity to the Divine will. There were times when the prophetic faith penetrated with its spirit and transfigured with its meaning the priestly system—and in this, their real Mosaic relation, they completed and complemented each other; but in the actual field of history and life their usual relation was one of antagonism and conflict. The prophetic was by its very nature qualified to be in all its splendid elements permanent and universal, but the priestly was designed and qualified to be at best typical and provisional. But the temporal, in its struggle to become eternally and universally valid, would not allow the eternal to be realized. The priests so tenaciously laboured to make their shadows the substance that the substance was hidden by the shadows, and it was against this sustained endeavour of theirs that the prophets so strenuously contended. But the weakness of man helped the priests. Hebraism remained an ideal, a faith too sublimely spiritual and ethical for gross and sensuous men; but Judaism became a reality, as was easily possible to a religion that translated the grand and severe idea of righteousness into the poor and simple notion of legal cleanness, and substituted the fanaticism of the symbol for the enthusiasm of humanity.

Two things need to be here noted. (1) The contradiction in the history of Israel between the political ideal, which was in its highest qualities prophetic, and the reality. The ideal was the Theocracy. The state was the Church, God was the king, the polity was the religion. Our modern distinctions were unknown; God penetrated everywhere and everything, and consecrated whatever He penetrated. The individual and the state were in all their modes of being and action meant to be religious. But to the realization of such an ideal, absolute freedom was necessary; a tyranny, either native or foreign, could only be fatal to it. If the state was not allowed to develop according to its own nature, its institutions spontaneously crystallizing round its central belief, it could not fulfil the end given in its very idea. And Israel had but seldom enjoyed the freedom his ideal demanded. He had often been the vassal, had even been the captive, of great empires. His struggle for political existence acted injuriously on his religious ideal—made him feel that to maintain national being was to fulfil his religious mission. And the patriotism evoked by the first narrowed to a miserable particularism the generous universalism that lived in the second. Israel believed that the states which were the enemies of his political being were the enemies of his religious mission, and so he hated his conquerors with the double hatred of the vanquished patriot and the disappointed zealot. If the alien refused to spare his freedom, he could refuse to distribute his light. The circumstances that did not allow him to realize his political ideal prevented him from fulfilling his religious mission.

(2) The contradiction in the life of Israel between the religious ideal and the reality. The two elements in the faith of Israel were, as above indicated, the sacerdotal and the spiritual, or the priestly and the prophetic. The one was embodied in the legal ordinances and worship, the other expressed in the prophetic Scriptures. The prophets represent the religion of Jahveh, not as realized in Israel, but in its ideal truth and purity. The priests represent it, not as it ought to have been, but as it actually was. It was possible to be most faithful to the sacerdotal, while most false to the spiritual element. Where the priest was most blindly followed the prophet was most obstinately disobeyed. Prophecy, neglected, died, but the priesthood, respected and revered, grew. While all that remained of the prophets was a dead literature, the priests lived and

multiplied, the soul of an active and comprehensive system. It has often been said that the Jews went into captivity polytheists and returned monotheists; that, before it, nothing could keep them back from idolatry, after it, nothing tempt them to it. But it entirely depends on the meaning of the terms whether the above statement be true. The Jews were as little monotheists, in the sense of the prophets, after as before the captivity. There is an idolatry of the symbol as well as of the image. The idol is a representation of God, the symbol a representation of the truth; and where the representation becomes to the man as the thing represented, there is idolatry—reverence of the sign instead of the thing signified. And the Jews were idolaters of the symbol. Their sacerdotalism was deified. Means were made ends, legal more than ethical purity, mint, anise, and cummin, more than righteousness, mercy, and truth. Priestcraft and legalism proved as fatal to the realization of the religious ideal as bondage to the realization of the political.

And these contradictions between the ideal and the real had reached their sharpest point when Christ came. Freedom, the necessary condition of greatness, whether of deed or endeavour, was unknown. The land was ruled by hated aliens. In things outer and social, indeed, the people seemed prosperous. New and splendid cities like Cæsarea were rising, aping the magnificence in architecture and vice, in law and license, of the famous and dreaded Capital in the West. In old cities like Jerusalem buildings were in process that eclipsed the greatest structures of ancient times, a temple splendid as Solomon's, monument of a man who mocked the faith it was meant to honour. While the people used the temple, they hated and feared its builder. For Herod was a double offence—a son of Edom, a hated child of hated Esau; and a vassal king, monarch of Judæa, but subject of Rome, one whose rule made the ruled slaves of a slave. On the religious side the people had been for centuries afflicted with barrenness. The Divine oracles were dumb, and in their place there had risen a forced and fantastic literature, visionary, turgid, that was to the prophetic what the spent echo, broken into confused and inarticulate sound, is to the human voice, full of soft music and sweet reason. The people were in the seat of their strength smitten with weakness, and at their heart the grim and terrible forces of dissolution were at work.

But the state of the people will become more evident if we analyze and describe the two great parties of Christ's day, the Pharisees and Sadducees. Ascetic and communist societies like the Essenes stood too remote from the national life and influenced it too little to be here of much significance. Our knowledge of the two great historical and politico-religious parties is still most imperfect, though clearer than it once was. The parallel suggested by Josephus between the Pharisees and the Stoics, and the Sadducees and the Epicureans, was as incorrect as unjust.[1] The popular notion, identifying the Pharisee with the formalist and the Sadducee with the sceptic, is no better. The two parties were at once political and religious, represented different ideas of the national polity, and different interpretations of the national faith. The Pharisees were a popular and democratic, but the Sadducees a conservative and aristocratic, party. The former represented a freer

[1] Josephus was indeed too careful to draw the parallel explicitly himself. He compares the Pharisees to the Stoics and the Essenes to the Pythagoreans (*Vita*, 2 ; *Antt*, xv. 10. 4) ; but while his exposition of Sadducean doctrine (*Antt.*, xiii. 5 9) suggests the Epicurean, he too well understood the thoroughly Jewish character of the party to compare it with any Greek school. Even as it is, his use of Greek terms is essentially misleading. There was no idea affirmed by the Pharisees and Essenes and denied by the Sadducees that could be fitly translated by Εἱμαρμένη.

THE HISTORICAL CONDITIONS.

and more individual movement, but the latter a hereditary and sacerdotal tendency. The Pharisees constituted a school or society, where the condition of membership was intellectual; but the Sadducees constituted a party, where the condition of membership was descent. The former was an association of the likeminded, but the latter a cluster of priestly and governing families. Each had a different interpretation of the past, present, and future of Israel; and their conduct differed with their interpretation. When the creative period in Israel ceased, the interpretive began. When the school of the prophets died, the school of the scribes was founded, and in the latter Pharisaism was born. The Pharisees were essentially interpreters; what had been written and delivered as law they lived to explain and obey.[1] Their ideal was to see every Israelite skilled in the law, and obedient to it, in order that man, by being faithful to the human conditions of the covenant, might enable God to fulfil His promise and restore the kingdom to Israel. Their notion of the law was broader than the Sadducean; comprehended not simply the priestly ordinances, but every statute or precept by lawgiver, prophet, or rabbi which related to the regulation of the individual or social life. Their notion, too, of reward or recompense was much more pronounced and powerful, bound all the promises of the Old Testament both to this life and one that was to come. The necessary counterpart of an obedient people was a faithful God; when the people did as God commanded, God would do as He had promised. So the Pharisaic zeal for the law but expressed the Pharisaic zeal for the future and triumph of Israel; and it at once rested on and addressed the deepest of Jewish hopes —the hope in the Messiah. Thus over against the Sadducean policy and position they placed the ancient national ideal, which was to be realized by obedience to the law the

[1] Jos., *Bell. Jud.*, ii. 8. 14; *Antt.*, xvii. 2. 4.

fathers had received and they interpreted. With the idea of interpretation came the idea of authority. The men that had been despised while living were revered when dead; and the interpretation became as authoritative and sacred as the interpreted, the oral as the written law. The former at once explained, modified, and enlarged the latter. The school became a sort of permanent lawgiver, augmenting the original germ by aggregation as opposed to growth or development. This process the Pharisees represented, but the Sadducees resisted. They stood by the old sacerdotalism, by the hereditary principle that secured sacerdotal functions and political authority to the old families. The prophecy their fathers had hated, they ignored. The later doctrines of angels and spirits, of resurrection and immortality, they denied. The oral law, the interpretations of the schools, they despised. And so they and the Pharisees stood in practical as in theoretical politics in antithetical relations. The Pharisee represented the patriotic view, developed Judaism, the theocratic belief in all its scholastic exaggeration and rigidity. But the Sadducees represented the standpoint of the politician, the creed of the ruling families, that know how calmly to accept the inevitable while preserving their prerogatives and privileges. Neither party was true to Hebraism, the universalism that lived in the prophets. Both were illustrations of how historical parties may be most false to history, to every great principle it expresses or contains. Judaism, as it then lived, was the antithesis and contradiction of Hebraism; the religion alike of Pharisees and Sadducees was the negation of the religion Psalmists had sung and Prophets preached.

Now, amid these and similar historical conditions Jesus lived. Could they make Him? Can they explain Him? There was a fine fitness in His being a Jew, a Son of Abraham the Hebrew. The supreme religious person of the race fitly came from its most religious family. He was the personalization of its genius, the heir of its work. It had created the history that made Him possible, the men to whom He was intelligible and through whom He could be revealed to the world. But He transcended its powers of production, was more and greater than what its native energies could create. The splendid religious genius of Israel had issued in Judaism, and which of its two great parties could produce a Christ? The Sadducees would not own Him. He belonged to no ruling family, had no priestly blood in His veins, was one whose very meddling with religion deserved nothing less than death. And Pharisaism was as incapable of forming Him. It was nobler than its rival, had loftier aims, truer ambitions, a sincerer spirit. But it was fundamentally increative, radically infertile. It could not be inventive, inward, spiritual, without being suicidal. The moment it had tried to transcend legalism and particularism, it had perished. All its wisdom is the wisdom of the interpreter, all its goodness the goodness of the School. But Jesus is throughout the very antithesis and contradiction of Pharisaism. He is the supreme religious spirit of history, the foremost creator of faith, the least bound by legalism, the most absolutely universal, rich in the most human wisdom, gracious with the most Divine goodness. It is a small thing to find among the sayings of Hillel or Shammai one curiously like a saying of Jesus. The great thing is the spirit of the men and the system. Common sayings can be claimed for neither Hillel nor Jesus, but what each can claim is his distinctive character and spirit. Hillel is a Jewish Rabbi, and could never have been a Universal Teacher; Jesus is a Universal Teacher, and could never have remained a mere Jewish Rabbi. But He could be the first only as He transcended the second, and his historical conditions, while equal to the making of a

Rabbi, were not equal to the creation of a Universal Teacher.

There is nothing so easy as to change conditions into causes, to mistake the enumeration of formal elements for the discovery of the plastic mind. What is dead and amorphous in Judaism was made living and organic by the touch of Christ. Judaism cannot show how His hand became creative, though the fact is indubitable that His hand did create. The maker of a great religion is no simple product which an exhausted faith suddenly and almost insensibly touched by other exhausted faiths may easily produce. The most hurried glance can see how complex and difficult the problem is.

Contrast Christ's day with ours. We are free, the children of a land where a man can speak the thing he will; but He was without freedom, the Son of a people enslaved and oppressed. We are educated, enlightened by the best thought of the past, the surest knowledge of the present; but His were an uneducated people, hardly knew the schoolmaster, and where they did, received from him instruction that stunted rather than developed. We live in a present that knows the past and is enriched with all its mental wealth—the treasures of India, from its earliest Vedic to its latest Puranic age—of China, of Egypt, of Persia, of Assyria; the classic riches of Greece and Rome; the wondrous stores accumulated by the Hebrews themselves and deposited in their Scriptures—all are ours, at our feet, in our heads, there to make the new wealth old wealth never fails to create. But Jesus lived in a present closed to every past, save the past of His own people. The common home-born Jew knew the Gentile but to despise him; the wisdom of Greece and Rome was to him but foolishness, best unknown; while the light that streamed from his own Scriptures could be seen only through the thick dark horn of rabbinical interpretation. We live in times when the world has grown wondrously wide and open to man; when nations beat in closest sympathy with each other; when the thoughts of one people swiftly become those of another; when commerce has so woven its fine network round the world that all its parts now feel connected and akin; but Jesus lived in a land which prided itself on its ignorance and hatred of the foreigner, where the thought of common brotherhood or kinship could only rise to be cast out and abhorred. In our day nature has been interpreted, the physical universe has become practically infinite in space and time, filling the soul with a sense of awe in its presence the earlier ages could not possibly have experienced; but in Christ's day and to His countrymen nature was but a simple thing, of small significance, with few mysteries. Ours is, indeed, a day that might well create a great man, a universal teacher, the founder of a new faith. Yet where is the person that thinks it possible for our historical conditions to create a Christ? Strauss did not think they could, for Christ was to him the supreme religious genius, unapproached, unapproachable, who must in His own order stand alone for all time. Renan does not think so, for to him Christ is a Creator, the Founder of the absolute religion, who did His work so well that it only remains to us to be His continuators. But if the creation of Christ transcends our historical conditions, was it possible to His own? Or does He not stand out so much their superior as to be, while a Child of time, the Son of the Eternal, the only Begotten who has descended to earth from the bosom of the Father, that He might declare Him?

II.

THE NARRATIVES OF THE BIRTH AND INFANCY.

THE sun while setting in the west often throws upon the eastern heaven a burnished shadow, the reflection of the golden glory in which he dies. So, many an infancy has been transfigured by the light of a great manhood, beautified by the marvellous hues shed back upon it from a splendid character and career. The childhood of Moses was to later Hebrew tradition a childhood of wonder and miracle. Ancient Greece made her heroes sons of the gods, men dear to heaven, for whom the Olympians plotted and schemed, and round whom they strenuously fought. The proud fancy of the Romans made Romulus the suckling of the she-wolf; the early history of his "eternal city" a history of marvel and miracle, of deeds and events prophetic of universal empire. The fame of the life reflected on the infancy may thus become in a creative imagination the fruitful mother of myths, credible in an age of wonder and childlike faith, incredible in an age of critical and rational thought.

Now, are the stories of Christ's birth and infancy but the luminous and tinted shadows of His marvellous manhood, the creations of intense and exalted dreamers who, bidden by their own fancies, made the child the father of the man ? So it has been thought and said. The narratives which describe the coming of Jesus have been resolved into myths, no more historical than the stories

THE BIRTH AND INFANCY.

which tell the adventures of the gods of ancient Greece. Yet on the surface one great difference lies, which may have no critical, but has some rational, worth. The Greek mythologies became incredible centuries since, faith in them died out and no man could revive it; but the story of Christ's birth and infancy still remains credible, need not offend the most cultured reason of the most cultured age. *They* were proved, by actual history too, creations of the childlike imagination, credible to the fanciful child, incredible to the rational man; but *it* has been proved, by long and extensive human experience too, to be as fit for belief by the man as by the child, to be capable of vindication before the calm and critical reason. In the presence of rational thought legends die but truths live, and in their respective fates their respective characters are revealed.

The story of the birth and infancy is told in the First and Third Gospels with a simple grace that excels the most perfect art. Its theme, hardly to be handled without being depraved, is touched with the most exquisite delicacy. The veil where it ought to conceal does not reveal; where it can be lifted, it is lifted softly, and neither torn nor soiled. There is as little trace of a coarse or prurient, as of an inventive or amplifying, faculty. The reticence is much more remarkable than the speech. Indeed, the distinction between history and legend could not be better marked than by the reserve of the canonical and the vulgar tattle of the apocryphal Gospels. These latter are, so far as they concern the birth and infancy, full of grossness and indecency, of rude speech as to things that become unholy by being handled. But our narratives are pure as the air that floats above the eternal hills; are full, too, of an idyllic sweetness like the breath of summer when it comes laden with the fragrance of garden and field. The lone, lovely, glad, yet care-burdened mother; the holy beautiful Child, bringing such unsearchable wealth of truth and peace to men; the meanness of His birthplace, the greatness of His mission; the heedless busy world unconscious of the new conscious life that has come to change and bless it; the shepherds under the silent stars, watching and watched; the angel-choir, whose song breaks the silence of earth with the music of heaven; the wretched and merciless Herod, growing in cruelty as he grows nearer death, a contrast to the gentle Infant who comes with "peace and good-will towards men;" the Magi, wanderers from the distant East in search of light and hope: and round and through all the presence in angel and dream, in event and word, of the Eternal God who loves the fallen, and begins in humanity a work of salvation and renewal—these all together make, when read in the letter but interpreted by the spirit, a matchless picture of earthly beauty and pathos illumined and sublimed by heavenly love. Whatever fate criticism may have in store for our narrative, it must ever remain a vehicle of holy thoughts to every mind that lies open to the spiritual and divine.

The narratives of the Birth and Infancy may be studied either on their critical and historical, or their ideal and intellectual, side. If on the first, the questions mainly concern their authenticity and trustworthiness; if on the second, the questions chiefly relate to their interpretation and significance. But while the two classes of questions are distinct, they yet interpenetrate. If the critical and historical questions are answered in a way adverse to the authenticity and credibility of the narratives, then they must be regarded as legendary, and explained as creations of a more or less childlike imagination. If, on the other hand, the ideal and intellectual questions can be so answered as to satisfy the reason, the answer may have considerable critical worth. It ought to show, at least,

THE BIRTH AND INFANCY. 33

that the narratives need not be rejected *a priori* as contra-rational, that they speak of matters the intellect can conceive and believe. It ought to show, too, that they are not explicable like ordinary legends, cannot be explained by the normal action of the mythical faculty, are due to other psychological factors than those that have produced the myths of the world's childhood. If so much can be shown, the objections taken *in limine* to these narratives must lose much of their power. It is our purpose to deal here with the phase of the subject last indicated, to endeavour to discover the psychological roots of the narratives, though within our limits but little can be done to determine at once their critical and intellectual worth.

There is a peculiar fitness in discussing here the problem just stated. There was no part of the evangelical history that so early fell under the charge of being mythical as the one now before us. Long before the days of Strauss its historical veracity had been doubted, and the readiness with which even orthodox theologians had confessed to its mythical or semi-mythical character helped to suggest to him his own distinctive hypothesis, which was but an extension to the entire history of a critical and interpretive principle that had been already applied to its introduction. Our problem, then, raises the question as to the mythical element in the Gospels at what may be regarded as the most cardinal point. Here the mythical theory has its strongest, as here it had its first, foothold; yet once established as to these narratives, it cannot be confined within their limits, must penetrate the whole body to which they belong. While the question is particular in its subject, it is general in its bearings. In determining whether our narratives are myths, we determine, in a sense, the far wider question whether our evangelical histories are mythical.

The narratives of the Birth and Infancy are peculiar to

our First and Third Gospels, and they stand in each with agreements and differences that are alike significant. In Matthew the Jewish, in Luke the Gentile, standpoint and purpose are apparent. Their influence is seen (1) in the genealogies. Matthew traces the descent of Jesus Christ, "the son of David, the son of Abraham;"[1] but Luke ascends higher, makes Jesus "the son of Adam, who was the son of God."[2] The difference is significant. Matthew the Hebrew, addressing Hebrews, presents Jesus as the Messiah, complying with the conditions necessary to the Messiahship that He may be qualified to fulfil the Messianic hopes. But Luke the Greek, addressing Greeks, presents Jesus in His common brotherhood to man and native sonship to God. In the one case He is incorporated with Israel, in the other with humanity. Both standpoints were universal, but with a difference. Matthew regarded Israel as a people existing for the world, their mission culminating in their Messiah, who, while of particular descent, was of universal significance; but Luke regarded the race that had grown from Adam as blossoming into Christ, who, while the flower of the old, was the seed of the new humanity. Matthew's genealogy is the vehicle of Prophetic, but Luke's of Pauline ideas. The first represents Christ as a redeemer of Abrahamic, a king of Davidic descent, appearing to fulfil the aspirations of the ancient people, and realize the theocratic ideal; but the second exhibits Him as through His descent from Adam the blood-relation, as it were, of every man, appearing that He may create in every man a no less real and intimate spiritual relation with God. And so, while Jesus is to Matthew the Messiah, He is to Luke the Second Adam, the Creator and Head of the new humanity, sustaining universal relations and accomplishing an universal work.

(2) In their modes of conceiving and representing the

[1] Matt. i. 1. [2] Luke iii. 23, 38.

THE BIRTH AND INFANCY.

Child Jesus. Both, indeed, know but the one cause of the Child's coming, the creative action of the Spirit of God. Matthew says, with significant modesty, Mary " was found with child by the Holy Ghost; " while Luke, with greater fulness but equal purity, says, " The Holy Ghost shall come upon thee, and the power of the Highest shall overshadow thee." It is possible that theologians have here personalized too much. The phrase " Spirit of God " often in the Old Testament denotes the Divine creative energy, the might of God, active and exercised, whether in the making and maintaining of the world, or the forming and direction of man. And so our Evangelists agree in representing Christ as the child of the Divine creative energy, find the cause of His becoming and birth in the action of God. But the agreement here gives point to the differences elsewhere. Matthew, true to his Jewish standpoint and purpose, finds the birth to be the fulfilment of a prophecy, and not satisfied with explaining the name Jesus in the sense Israel loved, describes and denotes Him by the prophetic title Emmanuel. But Luke, while he invokes no prophet or prophecy, and supplies no special interpretation of the name, significantly denotes the Child Mary is to bear as " the Son of God." The former is here true to the spirit and thought of Israel, but the latter to the theology of Paul. Luke had learned to read the Christian facts in the light of his master's ideas. The Divine Sonship of Christ was the foundation of the Pauline theology, and is here made the starting-point of the evangelical history that represents and embodies it. To the pupil as to the teacher the Second Adam could accomplish this work only as He was " the Son of the Highest."

(3) In the narratives of the Infancy, Matthew never forgets the kinghood of his Messiah—the theocratic character of His mission. The Magi come from the East in

search of Him "that is born king of the Jews;" their act is an act of fealty, of homage to rightful royalty. What Herod fears in the Child is a rival—a king of the ancient stock with claims he and his could not withstand. But though it is said that Christ "shall reign over the house of Jacob, and of his kingdom there shall be no end," Luke in his narrative hardly finds a place for the theocratic idea. The Child is set at once in His universal relations, a Saviour "to all people," "a light to lighten the Gentiles," "the dayspring from on high," risen "to give light to them that sit in darkness and in the shadow of death." The standpoint is throughout Pauline. The advent that is celebrated is the advent, not of a theocratic king, but of a Redeemer whose work is universal, who is essentially related, on the one hand to God as a Son, on the other to man as a Brother.

But while the Evangelists remain true to their respective standpoints and purposes, their narratives prove that they could transcend both. The one happily indicates the universalism of the ancient faith, the other the historical relations and reverence of the new. The Hebrew makes the heathen Magi the first to worship the newborn King; the Greek shows the beautiful love alike of parents and Child to the law, the temple, and the customs of the Fathers. In Matthew the Gentile comes from the East to claim his right to sit with Abraham, Isaac, and Jacob in the kingdom of God, and His right is as finely expressed as divinely recognized. In Luke the aged representative of the faith and hope of the past stands up in the temple to acknowledge the advent and proclaim the work of a Redeemer. And so each Evangelist in his own way approves the standpoint and ratifies the purpose of the other. Their differences are not disagreements, but means by which the varied phases of a history of universal and enduring import may be exhibited.

THE BIRTH AND INFANCY.

But now we must advance from what is formal to what is material in the narratives. What is cardinal to each is common to both—the Child that is born of Mary is the Son of God, the fruit of the overshadowing "of the Most High." Agreement on this point is not peculiar to our First and Third Gospels, but to the New Testament books as a whole. Though the detailed narratives are peculiar to the former, allusions to the real and ideal elements in the birth of Christ are common to the latter. Paul could speak of Him as "born of a woman," "of the seed of David according to the flesh."[1] Even the Fourth Gospel is most explicit in its recognition of His natural birth. In it His mother asserted her maternity, and He, in the most solemn moment of His life, confesses His sonship.[2] Philip says to Nathanael, "We have found him of whom Moses in the law, and the prophets, did write, Jesus of Nazareth, the son of Joseph."[3] The people of Capernaum are made to inquire, "Is not this the son of Joseph, whose father and mother we know?"[4] and in Mark we have the similar inquiry, "Is not this the carpenter, the son of Mary?"[5] But alongside this recognition of the real and material birth stands the common confession of a higher and diviner being. The birth, but not the parentage, is human. While born of Mary, He is the Son of God. The Fourth Evangelist conceives the coming of Christ as the becoming incarnate of the Divine and Eternal Word; while Paul in many a form expresses and emphasizes his belief in a Christ who, "being in the form of God, did not think equality with God a thing to be snatched at, but emptied Himself by taking the form of a servant, being made in the likeness of men."[6] Now, as the ideal Gospel, as well as the doctrinal Epistles, everywhere imply the human birth, and often refer to it, the narratives which describe this birth

[1] Gal. iv. 4; Rom. i. 3. [2] John ii. 3, 4; xix. 26, 27. [3] John i. 45.
[4] John vi. 42. [5] Mark vi. 3, cf. iii. 31-35. [6] Phil. ii. 6, 7.

more than imply the theory of His higher nature and relations developed in that Gospel and these Epistles. What is intellectually presented in the latter is historically exhibited in the former, and what we have to explain is, how men with the passions and prejudices, with the inherited tendencies and beliefs of Jews, could come to believe in what can only be described as an incarnation of Deity. The problem, which is one of deep and varied interest, must be rightly apprehended. In stating it we must carefully distinguish what is accidental and formal from what is essential and material. Mythical explanations have been mainly based on critical analysis of the form, on the discovery and proof of correspondences with Old Testament history and prophecy. In a monotheistic religion, God can have intercourse with the creature only through the agency of a special messenger, and the angel of the Annunciation is suggested by the histories of Israel and Ishmael, Samson and Samuel. The Song of Mary is a "plagiarism"[1] from Hannah. The birth at Bethlehem finds a double source in the history of David and the prophecy of Micah. The star in the east rises to fulfil Balaam's prophecy. Jesus as the Son of David becomes the possessor of the names and attributes of the Messianic King described in the second Psalm. And so our narratives are proved to be mythical by being proved to be fancies clothed in forms suggested by the Old Testament or borrowed from it. But this is so purely formal as to be entirely irrelevant. The really material point is this—the peculiar and specific character of the belief the narratives embody in its relation to the distinctive character of the men who entertain and embody it. The first Christians were Hebrews, their leaders men of intensely Hebraic natures; yet their fundamental and most distinctive doctrine was one profoundly offensive to the Hebrew mind and

[1] Strauss, *Das Leben Jesu*, § 58. Eng. Tr., II. 52.

THE BIRTH AND INFANCY. 39

faith. The problem is, How did such men come to entertain such a belief, to be the apostles of it, martyrs for it, so inspired by a Divine enthusiasm in its behalf as to be transformed from illiterate Jews into the founders of a new and beneficent religion? It is a small and simple thing to discover in their ancient literature anticipative affinities with the forms of their thought; the main matter is to discover the source and cause of the thought itself, which is but another form of our already indicated question as to the psychological roots of the belief embodied in the narratives of Christ's birth and infancy.

Can our narratives be explained through the Hindu mythologies? Can they be traced to similar psychical roots? Can they be resolved into creations of the mythopoetic faculty? Hindu mythology is an enormous growth, extending over many thousand years, and so far too immense and complicated to be compared with our short and simple narratives. All that can be done is to compare them where they seem to embody similar ideas, and discover whether the psychological explanation possible in the one case is possible in the other. Well, then, the idea of the incarnation of Deity is familiar to Hindu mythology. Brahmanism knows it, and so, in a sense, does Buddhism. Divine appearances or manifestations are common in the former system: incarnations of Buddha are frequent in the latter. But as Buddhism is nominally, though not really, atheistic, it wants one of the terms most essential for comparison, and so for our present purpose had better be dropped out of account.

The affinity of the Hindu and Christian ideas of incarnation has often been asserted, and the derivation, now of the Christian from the Hindu, and again of the Hindu from the Christian, has been confidently affirmed. Only a few years since a German scholar endeavoured to prove traces of Christian ideas both in the theology and ethics of the Bhagavad-gîtâ,[1] and the influence of the Orient in the schools of the apostolic and post-apostolic age is a commonplace of historical inquiry. But these inquiries have been due to affinities that are only apparent, that mask, indeed, the most radical antitheses. (1) The idea of incarnation is essentially different. In the Hindu system incarnations are many and frequent, but in the Christian there is but one. In the former they are transitory and occasional; in the latter it is permanent and providential, necessary to produce the well-being of man and accomplish the ends of God. The Hindu incarnations are often monstrous forms, effected to perform with immoral violence works that can hardly be called moral; but the Christian incarnation is human, rational, the moral means of achieving the greatest possible moral work. Multiplicity is essential to the first, but unity to the second. Unity would be fatal to the ideas expressed by the former, but multitude to those represented by the latter. Were the Hindu incarnation conceived as happening but once, it would lose its essential character; to conceive the Christian as happening oftener would be to abolish it. But (2) the Hindu and Christian incarnations express and repose on essentially different ideas of God. In India the belief in incarnation is the logical and necessary result of the belief in God. To the Hindu, God is no person, but the universal life, the inexhaustible energy that, unhasting, unresting, creates every change and exists in every mode and in all forms of being. As the particles that make up the water-drop may roll in the ocean, float in the vapour,

[1] Dr. Franz Lorinser, of Breslau. On the same side, though occupying a much more moderate and critical position, is Professor Weber, of Berlin. Very strongly on the opposite side is an eminent Hindu scholar, the most recent translator of the Bhagavad-gîtâ, Kâshinâth Trimbak Telang. Professors Monier Williams and Cowel lean favourably to the former opinion, without exactly adopting it; Dr. John Muir to the latter, yet without definitely pronouncing in its favour.

sail in the cloud, fall in the rain, shine in the dew, circulate in the plant, and return into the ocean again, remaining in all their apparent changes essentially unchanged, so the universal energy or life that is termed God assumes the infinite variety of forms that constitutes the world of appearances. But the Hebrew did not so conceive God. His Deity was a conscious Mind, a voluntary Power, the living Maker and righteous Ruler of nature and man. He was never confounded with the world or its life; He stood infinitely above both, the cause of their changes, not their subject. The Hindu could not separate, the Hebrew could not identify, God and nature. Incarnation was the logical correlate of the Hindu, but the logical contradiction of the Hebrew, idea of God. The one reached it by the simple process of logical evolution, unconsciously performed; but the other could·reach it only by a violent logical revolution. It was a native growth of the Hindu mind, especially as Brahmanism had made it; but it was utterly alien to the Hebrew mind, especially as it had been educated and possessed by Judaism. The law of natural mental development explains the rise of the belief in incarnations in India, but it cannot explain what so manifestly contradicts it as the rise of the belief in the Incarnation in Judæa.

Can our narratives be explained through the Greek mythology?[1] Can the psychological laws exemplified by the latter be applied to the former? The Greek mythology, while it had started from the same point as the Hindu, had yet had a very different development. The ideas it ultimately embodied were almost as unlike the distinctive ideas of the Hindus as of the Hebrews. It knew, indeed, many gods and sons of the gods, but in these the idea of incarnation was in no proper sense expressed. Gods and men were to the Greek alike created beings. They were

[1] Strauss, *Das Leben Jesu*, §§ 57, 60

akin, of a kind, and stood so near each other that the god was but a magnified man, the man a reduced god. The god lived a sort of corporate existence, needed food and drink; was immortal, not in his own right, but by virtue of the peculiar qualities of the things he ate and drank; was, too, a husband and father, capable of sustaining the same relations as man, of feeling and indulging the same passions. We can say, then, in a sense, that every Greek deity was incarnate, none lived an unembodied spiritual life. But incarnation so universalized ceases to have any significance; it belongs to the idea of deity, not to his acts; is a necessary quality of his essence, not a state voluntarily assumed. Where God is so conceived, Divine Sonship becomes as natural and proper to Him as to man. Belief in it is a logical necessity. Men feel that without it their notion of deity would remain inconsistent and incomplete. And so the theogonic myths, so far from offending, pleased and satisfied the early Greek mind, seemed to it a native and integral element of the conception of God. But the Hebrew, who conceived God as spiritual, invisible, lifted above every creature, everything creaturely, filling eternity, filling immensity, could not while his old idea stood conceive Him as becoming incarnate, or as sustaining the relation of a Father to a Divine yet human Son. Into the latter conception elements entered so abhorrent to the former that the one could live only by the death of the other. The conditions that allow the old and the new to be affiliated as parent and child are here absent.

The belief, then, embodied in our narratives was not a natural product of Judaism, and cannot be explained by any normal evolution of thought within it. Yet the men who made and first held it were Jews, and their two most creative personalities were men of intensely Hebraic natures. Paul was a strong type of the scholastic Jew, the man trained in the methods, skilled in the dialectic of

THE BIRTH AND INFANCY. 43

the schools; Peter was a thorough representative of the unlettered class, stalwart, robust in mind, faithful to ideas and duties consecrated by ancient custom, not very open in eye and heart to new lights and loves. Paul was possessed by the prejudices of the school, Peter by the prejudices of the people; and in the various orders of prejudices these may claim to rank as the most invincible. And if anything could have heightened the native Jewish aversion to the ideas of Divine Sonship and Incarnation, it must have been the life and death of Christ. The men who had known Him, who had seen His poverty, who had watched His sufferings, who had witnessed the agony and impotence of His tragic end, must have had these so woven into their very idea of Him, that He and they could never be conceived as dissociated or apart. Yet this was the very person they were to conceive as the Son of their awful and eternal God, as the manifestation in the flesh of their Almighty Maker and Lord of men. It is impossible that any imagination possessed by the Jewish conception of God, and filled by the recollection of the poverty, suffering, and crucifixion of Christ, could ever, by a process purely mythical, have placed that God and this Christ in the relations expressed by the terms Sonship and Incarnation.

The men, then, did not pass by an easy and natural transition from their old to their new belief. They were, we might almost say, driven to the new in spite of the old, and the forces that drove them were revolutionary. There occurred a great and creative change in their conception of God. The God of the Jews was eternal, almighty, august, yet He was the God of the Jews only, loved them, loved no other people. But the God the disciples came to know through Jesus Christ was the God of men, a Being of universal benevolence, of love that embraced the world and sought its good. He pitied like a

Father, was a Father, and every man was His child. But this new conception seemed to involve two great consequences, the first as to the nature of God, the second as to His relations to man. As to the first, it was seen that He could not be essential and eternal love and be essentially or have been eternally solitary. Love is a social affection, and is impossible without society. Love of self is selfishness, and so it was necessary to conceive a God who is love and loves as having another than Himself, who stood over against Himself, made society, received and reciprocated His affection. An object is as necessary to love as a subject, and so Divine love is possible only where there is Divine society; in other words, there can be no eternal Father unless there be an eternal Son, His mirror and reflection. But God so conceived ceases to be the barren and abstract God of Judaism, becomes the living Father in heaven, in whom, through Jesus Christ, we believe, and to whom He taught us to pray. And so from the first a second consequence followed—the Divine relation to man was conceived in a grander and sweeter and more perfect way. Man was God's child, owed Him a child's obedience and love ; was true to the Divine idea of His nature only as he gave to its Giver what was His due. His relation to God did not depend on his descent from a particular patriarch : everywhere and always he stood by obedience, fell by disobedience ; but even after and from his fall he could be saved by the grace, which meant the love, of God. And as He loved all, He loved to see none perish, to see all saved. He could do nothing else and nothing less, His nature being love. But since it was so He could not refuse sympathy, could not deny sacrifice, when by these alone men could be reached and saved. And so out of the new thought of God which came by Jesus Christ there issued by natural and necessary growth the belief in the only begotten Son in the bosom of the Father, who had come forth to declare Him. The relations of God to His world were the copy and counterpart of relations immanent and essential to God Himself; and the love in God to God which we express by the terms Father and Son became at once the source and image of the love expressed to man by the facts of incarnation and sacrifice.

The change thus effected in the fundamental conception of the disciples made its presence felt everywhere. It set the person, the life, the death of Jesus in a new light —created as to Him an order of ideas that can be understood only when the Prologue to the Fourth Gospel is made to underlie the opening narratives of the First and Third. It set Him, too, in a new relation to man, made Him the centre and head of humanity, to whom the past centuries had pointed, from whom the coming centuries were to flow. His appearance was no accident, no Divine chance, the more miraculous the less designed; but the fulfilment of a gracious Divine purpose, or rather a sublime Divine necessity, which was yet but the means to highest Divine ends. And so the new faith was at once transforming and transfiguring, made the poverty of Christ the wealth of the world, the humiliation of the Son the condition of glorifying the Father, and His death the power of God unto our salvation.

III.

THE GROWTH AND EDUCATION OF JESUS: HIS PERSONALITY.

THE Person of Christ is the perennial glory and strength of Christianity. If the life of our faith had depended on its signs and wonders, it had perished long ago. If they win the ages of wonder they offend the ages of inquiry; and as the world grows in years credulous spirits die and critical spirits increase. But the Person that stands at the centre of our faith can never cease to be winsome while men revere the holy and love the good. His moral loveliness has been as potent to charm the human spirit into obedience as the harp of the ancient mythical musician was to charm nature into listening and life; has by its soft strong spell held the wicked till he ceased to sin and learned to love, and the tender and guileless heart of a child began to beat within his breast.

The Person of Christ makes the Christian faith, is its sacred source and highest object. In it lie hidden the causes of what He afterwards became. Circumstances did not make Him; God did. Thousands lived under the same conditions, in the midst of the same society, under the same heaven, in communion with the same nature, were born in the same faith, nurtured in the same schools and under the same influences; yet of these thousands not one can be named with even the most distant claim to be compared or matched with Jesus.

And why from among the many millions living in His own land and time did He alone become the Christ? The ultimate answer must be sought in His nature, in His person. That was His own, not given by man, but by God, full of the potencies that have blossomed into the glorious Being that has overlooked and ruled the ages. Education can educe, but cannot produce; circumstances may plant and water, but they cannot create; the increase must be given of God. Where the eminence is so pre-eminent and peculiar, the name that best expresses the nature and relations of Him who achieved it is the one proper to Jesus alone among men, "the Son of God."

The Person of Jesus stands in the most intimate and organic relation with His words and acts. Here the speaker and thing spoken are, while distinguishable and different, inseparable. The teaching of Jesus is His articulated character, His Person the realized religion of Christ. The more the Person is studied the better should the religion be understood; in the former the latter finds its creative source. Of the works Jesus performed, the greatest must ever remain Himself, since beyond all question the grandest element in Christianity is Christ. But if we are to know what He was as a result, we must, in some measure at least, know how He became it. He was not an abnormal being, an artificial or mechanical product, but a growth. His manhood developed out of a youth which had beneath it boyhood, childhood, and infancy. For the perfect man could be perfect only as His becoming was throughout human. A being sent full-formed into the world had been a monstrosity—a stranger to our kind, like us, perhaps, in form, unlike us in everything essential and distinctive. But He who came to lift us from our evil came to do it in and through our nature, and in Him it orbed into the one perfect Person that has at once dignified and redeemed humanity. And so He has made the world feel that while He hates evil He loves man, and men can cry to Him—

> Be near us when we climb or fall ·
> Ye watch, like God, the rolling hours,
> With larger, other eyes than ours,
> To make allowance for us all.

The growth of Christ must, then, be considered natural: strictly so alike in its physical, intellectual. and ethical aspects. His manhood can be real only as it remains a manhood realized within the limits necessary to man. The supernatural in Jesus did not exist for Jesus, but for the world. What He achieved for others might manifest the superhuman; what He achieved in Himself showed the human — humanity under its common conditions, obedient to its own, or rather its Maker's laws, become perfect, the realization of its eternal ideal or archetype as it exists in God. But one so conceived is not remote from God—rather is penetrated and possessed by Him. His humanity is full of the Divine—is a Divine humanity. Yet it is so for moral rather than physical reasons, because of spiritual rather than essential relationships. Were His humanity but a mask for His divinity, it would be illusive, without the meaning that belongs to truth, or the strength that belongs to reality. But if we must hold the reality of His manhood we must not shrink from the idea of His growth. Luke, at least, did not. He[1] exhibits the marvellous boy as increasing in wisdom and stature, and in favour with God and man.

But this growth cannot be well conceived apart from the scenes and influences amid and under which it went on. These, therefore, need to be collected into a more or less coherent picture. We must begin with His Home. It was at Nazareth, a town which survives almost un-

[1] Luke ii. 52.

HIS PERSONALITY.

changed to this day. Its narrow streets, tall houses, here and there almost meeting overhead, its still life, flowing undisturbed by the thoughts that move and the fears that agitate the great world, are now much as they were then. The home was poor. Joseph was an artizan, and Mary, woman of all work as well as mother. Their house would be of the common Eastern type, house and workshop in one, lighted mostly by the door, the light showing curiously mingled the furniture of the family and the tools of the mechanic.[1] The daily fare would be humble enough; everywhere the signs of less meanness perhaps, but more poverty than need be found in the home of our modern carpenter. The circumstances were not propitious to magnanimity, to wealth and majesty of soul. Town and home were alike insignificant, poor. Nazareth was a remote place, neither loved by the Jew nor admired by the Gentile. It was not a centre into which the wise of many lands gathered, where the words of the mighty dead were studied, and their spirits unsphered. Small as to population, secluded as to position, it nestled in its quiet nook, undisturbed by the march of armies, or the stiller but grander march of mind. There Jesus grew, His genial soul making the soil genial, unwatered by strange dews, unwarmed by alien suns, in breeding, a Child of Moses, in birth, "the Son of God."

But the home is made by the Parents; they determine its ethical and intellectual character. For the Hebrew the home had pre-eminent sanctity; his religion dignified and blessed it. Paternity was honourable, the sign of Divine favour, children being "the heritage of the Lord." Honour to parents was the highest and best rewarded human duty, stood second only to the honour due to God. The children God gave man was to teach; He who made the family was to receive its homage. And so the home

[1] Renan, *Vie de Jésus*, c. ii.

was to be a school for religion : the father was to instruct his children, and command them that "they shall keep the way of the Lord, to do justice and judgment."[1] Parents and children in Israel had thus a sanctity to each other unknown to the men of Greece and Rome; their relations were throughout religious, consecrated by God and defined by His law. And if we may interpret the home at Nazareth through the mind and speech of Jesus, it must have been an ideal Hebrew home. It is but reasonable to suppose that in His later teaching His earlier experiences are in part reflected. "Father" is a name He so uses as to show that for Him it was steeped in the fondest and tenderest associations, was the symbol of loved memories and endeared relationships. In the picture of the father who cannot resist his child's pleading,[2] or the still grander picture of one who knows how to forgive and restore a penitent son, and how to rebuke and forgive a son hyper- because hypo- critical,[3] we seem to have features that could be painted only by a hand guided by a heart that had known before the imagination had created. Even within "Our Father which art in heaven" there may live a transfigured earthly reminiscence, the recollection of a father who had passed into the heavens. Childhood, too, is beautiful to Jesus, the manifest image of a time when He lived, sheltered and tended by prescient love.[4] Years that were so sunny to memory could not have been bitter to experience, must have been possessed of the light and love that are to the heart of man as the life of God. Then He learned the value and the strength of human affection, the holy and beautiful love that in the child responds to the brooding and creative love of the parent.

Beside the home there stood the School. The Jew loved education, to him instruction in the Law was the

[1] Gen. xviii. 19.   [2] Matt. vii. 9-11.   [3] Luke xv. 11, ff.
[4] Matt. xviii. 1-6, 10-14, xix. 13-15.

HIS PERSONALITY.

most important concern in life. Josephus boasted that the study of it commenced with the first dawn of consciousness, and was so conducted as to involve both knowledge and action.[1] While the Spartans were anxious about practice, and the Athenians and other Greeks about theory, the Hebrew Lawgiver had so carefully bound both together, that to be well instructed in the Law was not only to know its doctrine, but to observe its precepts.[2] He declared that He had had so full and accurate a knowledge of the Law in His fourteenth year, that He was consulted by the chief priests and first men of the city.[3] Philo, too, says that the Jews were from their earliest youth so instructed in the Law as to bear in their souls its very image.[4] This love of education, this zeal for instruction in the Law, was one of the most distinctive features in Judaism. And so it was a favourite axiom, " He who knows not the Law is accursed."[5] Rabbi Hillel had said, "An ignorant can never be a really pious man;" and "the more instruction in the Law, the more life, the more of the great school, the greater the wisdom; the more counsel, the more reasonable the conduct. He who attains knowledge of the Law, gains life in the world to come."[6] Rabbi Chananya ben Teradyon said, " If two sit together and speak not of the Law, then are they a company of mockers, of whom it is said, ' Sit not where the mockers sit.' But if two sit together and speak of the Law, then is the shechina present with them."[7]

Since enthusiasm for the Law and its study so possessed the Jew, Jesus could not have remained uninstructed. Schools, indeed, in the modern, or in any formal sense, He could hardly have known. There were, indeed, famous schools in Jerusalem, but no evidence that in the

[1] *Contra Apion*, II, 18. [2] Ibid. II, 16, 17. [3] *Vita*, 2.
[4] *Legat. ad Cajum*, § 31; Ed. Mang., II. 577.
[5] John vii. 59 [6] *Pirke Aboth*, II 5, 7. [7] Ibid. III. 2.

time of Jesus any existed in Nazareth. The wonder both of Nazareth and Jerusalem as to how He had come by His wisdom, and as to how He knew His letters,[1] proves that He had not been educated in any school. Yet He must have had teachers. He knew letters, could read the Scriptures, was familiar with the interpretations of tradition and the school.[2] We may well believe that His parents had been His earliest teachers. An authority no Hebrew could despise bound them to teach their children the law and the words of God.[3] The proverbs the Jew loved, the short pregnant sayings into which were condensed the experience and wisdom of the ancients, were taught the child by father and mother alike.[4] Then there was the synagogue, which, as Philo says,[5] was everywhere an "institution for teaching prudence and bravery, temperance and justice, piety and holiness; in brief, every virtue which the human and Divine recognises and enjoins." Here Jesus must often have been, and here His wondrous open soul must have learned by every sense. In the society of the worshippers He would enter into the fellowship of Israel, become conscious of affinities that would awaken many sympathies, especially with the sins, the sorrows, the hopes, the aspirations of man. There, too, as He listened to the skilled yet childish interpretation of the Law, as He watched the masked yet apparent struggles for place, He may have learned to understand the scribes and Pharisees. The synagogue may have been the school that instructed Him in the *idola* of the human heart, showed Him how man could be so loyal to his own dreams and doctrines as to be faithless to Divine realities and truths. But with Him to see the folly and weakness

---

[1] Matt. xiii. 54; Mark vi. 2; John vii. 15.
[2] Matt. xii. 3, xix. 4; Luke iv. 16; Matt. xv. 1-9, xxiii. 2, ff., v 17-20; Mark xii. 35.
[3] Deut. xi 19.   [4] Prov. 1 8, xxxi. 1.
[5] *Vita Moses*, lib. iii § 27, Mang., ii. 168.

of man was only the better to know the wisdom and strength of God. As He sat listening to the voices of heaven and earth, now blending in strange sweet music, and again meeting in sad deep discord, what thoughts, what visions of man's struggle towards God and God's endeavour to reach man must have come to Him! In experiences like these the Christ would find teachers qualifying Him to be a merciful and faithful High Priest, compassionate to the ignorant while dutiful to righteousness and truth.

Then, His study of the Scriptures must have been an eminently educative study. His knowledge of them was so great as to astonish the scribes and Pharisees, as well as the people. Such knowledge was possible only to years of study and meditation, and years so spent must have been full of the noblest formative and informative influences. Those old Hebrew books, with their great thoughts as to God, their strong faith in His righteous rule and high purposes, their record of man's sin and error, yet resolute and pathetic endeavour after the light, must have enabled the mind of the Christ to penetrate as from below the mysteries of the Divine nature, to see as from above the miseries of the human. And as He became conscious of their meaning, He must also have discovered that light did not always signify sight, that in man false or half-vision often made the luminous worse than the dark. And so the Scriptures would awaken Him to the unity of the ages, the kinship of the earliest with the latest, the grand Divine purpose that man in all his times and families was fulfilling, though seldom with the consciousness that his acts were being used to promote, the ends of God. He has been to us the interpretation of the Scriptures, the fulfilment of the Law and the Prophets; but before He could be so to us they must have been as an interpreter to Him, revealing Himself to Himself, translating, as it were, reminiscence into knowledge. Study of the written word became fellowship with the Living Will, and the visible Son rested consciously in the embrace of the invisible Father.

But Nature is to the spirit that loves her as great an educator as the Scriptures. The modern poet that knew and loved her best has made us feel how she can teach and exalt, creating

> sensations sweet,
> Felt in the blood, and felt along the heart,
> And passing even into our purer mind,
> With tranquil restoration;

how in her presence one can hear " the still sad music of humanity," and enjoy

> that serene and blessed mood
> In which the affections gently lead us on,
> Until the breath of this corporeal frame,
> And even the motions of our human blood,
> Almost suspended, we are laid asleep
> In body, and become a living soul.

Now, the purest, calmest Spirit earth has known could not but find nature a translucent veil revealing the Father it seemed to conceal. Nazareth is said to lie amid beauties. The hill which rises behind the city looks upon a scene of rarest loveliness; mountains that uplift their snowy heads to a heaven that stoops to kiss them; valleys fruitful, vineclad, swelling into soft ridges, melting into a plain that slopes in lines of rich beauty to the distant sea. And the scene must have been familiar to His eye, all its objects terms in which He and heaven could speak to each other, its moods moments when Father and Son could stand, as it were, face to face. His words show how full His mind was of Nature and the truths she teaches to those that in loving her love her Maker. The brooding heaven, so distant yet so near, where shone the sun that

HIS PERSONALITY.

enlightened the earth, whence came the rain and the heat that fertilized it, was at once the home and symbol of His Father.[1] The lily, clothed with a loveliness which shamed the splendour of Solomon; the skimming swallows by dutiful diligence to-day making care for to-morrow vain and undutiful; the sparrow that, while unloved of man, yet lived and multiplied; the sower going out to sow; the green blade breaking through the dark soil; the fields yellowing for the sickle; the fig-tree throwing out its leaves; the vine, with its hanging clusters and grateful juices,[2] had attracted His eyes, filled Him with a sense of the beauty that is everywhere in nature, of the Divine care that pervades everything and protects all life. Nature bears to us another and nobler meaning since He lived, and the meaning He found for us He must have first found for Himself. As He walked, "in pious meditation, fancy fed," on the hill that overlooks Nazareth, through the vineyards and corn-fields that clothe its slopes; as He stood on the shores of Gennesareth, watching the calm heaven mirrored in the calm lake, His spirit in the degree that it opened to nature opened to God, and humanity became in Him conscious of its Divine affinities, at one with the Father.

But man cannot be educated without Society; his nature cannot develop all its energies or breathe out all its fragrance in solitude. The teacher of man must know men, must be taught of men, that he may teach man. And Jesus was not denied the education society alone can give. He had the discipline that comes of social duty. He was a Son and Brother, fulfilled the duties proper to relations so near and tender, experienced and enjoyed the affections

[1] Matt. v. 34, 45; vi 9.
[2] Matt. vi. 25, 26, 28-30, x 29, 31; Luke xii. 6, 7; Matt xiii. 3, ff; Mark iv. 28; John iv. 35, Matt xxi. 19, xxiv 32, xxvi. 21; John xv. 1, ff.

that brighten the home. He was not a father, yet it is almost certain that He knew paternal cares. He was the first, but not the only child of Mary; and it is more than probable that Joseph died during the youth or early manhood of Jesus. On the death of the father, the eldest Son would inherit his responsibilities, become the guardian and bread-winner of the family. And so to Him was granted the Divine discipline of toil, of labour for the bread that perisheth, yet undergone because of relations that are imperishable. Work for home is a noble education. It makes man forethoughtful, unselfish, dutiful to the weak, tender to the sorrowful, mindful of the loving. It had been a calamity to Himself and His mission had our Christ been deprived of so grand yet so universal a discipline. He was not, and it was, perhaps, the condition of His sympathy with poverty and toil. His own mother may have been the widow that cast her mite into the treasury,[1] and his own may have been a heart pierced and touched by a child's cry for bread.[2] The education of Christ has been the education of man. What He learned in society and the home has helped Him to soften the heart and sweeten the relations of society throughout the world.

But we must now study the Personality formed under these varied influences. It was unique, a new embodiment of humanity, unlike anything that had been realized in Israel, or indeed in the world. He was no scribe or Pharisee, no shining example of conventional goodness or the traditional in character and conduct. While He had been educated in Galilee and within Judaism, He was no Jew, transcended in every way the moral and historical ideals of His race. The ideal of the scribes was narrow enough to be easily imitable in the schools; and the virtues they practised but reflected and expressed the law they studied and praised. Their characters were often very

[1] Mark xii 42.   [2] Matt vii 9.

HIS PERSONALITY.

beautiful, marked by a fine simplicity and truth which adorned and illustrated their homely wisdom. Thus Hillel, zealous in his study of the law, but too poor to pay the entrance fee to the Beth-ha-Midrasch, clambers in the cold winter season up to the window sill, that he may there listen to the voice of the instructor within, and listens till he is found stiff with cold by the astonished teacher and scholars.[1] So his distinguished rival, Schammai, thinks the fit celebration of a feast a matter so vital that when his daughter-in-law bears a boy during one, he has her bed made into the likeness of a tabernacle in order that the new-born child may keep the feast after the manner prescribed in the law.[2] And these are typical cases. The pre-eminent virtues are zeal to know what has been delivered and scrupulous obedience to it. Knowledge of the law is the chief good; a conformity to it that knows no distinction between great and little, essential and accidental, the noblest virtue. But this ideal involves an increative particularism; the new is the false, the original the wrong. The knowledge most prized was remembrance —Rabbi Eliezer was praised as "a well-trough that loses not a drop of water;"—the moral faculty most esteemed the ability to imitate or reproduce. So peculiar and particular was the ideal of the schools that it could not have been either understood or realized outside Judaism. The man perfect according to the rabinnical standard could not have been defined as a man, but only as a Jew, had been no citizen of the world, but only a child of Moses or son of the Law. But Jesus was the opposite of all this, of a character so universal that He can only be described as the Man, of a nature so humane that He is to us as realized humanity. He created a type of manhood so absolutely original that it had no fellow in his present or past; yet so absolutely

[1] Delitzsch, *Jesus und Hillel*, pp. 9-11.
[2] *Sukka*, 11, 8.

true that the world has ever since said, "If man is ever to be perfect, he must be as Jesus was." And so He is as little of a Greek as of a Jew, He can be placed in no one of the ethico-national categories of His own or any time. He does more than embody Plato's dream of the righteous man, for His righteousness far exceeds the righteousness imagined by the Greeks. It was but conformity to the instituted, obedience to the laws established by man and approved of God; but Christ's was a creative type, great by its very transcendence of what had been instituted and its might to institute what was to be.

In studying the Personality that developed under the agencies and influences just described, we are thus forced to see that they were not creative or constitutive, but only occasional or conditional. It was too transcendental a product to be the work of a mere empirical factor, and finds its material cause in the living Person, though its formal in the conditions under which He lived. And this becomes the more apparent when we analyze its contents and qualities. We cannot, indeed, see the process, only the result. The man in germ, the Personality in the making, we see but once,[1] yet the once is almost enough. The Child has come with His parents to Jerusalem. The city, the solemnities, the temple, the priests, the sacrifices, the people, have stirred multitudinous new thoughts in the marvellous boy. He becomes for the moment forgetful of His kin, conscious of higher and diviner relations, and seeks light and sympathy where they were most likely to be found—in the temple, and with the doctors. It is an eminently natural and truthful incident. The ideal Child, wise in His innocent simplicity, seeks the society of simple but learned age, feels at home in it, wonders only, when sought and found, that it could be in His mother's mind other than it was in His own. The light that streams from the question,

[1] Luke ii. 41, ff.

"'Wist ye not that I must be among my Father's matters,' in his house, in search of his truth, mindful of his purposes?" illumines the youth, and makes Him foreshadow the man. For He who as boy was anxious to be absorbed in His Father and His Father's affairs, became as man the conscious abode of God. Here, indeed, emerges the sublimest and most distinctive feature of His Personality. In Him, as in no other, God lived; He lived as no other ever did in God. Their communion was a union which authorized the saying, "I and the Father are one;" "He that hath seen me hath seen the Father." His consciousness was full of God, was consciousness of God. Fellowship with man did not lessen it; solitude only made it more real. The society of the sinful did not disturb his serene certainty, or becloud for a moment His sense of the indwelling Presence. Amid faithless friends and bitter foes, in the shadow of His doom and the exhaustion of His great sorrow, in the agony of the garden, the desertion and death of the cross, He was never without the clear and certain consciousness of the Father's presence. And this so distinctive feature of His Personality has made Him of pre-eminent religious significance. Since Jesus lived, God has been another and nearer Being to man; and the reason lies in that universal and ideal significance of His Person which made it a symbol as well as a reality, and a symbol which showed that what God was to Jesus He might be to every man, what Jesus was to God every man ought to be. He who sails across an unknown sea and finds beyond it a continent is named a discoverer; and so Jesus, in the region of the Spirit, standing where no one in human form ever stood before, found a new relation to God, and became the Founder of a new religion for man. His Personality became the creative type of a new and more filial relation to God: since His day we have inherited the spirit of sons, and can cry, "Abba, Father."

But His relation to Man was in its kind and degree as perfect as His relation to God. It rested on a conception, at once truthful and generous. He conceived God as He is, and loved Him because He is Love; He conceived man as he ought to be, and loved him for the sake of the Divine ideal hidden under the depraved reality. Jesus loved holiness and hated sin. Evil was not in Himself, and His aversion to it was the radical and invincible aversion of a whole and holy nature. Yet He did not allow His hatred of the sin to become hatred of the sinners. He discovered within the evil a soul of good, and, what was even more, made them conscious of the discovery and the promise it contained. Men offensive to the traditional and typical religious character are seldom treated with mercy. A double and ineradicable suspicion almost always stands in the way of reaching and restoring outcasts— their suspicion of the respectable and the religious, and the suspicion the respectable and religious have of them. A studiously correct society has ever found excommunication and exclusion of the evil easier and safer than reconciliation and restoration. But Jesus made His way to the outcasts, became their Friend in order that they might become His, and as His, friends of righteousness. Men whose goodness was of the conventional type thought they had condemned Him when they had named Him "the friend of publicans and sinners." But His friendship was justified by its results; it did not make *Him* a publican and a sinner, while it made men who were either or both friends of righteousness and truth. His relation to the evil was absolutely unique. He did not satirize or sneer at the sins and follies of men, like the cynic. Cynicism does not so much hate evil as despise folly; and, while it may keep the respectable from open vice, it can never restore the vicious to virtue. He did not, like the conventional moralist, hold Himself aloof from the fallen.

The separation he enjoins may prevent the deterioration of the good, but can never promote the amelioration of the bad. Jesus, on the other hand, did not allow the man's evil to hide the man—saw that he was a man in spite of the evil. In every one there was an actual and an ideal—the actual might be His own, but the ideal was God's. Whatever the man might have made himself, there still remained the possibility of his becoming what God had intended him to be. And this belief of the Divine possibility within the depraved reality made Jesus seek, that He might save, the lost. The goodness He incarnated could vanquish man's evil, while the evil could not vanquish it. He had the purity which could see the best things in the worst man as well as the holiest and loveliest things in God; and when purity is hopeful of the impure, the impure themselves can hardly despair. And so the hope that lived in the Saviour was planted in the lost; what He believed possible they too came to believe, and the belief was at once translated into sublime and singular reality—the lost were saved.

But the relation of Jesus to Righteousness was as perfect as His relation to God and man. His moral ideal was the highest. He lived to do the will of God. His beatitudes were moral, the good was the blessed man. But it is significant that one whose ethical ideal was so exalted had Himself no consciousness of sin, confessed to no sense of guilt, to no failure in obedience. In one constituted like Jesus, to be without the sense of sin was to be sinless, to be conscious of no disobedience was to have always obeyed. And this becomes the more evident when His goodness is seen to be spontaneous, without effort, the free and joyous outcome of a nature so happy as to have been always holy. His calm and serene soul knew no struggle, no conflict of the flesh and spirit such as made the experience of His greatest apostle so tragic. He knew sorrow, but it was the sorrow of the heart that weeps for sin, not of the conscience that reproves it. And the character that expressed this spontaneous obedience was a harmony of blended opposites. He was so gentle as to draw the love and trust of little children, as to conquer the suspicion and fear the fallen ever feel towards the holy; but He was so stern as to rebuke hypocrisy in words that still burn, so strong as to resist evil till it vanquished His life in revenge for its failure to vanquish His will. He was " meek and lowly in heart," had no love for place or power, no lust of wealth or position, no craving for the fame that is the last infirmity of noble minds; but yet He claimed a majesty so august that beside it Cæsar's was the merest mock royalty. He had singular independence, a will so strong that nothing could unfix its resolution or divert it from its chosen path; but yet He was so dependent that in His deepest agony He sought the sympathy and presence of man. These features of His character are but phases of His obedience. The principle that rules Him is one, the forms which express His loyalty to it are many. His nature is good, and His goodness spontaneous, but it ever assumes the aspect appropriate to the moments of His many-sided and significant life.

These phases and features of His Personality emerge in His teaching, give to it its most distinctive characteristics. His words as to God but express truths represented in His own relation to the Father. The love from heaven that filled and surrounded His soul became articulate in His sayings and parables. What He experienced He expressed; the God He knew He made known; and as we enter into the truth He embodied and revealed, we enter into a relation to the Father akin to His. And as He thought, felt, and acted towards man, so He taught concerning Him. His words witness to His faith in the Divine possibilities that still live in the most depraved man, and witness, too,

HIS PERSONALITY.

to the yearning of the Supreme Goodness we call God after His broken and buried image. The parables that speak of the shepherd that seeks till He finds His lost lamb; of the woman that lights the candle and searche for the coin she can ill spare; of the father who watches for the return of the prodigal, and receives him with weeping joy; represent the Divine side of His mission, the attitude of His own unique Personality to the fallen and outcast. And the sermons and parables that enforce and illustrate the righteousness He loved, the virtues He instituted or made possible, obedience of the one righteous Will, imitation of the perfect God, forgiveness, prayerfulness, truthfulness, purity, faith, charity, love to the stranger, sympathy with the suffering, tenderness to the fallen, only describe and enjoin the ideals He had realized, the graces that were personalized in Him. He who rightly apprehends the relation of the Personality to the teaching of Christ will understand why He was and is " full of grace and truth."

IV.

THE BAPTIST AND THE CHRIST.

NATURE begins and perfects her finest works in secrecy and silence. No eye has yet seen the subtle agents at work which weave for her the rich-coloured sweet-smelling garments of summer, or strip her naked and leave her desolate in the cold and gloom of winter. No ear has heard the footsteps or the swift-moving tools of the mechanics who in her secret yet open workshop build minute crystals or mighty mountains, or those varied and wondrous organisms that make up our living world. Nature is here but the mirror or parable of mind ; its growth is a silent process, the swelling till it bursts of the bud under the soft but potent pressure of forces that struggle from without inwards, only that they may the more harmoniously work from within outwards. So in a pre-eminent degree was it with Christ. We can study and describe His historical appearance, can analyze and estimate the educative influences that surrounded His boyhood and youth ; but we cannot see the mysterious personal force that at once used and unified these influences and created that appearance. Yet the forces active in the process become manifest in the result, and from it we can infer what kind of architects and builders were needed to plan and rear the substructure of the splendid moral edifice that, as the sinless Man, commands humanity. What was apparent had its source in what was veiled, and revealed it, just as the roots of the glorious flower are bedded deep in the sapful soil; but the thing of beauty and of fragrance into which they blossom tells of the wondrous alchemy that has in silence and in darkness been changing the juices of earth and the sunbeams of heaven into an object of sweetness and delight.

The growth of Jesus was not hurried and forced, but slow and natural. For more than thirty years He tarried at Nazareth, waiting till His strength had matured and His manhood was complete. Then His hour was struck in tones audible to Himself and His people. The tongue that told it came from the banks of the Jordan and the waste places about the Dead Sea. There a New Prophet had appeared, ancient in manners and spirit, modern in speech and purpose. No sleek scribe, no pompous priest, or courtier clad in soft raiment was he; but a son of the desert, clad in garments of coarse camels' hair, bound round him by a leathern girdle, seeking his food from the rock where the wild bee left its honey, and the locust came—a man full of the stern spirit of solitude and the thoughts God speaks to the soul that can dare to be alone. He called himself a Voice, but he was not like the still small voice the Prophet had heard in his mountain cave; he was rather like the wind and the fire that broke in pieces the rocks, heralds as they were of the low sweet voice that was to come out of the silence they left. People from the banks of the Jordan crowded to hear him. His fame reached Jerusalem, and Sadducees and Pharisees, scribes and priests, publicans and sinners, went forth to listen, and be awed into a passing reverence and faith. West and east, south and north, the tidings spread, reached remote Nazareth, and woke great emotions in the home of the Carpenter there. He who had become, since Joseph was not, the head and bread-winner of the little family, knew that His hour was come, and went forth, the son of Joseph, to return the Messiah of God.

Now, this New Prophet is full of the deepest and most varied significance for the history of Christ. He not only marks the moment of His emergence from obscurity, but is, as it were, its occasional cause. The only historical authority that does not recognize this relation is Josephus, whose silence as to Jesus is the most eloquent tribute of Jewish antiquity to the transcendent, and to it inexplicable, importance of our Christ. Our other authorities show us Jesus coming, obscure, undistinguished, to John, mingling with the crowds that throng the banks of the Jordan; but when the wave of excitement subsides, John has vanished, Jesus alone stands, the end for which the Baptist has lived, the fulfilment of his prophecy and completion of his mission.

The Baptist is one of the greatest of the minor characters in either the Hebrew or Christian Scriptures. His career is short, and his work transitional, but his influence is at once penetrative and permanent. His ministry exercised an immense power—made, while it lasted, Judæa contrite and earnest, Galilee penitent and wistful; remained, when it had long ceased, a memory so moving, as to touch the courtier heart of Josephus with reverence and admiration. Each of our Gospels is a witness to his eminence. Love of him distinguished alike Jesus and the Jews. To Jesus he was the very greatest of the prophets.[1] His name was so potent as to subdue the arrogance, if it did not extort the respect, of the Pharisees;[2] so noble as to rouse and retain the devotion of the crowd.[3] So full was he of the inspiration of God, that he not only dared to be a prophet in an age of priestcraft and formalism, but even compelled it to listen to him.[4] So possessed was he of a lofty humility, that he retired before a greater, proudly confessing that he was, and had lived to be, superseded.[5]

[1] Matt. xi 9–11. [2] Matt. iii. 7; John i 19–25. [3] Mark xi. 30–32.
[4] Matt iii 5. [5] Matt. iii. 11, John iii. 27–30.

He evoked from the Old Testament the spirit that inaugurated the New, and so became the meeting-point of both, a symbol of the dawn, which is at once the death of the night and the birth of the day. So the man and his mission must be studied if the Christ is to be understood.

There is no need to discuss here the story of John's birth. Enough to say, he sprang from an old priestly stock, both parents being of Aaronic descent. He was a child of age, and there is in age a simplicity that may make its home more sweetly child-like than the home of youth. His birthplace was a city in the hill country of Judæa, possibly Hebron, the old regal and priestly city of Judah. There a simple and sincere faith would live, utterly unlike the formal and official religion that reigned at Jerusalem. If the father may be interpreted through the son, we can say that Zacharias was no priest of the Saducean type, apt at clothing secular ambitions in sacerdotal forms; no scribe too well skilled in tradition to be familiar with the spirit and the truth that lived in the ancient Scriptures. His son at least was no child of policy and tradition, but of prophecy and freedom. He was not trained in the schools of his people. One authority[1] represents him as passing his youth in the desert, and his speech seems to breathe its atmosphere and reflect its images—the stones that mocked the culture of man, but illustrated the creative power of God; the viper-brood curled and concealed among the rocks; the olive-trees, sending their roots far into the dry and stony soil, without finding moisture enough to become fruitful. His bearing, too, and spirit are of the desert. He was scornful of society, independent of its companionships and comforts;[2] was not clad in soft raiment, or distinguished by supple and courtly grace; was no reed shaken by the wind, but a

[1] Luke i. 80. [2] Luke vii. 33

gnarled oak the wind could neither bend nor break.[1] Yet his solitude was society: it enabled him to escape the Rabbis and find the Prophets. The priest by birth became a prophet by Divine nurture, so steeped in the thought and speech of the ancient seers as to seem, alike to the faith and imagination of his time, the greatest of them resurgent. He so speaks the language of Isaiah as to show who had been the great companion of his solitude.[2] His ideas of repentance, the kingdom, judgment, righteousness, were prophetic, not priestly; and the emphasis with which he declared himself a "Voice" showed that in him the ancient *Nabi*, the speaker for God, had revived. And this prophetic nurture and character sets him in radical antithesis to the ascetic fraternities of his time. He is no Essene—can be as little relegated to an anchorite as to a Pharisaic order. He was no selfish lover of his own soul, too fearful of pollution to touch society, but a magnanimous reformer, great in his love alike of man and of righteousness. The Essene hated flesh, but John ate without scruple the locust of the desert. The ascetic communities were great in ablutions, but John had only his baptism, an ablutionary rite but once administered, and without meaning, save as expressive of a moral change and prophetic of the baptism of Him who was to baptize with the Holy Ghost and with fire. He did not believe in regeneration by separation, in saving the soul by forsaking the world. That to him was but a deeper loss. He believed in a kingdom of heaven which was a kingdom on earth and of men, a society of God, to be realized in the homes they had formed and the cities they had built. And so he was too much the pupil of Divine freedom and discipline to be the child of any school, the spokesman of any sect. His faith was the fruit of inspiration as opposed

[1] Luke vii. 24, 25, Matt xi 7.
[2] John i. 23. Cf Matt iii 3, Mark i 2, 3; Luke iii 4–6.

THE BAPTIST AND THE CHRIST. 69

to experience. Contact with hard human realities had not dulled his enthusiasm, or changed his belief in the practicability of the old theocratic ideals into a belief in the wisdom and omnipotence of expediency. His education made him a preacher who lived as he believed, possessed of the courage to summon men to a like faith and life.

Distance makes many things clear. The air of the desert was more favourable to penetrative spiritual vision than the atmosphere of the city. In the desert John came to understand the past of his people as his people did not, and through it their present needs, their present duties, and the possibilities of their future. He looked at the men of his age and their needs through his great beliefs, his exalted ideas; and the contrast of the ideal and the possible with the real and the actual made the student of the desert into the Baptist and Preacher. Had Israel realized the kingdom of heaven? Did the people of God embody and fulfil His righteousness? Were they a society of brethren, dutiful, merciful, kind? Were they, by their lovely and honourable manhood, making the name of God loved and honoured? Were they making His faith so beautiful and glorious as to be a joy and attraction to the Gentiles? Nay; everywhere and in everything it was the reverse. Israel seemed farther than ever from realizing the visions that had inspired the exalted spirit of the later Isaiah; the sins that had so moved the soul of the earlier still lived, only in prouder and more magnified forms. The "new moons," the "Sabbaths," the "appointed feasts," were still celebrated, the "multitude of sacrifices," the "many prayers," the "incense," were still offered, but less than ever was the command obeyed, "Wash you, make you clean; put away the evil of your doings from before mine eyes; cease to do evil;

learn to do well; seek judgment, relieve the oppressed, judge the fatherless, plead for the widow."[1]

With the decay of prophecy had come the degeneracy of Israel. The priesthood was left free to develop the ritual to the injury of religion, the scribe to create artificial sins and an artificial conscience, the passion for ceremonial purity which is so fatal to the nobler and more generous virtues. The Sadducee said scornfully, "The Pharisees will soon clean the face of the sun;" and in his scorn he expressed this truth, that there is no surer sign of a decayed ethical and religious sense than the endeavour to cleanse what is naturally pure. The universalism of the prophets had been quenched by the particularism of the priests; the humanity of Hebraism had been buried under the nationality of Judaism. The curse of perverted being was on Israel. The law which bound to the service of man was used to create division and isolation. Even within the nation the spirit of separatism reigned. Caste is but a sacerdotal translated into a social system, and is only possible where the accidents have been turned into the essential qualities or elements of religion. The Pharisee could not touch the publican, and be clean; the priest could not help the Samaritan, and be holy. To be one of "the lost sheep of the house of Israel" was to be an outcast, and an outcast is worse than a heathen. Hillel might say,[2] "Belong to the disciples of Aaron (the meek); love peace and seek after it; love mankind and bring them to the law;" but the people, with the fanaticism of the letter, without the enthusiasm of the spirit, believed in the divinity of custom and obeyed it.

Now John emerges from his solitude, no Priest or Rabbi, but a Prophet, with a consciousness of authority

[1] Isaiah i. 16, 17
[2] *Pirke Aboth*, i. 12-14. Cf. Delitzsch, *Jesus und Hillel*, pp. 17, ff.

so clear and intense as to disdain expression. There is, indeed, in the man a wonderful self-abnegation. He never speaks of his own claims, only delivers his destined message. He is but a " Voice ; " the word it utters alone deserves thought and demands faith. When the people —anxiously curious, prepared to believe almost anything as to the new preacher — inquire, " Who is he ? the Messias ? Elias ? the prophet like to Moses ? " he has but one answer, " I am not. What I am matters nothing; what I say is matter enough."[1] But this silence as to himself is eloquent as to his greatness. The man who is, as it were, annihilated by his mission, is most magnified by it ; he becomes an organ of Deity, a voice of God, altogether silent as to his own claims, concerned only with God's. He who is so divinely possessed is insensible to the strength of the resistent forces, does his work by a kind of inspired necessity, and once it is done is content to die, or be forgotten—to decrease, that a greater may increase.

In this New Prophet, so divinely unconscious of himself, so divinely conscious of his mission, there revived the ancient conflict of his order against the ritualism of the Temple and the legalism of the Schools. He was a sort of personified revolt against the law, written and oral. The image and authority of Moses do not seem to exist for him; but the prophets, with their scorn of legal pride and privilege, ceremonial purity and observances, with their faith in the reality of righteousness and retribution, are so real to him, that he appears the very incarnation of their spirit, the embodied voice of their God. Hence his message is moral, not political. His relation to the Roman cannot be directly determined; his relation to the Jew is apparent enough. He does not think that Judaism is

[1] John i. 19–23.

the religion of Jahveh, or that Israel needs only freedom to be perfect. He can hardly be named a patriotic Jew; that is, if patriotism be fidelity to what his countrymen passionately revere. To him their national idea is abhorrent, and the attempts at realization but prove its evil. He thinks that people and rulers are alike guilty, that their supreme need is repentance, and the regeneration repentance alone can bring. The priest and the scribe had made the people of God the people of form and privilege; the prophet appears that he may command the people of form and privilege to become the people of God. National was possible only through individual regeneration. The mass could be made holy only by the units becoming holy. And the change must be immediate. The God who had borne so long with their evil would bear no longer. The kingdom of heaven was at hand;[1] its dawn stood tip-toe on the mountain top. And the King was a Judge, coming to do His own will, not the will of the Jews. What He needed was a prepared people; what He would find was a brood of vipers. To Him purity of blood was nothing, purity of heart alone was good. He was coming, fan in hand, to divide the chaff from the wheat, to gather the one into His garner, to burn up the other with unquenchable fire.

John's spirit was thus essentially ethical, and his attitude one of essential antagonism to the unethical spirit of Judaism. The people, so far from realizing, had corrupted the theocratic ideal, and had, in depraving it, depraved themselves. Hence his preaching had in its earliest form a twofold character, a minatory and a hortatory, threatened with punishment, and exhorted to repentance. "The axe was laid to the root of the tree, and the tree must either become fruitful or be hewn down."[2] But his general principles received most particular and direct application.

[1] Luke iii. 7-9, Matt iii 10. [2] Luke iii. 7-9, Matt. iii. 10.

THE BAPTIST AND THE CHRIST. 73

To the Sadducees and Pharisees, the priests and teachers of the people, responsible in the most eminent degree for the worship and faith, manners and laws, of the nation, his speech was plain and severe. They were a " generation of vipers," seeking his baptism in the hope of escaping " the wrath to come." They were foolishly proud of their Abrahamic descent, but were warned not to trust it. God was able, out of the dry stones of the desert, " to raise up children unto Abraham." [1] The advice was unsought, and the warning was unheeded. But the people were more tractable than their priests and rabbis. They asked the stern preacher, " What shall we do ? " [2] and the answer, so needed by a broken and divided nation, was, " He that hath two coats, let him impart to him that none; and he that hath meat, let him do likewise." To the publicans, who answered exclusion by extortion, he said, " Exact no more than what is due ; " to the soldiers, " Do violence to no man; accuse none falsely, and be content with your pay." These were words that became a prophet—echoes of those spoken long before. " Is not this the fast that I have chosen ? to loose the bands of wickedness, to undo the heavy burdens, and to let the oppressed go free, and that ye break every yoke ? Is it not to deal thy bread to the hungry, and that thou bring the poor that are cast out to thy house ? when thou seest the naked, that thou cover him ; and that thou hide not thyself from thine own flesh ? " [3]

But John was not satisfied with a preaching that was simply minatory and hortatory : he determined to institute a society of the penitent and reformed. It was but according to Oriental ideas that entrance into the society should be signified by a symbol. Hence the command to repent was supplemented by the command to be baptized.

[1] Matt. iii 7-9.   [2] Luke iii. 10-14.
[3] Isaiah lviii. 6, 7.

If in his preaching he far transcended Judaism, in his baptism he proved himself a true child of Judæa, a believer in the Divine worth and significance of symbols. The symbol must be interpreted by the circle of ideas in which he moved and which he variously expressed. Its suggestive cause is as hard to determine as it is unimportant. The rite may have formal affinities with the lustrations of the Essenes or the ablutions of proselytes, but it has a material significance of his own. John placed it in a relation with confession of sin and repentance that made it the symbol of certain spiritual realities—evil recognized and repudiated, good perceived and chosen. In this connection its use may have been suggested by such words as, "Wash you, make you clean;"[1] or, "In that day there shall be a fountain opened to the house of David and to the inhabitants of Jerusalem for sin and for uncleanness."[2] But his baptism was a symbol of another and no less significant fact; the baptized were not simply the penitent, but the expectant, men consecrated to a great hope. They formed a community that had renounced with their sins the older Judaism, with its civil kingdom and political Messiah, and stood expectant, waiting the coming of Him who was to baptize with the Holy Ghost and with fire. Under this aspect his baptism had affinities with events and customs dear to the Hebrew. When Moses descended from the mount to sanctify the people, he made them "wash their clothes."[3] When the Gentile became a Jew he was purified by water. What is to us a sensuous symbol was to him a translucent form of an eternal truth. What he always loved he loved most of all when it had a national significance, expressed some truth as to the relation of the people and their God. And so John was but true to the best genius of his people when he made

[1] Isaiah i. 16   [2] Zech xiii 1.   [3] Exod xix 10-14.

his baptism represent, not simply an individual change, but a social fact—entrance into a society prepared for the kingdom which was at hand. The "baptism unto repentance" was also a baptism unto hope: as the first, it was the sign of a renounced past, as the second, it was the symbol of a new future.[1]

The Baptist's idea of this new future was embodied in the phrase "the kingdom of heaven." This kingdom he interpreted in the prophetic sense as the realized reign of the righteous God. It was because his conception of the kingdom was so ethical that his condemnation of unethical Judaism was so vehement and unsparing He believed that a Divine society could be constituted only by men who were penetrated and possessed by the Divine. So his cry to his evil generation was, "Confess your sins, repent, be baptized; and, so prepared, await the coming of the day whose dawn we see." But the Kingdom implied a King. The prophets when they dreamed of the golden age dreamed of it as instituted by a Divine Prince, a Messiah. In the Messiah the hopes of Hebraism culminated; for Him it had lived, without Him its faith had died. In the days of a wicked tyranny, men could not have believed in the eternal righteousness unless they had at the same time believed in a day of victory and retribution. To the prophet the present might be man's, but the future was God's; in it He would see that right reigned and good triumphed. The Messiah personified to the prophetic spirit the Divine judgment against wrong and vindication of right; He was to live to do the will of God, and cause it to be done. The ideas of the king and the kingdom, thus inseparably blended in prophecy, appeared as indissolubly connected in the mind of John. He could indifferently say, "The kingdom of heaven is at

[1] In the interpretation of John's baptism the words of Josephus (*Antiq.*, bk. xviii. c. v. § 2) are of great importance.

hand;" and, "After me cometh one mightier than I."[1] He loved, indeed, to contrast his own meanness and the King's greatness. He was not worthy to bear His sandals, to loose His shoe's latchet. He was but the friend of the Bridegroom: the Bridegroom was to come. He only baptized with water, the mighty One who was coming would "baptize with the Holy Ghost and with fire." He was but a preacher, only a "Voice." He whose foot was on the threshold was a Divider, wielding a winnowing fan. He himself could but urge men to flee from wrath and seek life; but the King, at once a Saviour and Judge, was able "to gather the wheat into his garner, to burn the chaff with unquenchable fire."[2] The preaching of John was thus essentially concerned with the coming of a Person: the King made the kingdom. Without Him it could not be: with Him it was a necessity. In His prophetic word ancient prophecy lived again, and waited to welcome Him who was to fulfil its hopes and realize its truths.

The Great Prophet did not prophesy in vain. He moved Israel as Israel had not been moved for centuries. New hopes, new fears, awoke in Judæa. The people became conscious of sin, conscious of their failure to be the people of God. The voice from the banks of the Jordan awed the heart of Jerusalem, and stilled the conflicts of priests and scribes. For one splendid moment the nation awoke to the meaning of its singular and sublime faith, forgot its struggles against the eagles and images of Cæsar in its consciousness of the reign and righteousness of God. Crowds from the cities and villages, from Judæa and Galilee, Peræa and the land east of the Jordan, Pharisees and Sadducees, priests and Levites, scribes and elders of the people, publicans and proselytes, warriors from the

[1] Matt. iii. 2, Mark i. 7.
[2] Matt. iii. 11, 12, Luke iii. 16, 17, John i. 27, iii. 29.

Roman and Herodian armies, came to hear the prophet, to confess their old sins, and be baptized into his new life. And with a band from distant Nazareth came one who had hitherto been known as Jesus the carpenter, who was henceforth to be known as Jesus the Christ. How He was touched by the multitude, by the preacher, by the sense of sin that had seized the people, by the hope that was expressed in the baptism, we do not know. We only know that here He becomes conscious that His hour had come, that His happy obscurity must end, His mission of sorrow and glory, death and life, begin. What was certain to Himself was no less evident to John. Apparently they had never met before; but to two such spirits, to meet once at such a time and place was enough. Outwardly the two were most unlike. The son of the priest was in all things singular, in home, in dress, in food, in speech, a man of weird aspect, of spirit that disdained the common ways and life of man. The Child of the carpenter was, if not undistinguished, inconspicuous, familiar with society, the city, the home and his duties to it, the weariness and the tameness of common earth and common day. Yet the accidents of their respective aspects could not hide the Prophet and the King from each other. Spirit answered to spirit, and in the answer the revelation came. The hour of recognition might be brief, but it was in its meaning and issues eternal. Months after, John in Machærus, a prisoner, living by the grace of a lustful tyrant, at the mercy of a cruel and vengeful woman, compared his ideal and hope of the King with the gentle and peaceful Teacher who lived so humbly in Galilee; and clinging to his earlier faith as diviner than the Divine reality, fearing that his inspiration had been but illusion, he sent to ask, "Art thou he that should come, or do we look for another?"[1] About the same time the scene on the banks of

[1] Matt. xi. 2, 3; Luke vii. 19, 20.

the Jordan rose before the imagination of Jesus—the curious crowds streaming out to see and hear the prophet, the reeds by the river side bending before the wind, the great prophet unbent, inflexible, speaking the word God gave him; and as He compared the man and work, He declared him the greatest of prophets,[1] the one who not only prophesied the coming of the King, but had proclaimed Him come. The contrast is significant. Jesus did not altogether fulfil John's ideal, but the very degree in which our Christ differed from his King makes his recognition the more prophetic, less the fruit of design, more the child of inspiration. What the Baptist in that hour discovered and declared the experience of eighteen centuries has but confirmed.

The recognition over, the baptism ended, Jesus retired to the wilderness, full of the great consciousness that involved His conflict with the devil; but John remained by the Jordan, to fulfil his now almost completed mission. The meeting with Jesus seems to have worked a great change in the mind and speech of the Baptist. His preaching appears to have become less predictive and more declarative—less prophetic of Him who was to come, and more indicative of Him who had. So much at least seems to be involved in the deputation from Jerusalem.[2] They do not go, like those mentioned in the older narratives,[3] to his baptism, but to ask, "Art thou the Christ? Elias? that prophet?" The problem has now changed —is not, What mean his confession, repentance, baptism? but, Who is he? What means his saying about the Christ who is come? Men are eager, not to show their penitence and share his hope, but to possess his knowledge and discover his Messiah. And within this change there is another, still more significant. His preaching has become

[1] Matt. xi. 7, 14; Luke vii. 24–29. [2] John i. 19–24.
[3] Matt. iii. 7.

sweeter in tone, softer in spirit, materially unlike what it had been. He does not now speak of the unsparing Judge, axe or fan in hand, hewing down the fruitless trees, burning the vacant chaff; but of the "Lamb of God," devoted to meek silence and sacrifice. He does not threaten the multitudes with an avenger of sin, but points to One "who bears the sin of the world." The Synoptists show the Baptist before he saw Christ and when he first saw Him; but the Fourth Gospel shows him after he had known Christ, changed into a meeker, sweeter, nobler man, softer in speech and in spirit, with a diviner notion of the Messiah, a more hopeful and helpful word for man. And so, when the Christ returned victorious from the conflict, the preacher beside the Jordan hailed Him, not as He of the winnowing fan, but as "the Lamb of God," and turned the eyes of the crowds his voice still held together to One who stood among them, who had come to declare the Father and bear the sin of man. And the new faith mellowed the great preacher, made him feel that his work was done, that it was a glory to be so superseded and eclipsed, and so enabled him to make his last his most beautiful words: "Ye yourselves bear me witness, that I said, I am not the Christ; but that I am sent before him. He that hath the bride is the bridegroom: but the friend of the bridegroom, who standeth and heareth him, rejoiceth greatly because of the bridegroom's voice: this my joy therefore is fulfilled. He must increase, but I must decrease.[1]

[1] John iii. 28-30.

V.

THE TEMPTATION OF CHRIST.[1]

How is the Temptation of Christ to be understood? As a history, a parable, a myth, or an undesigned, though not accidental, compound of the three? If real, was its reality actual, a veritable face-to-face struggle of opposed persons, with personalities no less real that they represented universal interests, and, by their conflict, determined universal issues? Or was its reality ideal, subjective, a contest of rival passions, principles, and aims? If not real, whence came the narrative? From Jesus or His disciples, or, in a manner more or less unconscious, partly from both? Did He clothe a general truth or a mental experience in the drapery of historical narrative? Or did they mistake a parable for history? Or, with imaginations dazzled by His person and transfigured by His words and works, did they either simply create or expand from a small germ this, while mythical, symbolical and ideally true tale of the struggle of celestial light and strength with infernal darkness and subtlety?

These questions confront us the moment we attempt to understand the story of the Temptation. It has been interpreted by a rigid realism, which, unable to conceive any except a formal and apparent reality, has bravely embodied the Devil, and introduced him, now as a venerable sage, now as a friend, and again as a member of the Sanhedrin, or a high priest; or, as Bengel naively thinks,

[1] Matt. iv. 1–11; Mark i. 12, 13, Luke iv. 1–13.

"Sub schemate γραμματέως, quia τὸ γέγραπται ei ter opponitur." Since Origen, an idealism, more or less free, has resolved the Temptation, either in whole or in part, into a vision, now caused by the Devil, now by God, and now by the ecstatic state of Christ's own spirit. Within our own century Schleiermacher has explained it as a misunderstood parable; Strauss, as a pure myth; De Wette, as the expansion of an historical germ; and subsequent scholars have variously combined these with each other or with the older views. If variously interpreted means well interpreted, then certainly our narrative may be said to stand here pre-eminent. But, at least, the variety indicates the strength of the desire and the determination to understand it, and of the belief that within it are truths worth knowing, and certain, when known, to increase our knowledge of Christ.

To discuss the many critical and exegetical problems involved in the questions just stated, is, for our present purpose, unnecessary. Our design is rather to approach the subject from what may be termed the personal or biographical side, and from the standpoint thus gained make an attempt to understand the narrative.

Let us begin, then, with what ought to be a self-evident proposition. As Jesus was a moral being, whose nature had to develop under the limitations necessary to humanity, we must conceive Him as a subject of moral probation. He could not escape exposure to its perils. "It behoved him in all things to be like unto his brethren,"[1] and so to be "in all things tempted as they are."[2] He obeyed by choice, not by necessity; His obedience was conscious and voluntary, not instinctive and natural. It might be from the first and at every moment certain that He would achieve holiness, but could never be necessary. He could have been above the possibility of doing wrong only by

[1] Heb. ii. 17. [2] Heb. iv. 15.

being without the ability to do right. Obedience can be where disobedience may be, and nowhere else. God is too high to be tempted. He neither obeys nor disobeys, but acts wisely or righteously. We cannot say, "He is sinless;" must say, "He is holy." We speak of Him in words that imply He cannot err or fall, not in words that imply He may. A brute may be provoked, but cannot be tempted. It is too low, is beneath temptation, and so we think of it as neither sinful, nor sinless, nor holy, but simply as natural—an unmoral creature. But man can be tempted, is a being capable of obedience, capable of disobedience, limited in knowledge, free in will. And Jesus as Son of Man was the true child of humanity, an universal ideal man, wanting in no quality essential to manhood. He had a free will, an intellect which grew in capacity and culture, knowledge now more, now less, imperfect. Limitation, Leibnitz notwithstanding, is no physical evil, and imperfection no moral wrong, but they involve possible error in thought and possible sin in action. Hence Jesus was, by the very terms of His being, temptable. Where life is realized within the conditions of humanity there must be probation, and probation is only possible in a person who can be proved.

But again: we must here conceive the temptable as the tempted. In the person and life of Jesus there was no seeming. A drama where the face within the mask is placid, where the voice is outside the soul, where the person but personates an idea, is not to be here thought of. Now a real humanity cannot escape with a fictitious temptation. Where sin is universal, it cannot but be a greater and subtler force than were it embodied in a single being, more difficult to detect, less easy to resist. Every man becomes then, in a sense, an agent—one in whom it has a foothold and through whom it works. Hence Christ's struggle against sin could not but be persistent; the battle extended along the whole line of His life, and became a victory only by His death. And so, though our narrative may be termed by pre-eminence The Temptation, it was not simply then, but always, that Jesus was tempted. The devil left Him only "for a season;" returned personified now as Peter, now as Judas, and again as the Jews; met Him amid the solitude and agony of Gethsemane, in the clamour, mockery, and desertion of the cross. And so Milton's grand picture of the "patient Son of God" represents, not one moment, but every moment, in His glorious but perilous career:

> Infernal hosts and hellish furies round
> Environed Thee. Some howled, some yelled, some shrieked,
> Some bent at Thee their fiery darts, while Thou
> Satt'st unappalled in calm and sinless peace.

But this very word "sinless" starts another set of questions. How could Jesus be "tempted in all things, like as we are, yet without sin"? Is not temptation evil? Can a tempted soul be still a sinless soul? If a man becomes conscious of sin, though only to resist it, does he not lose the beautiful innocence, the white and sweet simplicity of spirit, that is, as it were, the heart of holiness? We must then consider how the tempted could be the sinless Christ. And—

1. What is Temptation? Seduction to evil, solicitation to wrong. It stands distinguished from trial thus: trial tests, seeks to discover the man's moral qualities or character; but temptation persuades to evil, deludes, that it may ruin. The one means to undeceive, the other to deceive. The one aims at the man's good, making him conscious of his true moral self; but the other at his evil, leading him more or less unconsciously into sin. God tries; Satan tempts. Abraham was tried when his faith was proved, Job when successive calamities made it manifest that he served God for nothing save the duty of the

service and the glory of the Served; but Eve was tempted when persuaded to sin by the promise of becoming a god; David when, blinded and enticed by lustful desire, he plunged into the crimes that were so terribly punished and so grandly confessed and lamented. And so here emerges another distinction—in trial the issues are made fairly apparent, in temptation they are concealed. Evil in the one case is, in the other is not, disguised. The wrong seems to the tempted the desirable, and the extent to which the desirable hides the wrong measures the strength of the temptation. And so there needs to be adaptation between means and end. What tempts one mind may only offend another. Some men are too coarse to perceive the finer forms of evil; others so refined as to be shocked by the grosser sins. Mephistopheles is one being to Faust, another to Margaret, and even to the Scholar he is inflexibly accommodating, full of changes to suit the many phases of the mind he leads. And so the tempted is the solicited to evil by evil, but by evil so disguised as to be winsome, as, if possible, to make desire victorious over conscience and will.

2. The Forms of Temptation. It may be either sensuous, imaginative, or rational, *i.e.*, a man may be tempted through the senses, the imagination, or the reason. If through the senses, then it appeals to greed, appetite, lust, or any one of the passions that bestialize man and create our grosser miseries and crimes. If through the imagination, then it dazzles to betray, comes as pride, ambition, or any one of the graceful and gracious forms that can be made to veil vainglorious, though Protean, egotism. If through the reason, then it comes as doubt of the true, suspicion of the good, or in any of the many forms in which intellect protests against the limits it so wishes, and yet is so little able, to transcend. Temptation may thus assume shapes akin to the highest as to the lowest in man,

but the forms most distinct often subtly meet and blend. Perhaps it is never so powerful as when its forces approach the mind together and at once through the senses, the imagination, and the reason.

3. The Sources of Temptation. It may proceed either (1) from self, or (2) from without self. If the first, the nature must be bad, but not of necessity radically bad; if the second, it may be innocent, but must be capable of sinning and being induced, or drawn, to a given sin. A thoroughly bad being may tempt, but cannot be tempted. The nature has become essentially evil, and so sin is natural. A sinless being may be tempted, but cannot tempt—even himself. Where inclination and will, conscience and passion, are in harmony, there can be no lust to entice or evil tendency to beset and ensnare. A being of mixed qualities and character can both tempt and be tempted, his baser can tempt his better nature, a worse creature can seduce him to deeper sin.

Now it is evident that temptation from within is a confession of sinfulness, the endeavour of depravity to become still more depraved. The self-tempted can never be the sinless. Tendencies that solicit to evil are evil tendencies. The Hunchback King, as conceived by Shakespeare and represented in the most tragic of his historical plays, is a man drunk with ambition, made by it false, perfidious, cruel. He knew that murder was a crime, eminently so where the murdered stood related to him as did the little orphans in the Tower, who seemed so beautiful and strong in their very helplessness to the hired and hardened villains who saw them—

> Girdling one another
> Within their innocent alabaster arms;
> Their lips like four red roses on a stalk,
> Which, in their summer beauty, kissed each other.

But where the ruffians had pity, Richard had none. Ambition had vanquished pity and, for the time being, seared conscience. His worse triumphed over his better nature. The temptation came from himself, and so condemned himself. The nature that produced it was bad, and its victory made the nature worse. The ability to tempt implies sinfulness, is impossible without it.

If, now, the temptation comes from without, three things are possible—it may speak either (1) to still fluid evil desires, and make them crystallize into evil action; or (2) to innocence, and change it into guilt; or (3) supply it with the opportunity of rising into holiness. A word or two illustrative of these three possibilities. The Macbeth, not of history, but of the drama, may stand as an illustration of the first. He is a man full of ambition, but also

> Too full o' the milk of human kindness
> To catch the nearest way.

He would be great, but guiltlessly; what he would highly, that would he holily:

> Would not play false,
> And yet would wrongly win.

And this man has a queen, with his ambition, without his scruples, strong, passionful, pitiless; and she, unsexed, filled, from crown to toe, top-full of direst cruelty, becomes the temptress, works upon her husband, now on his strength, now on his weakness, till he goes to his fatal crime and still more fatal remorse. There is evil beforehand in both, evil irresolute desires in the man, evil resolution in the woman, and the strength forces the weakness to incarnate itself in deeds conscience will not let die.

The second possibility—temptation coming to innocence and changing it into guilt—we may find illustrated in the splendid scene in "King John," where the King says to Hubert—

> If the midnight bell
> Did, with his iron tongue and brazen mouth,
> Sound one into the drowsy ear of night;
> If this same were a churchyard where we stand,
> And thou possessed with a thousand wrongs;

if, indeed, Hubert could see without eyes, hear without ears, reply without a tongue, the King would, " in despite of brooded watchful day," have poured into his bosom the thoughts that filled his own. The word murder remains unspoken, but the thing is suggested. By voice and look and fawning flattering speech, the honest tender-hearted Hubert is betrayed into a promise against the life of the boy he loved. And so the tempted falls, the innocent is made the guilty.

The third possibility—innocence raised through temptation into holiness—is, perhaps, nowhere better illustrated than in the beautiful creation which, like the genius of chastity and all that is winsome in woman, has been, as it were, enshrined in " Measure for Measure," the play that so well expounds its own saying—

> 'Tis one thing to be tempted, Escalus,
> Another thing to fall.

Isabella, lovely as pure, most womanly in her unconscious strength, stainless among the stained, loving her doomed brother too well to sin for him, triumphs over his tears and entreaties, the wiles and threats of the Deputy, and emerges from her great temptation chaster, more beautiful in the blossom of her perfect womanhood, than she had been before. The fierce fire refined, and what issued from it was a being purified, not simply innocent, but righteous, clothed in the invisible but impenetrable armour of sweet and conscious simplicity.

We are now in a position to consider the Temptation of Christ in relation to His sinlessness. Temptation implies (1) ability in the tempted to sin or not sin. Jesus had, to speak with the schoolmen, the " posse non peccare," not the " non posse peccare." Had He possessed the latter, He had been intemptable. (2) Evil must be presented to the tempted in a manner disguised, plausible, attractive. It was so to Jesus. When He was hungry, it was sensuous in its form; when He stood on the Temple tower, whether in body or in vision it matters not, it was imaginative; when He was offered the kingdoms of the world if He would worship Satan, it was rational. Each temptation appealed to a subjective desire or need. (3) The tempter must be sinful, the tempted may be innocent. And Christ was the tempted. The temptation came to Him, did not proceed from Him, yet performed a high and necessary function in His personal and official discipline. Whether the innocent become righteous or guilty, holy or depraved, temptation alone can reveal. The untried is a negative character, can become positive only through trial. Till every link in the chain that is to hold the vessel to its anchor be tested, you cannot be certain that it is of adequate strength. Till the bridge over which myriads are to sweep in the swift-rushing train be proved of sufficient strength, you cannot regard it as a safe pathway. So, till the will has been solicited to the utmost to evil, its fidelity to righteousness cannot be held absolute. The way to obedience lies through suffering. The inflexible in morals is what will not bend, however immense and intense the strain. Only a Christ tempted, "yet without sin," could be the perfect Christ. What He endured proved His adequacy for His work; and out of His great trial He emerged, not simply sinless, which He had been before, but righteous— that most beautiful of objects to the Divine eye and most winsome of beings to the human heart, a perfect man, " holy, harmless, undefiled, and separate from sinners."[1]

Our discussion conducts, then, to but one conclusion:

[1] Heb. vii. 26

temptation was not only possible to the sinlessness, but necessary to the holiness, of Christ. Yet this conclusion is but an introduction, only clears the way for the study of what we term the Temptation. And here we may remark that the place where it happened is not without significance. Into what wilderness Jesus was led to be tempted we do not know—whether the wild and lonely solitudes watched by the mountains where Moses and Elijah struggled in prayer and conquered in faith, or the steep rock by the side of the Jordan overlooking the Dead Sea, which later tradition has made the arena of this fell conflict. Enough, the place was a desert, waste, barren, shelterless, overhead the hot sun, underfoot the burning sand or blistering rock. No outbranching trees made a cool restful shade; no spring upbursting with a song of gladness came to relieve the thirst; no flowers bloomed, pleasing the eye with colour and the nostrils with fragrance: all was drear desert. Now, two things may be here noted—the desolation, and the solitude. The heart that loves Nature is strangely open to her influences. The poet sees a glory in the light of setting suns, and the round ocean, and the living air, which exalts and soothes him; but a land of waste and cheerless gloom casts over his spirit a shadow as of the blackness of darkness. And Jesus had the finest, most sensitive soul that ever looked through human eyes. He loved this beautiful world, loved the stars that globed themselves in the heaven above, the flowers that bloomed in beauty on the earth beneath, the light and shade that played upon the face of Nature, now brightening it as with the smile of God, now saddening it as with the pity that gleams through a cloud of tears. Think, then, how the desolation must have deepened the shadows on His spirit, increased the burden that made Him almost faint at the opening of His way. And He was in solitude—alone there, without the comfort of a human presence, the fellowship of a kindred soul. Yet the loneliness was a sublime necessity. In His supreme moments society was impossible to Him. The atmosphere that surrounded the Temptation, the Transfiguration, the Agony, and the Cross, He alone could breathe; in it human sympathy slept or died, and human speech could make no sound. Out of loneliness He issued to begin His work; into loneliness He passed to end it. The moments that made His work divinest were His own and His Father's.

But much more significant than the scene of the Temptation is the place where it stands in the history of the life and mind of Jesus. It stands just after the Baptism, and before the Ministry; just after the long silence, and before the brief yet eternal speech; just after the years of privacy, and before the few but glorious months of publicity. Now, consider what this means. The Baptism had made Him manifest as the Messiah. In the Baptist emotions inexpressible had been awakened. His newborn hopes made him a new man, lifted him into the splendid humility which rejoiced to be, like the morning star, quenched in the light of the risen Sun. But John was here a pale reflection of Jesus. The one's emotions were to the other's as "moonlight unto sunlight, and as water unto wine." We must not imagine that every day was the same to Christ, or Christ the same on every day. He had His great moments as we have. We may call the supreme moment when the soul awakens to God, and the man realizes manhood, conversion, the new birth, or what we please. What the experience we so name signifies to us, the moment symbolized by the Baptism signified to Jesus, only with a difference in degree which His pre-eminence alone can measure. It marked His awakening to all that was involved in Messiahship, and such an awakening could not come without

THE TEMPTATION OF CHRIST.

utmost tumult of spirit—tumult that only the solitude and struggle of the wilderness could calm. The outward expresses the inward change. Before this moment no miracle; after it the miracles begin and go on multiplying. Before it no speech, no claim of extraordinary mission, only Divine and golden silence; after it the teaching with authority, the founding of the kingdom, the creating of the world's light. Before it the Carpenter of Nazareth, the son of Joseph and Mary, doing, in beautiful meekness, the common duties of the common day; after it the Christ of God, the Revealer of the Father, the Life and the Light of men. Now, He who became so different to others had first become as different to Himself. What was soon to be revealed to the world was then made manifest to His own soul. And the revelation was dazzling enough to blind, was so brilliant as to need a solitude where the senses, undistracted by society, could be adjusted to the new light and perceive all it unveiled. And so the Spirit which in that glorious hour possessed Him, drove Him into the wilderness to essay His strength and realize the perfect manhood that was perfect Messiahship.

We must, then, study the Temptation through the consciousness of Jesus. Only by the one can the true significance of the other be revealed. The mind that can for forty days be its own supreme society is a mind full of fellest conflicts. We have seen how much the Baptism signified for Christ, how for Him it had ended an old and inaugurated a new life. Now observe, in our greatest and most decisive times the Divine and the devilish lie very near each other; supernal and infernal courses both seem so possible as to be almost equal. And the two appear to have been for the moment strangely mingled in the consciousness of Christ. Matthew says, " He was led up of the Spirit into the wilderness, to be tempted of the devil;"[1]

[1] Matt. IV. I.

and Mark, "immediately the Spirit driveth him into the wilderness.[1]" He was, therefore, the subject at once of Divine possession and demoniac temptation. And the two were in a manner related, the one involved the other: the first could become perfect only by the defeat of the second. To Him the great moral alternatives came as they had never come to any one before, as they can never come again. The forty days were not all days of temptation—were days of ecstasy and exaltation as well. Sunshine and cloud, light and darkness, fought their eternal battle in and round His soul. When the battle ended, the sunshine and light were found victorious; the cloud and the darkness had to leave the field broken, vanquished for evermore.

The Temptation and the assumption by Jesus of the Messianic character and office are thus essentially related. The one supplies the other with the condition and occasion of its existence. The office is assailed in and through the person. These indeed, blend in Jesus. Had He ceased to be the person He was, He had ceased to be the Messiah. Had He not been Jesus, He could not have been the Christ. Hence, had the person been ruined, the office must have perished; or had the office been depraved, the person must have failed in character and in work. The temptations aim at a common end, but by different means, appeal now to Jesus and again to the Christ. When He was driven into the wilderness three points must have stood out from the tumult of thought and feeling pre-eminent. (1) The relation of the supernatural to the natural in Himself; or, on the other side, His relation to God as His ideal human Son. (2) The relation of God to the supernatural in His person, and the official in His mission; and (3) the nature of the kingdom He had come to found, and the agencies by which it was

[1] Mark 1 12

THE TEMPTATION OF CHRIST.

to live and extend. And these precisely were the issues that emerged in the several temptations. They thus stood rooted in the then consciousness of Christ and related in the most essential way to His spirit. How, and to what extent, a word or two of exposition may make more apparent.

1. The First Temptation. Though in form sensuous, it is in essence moral or spiritual. Observe, the language is hypothetical, "*If* thou art the Son of God," and is subtly meant to express real but removable doubt in the mind of the tempter and to insinuate doubt into the mind of the tempted. It says, as it were, on the one side, "You may, or may not, be the Son of God; I cannot tell. Yet I am open to conviction; convince me;" and suggests, on the other, "Your consciousness of Messiahship may be illusive; you may be the victim of the Baptist's enthusiasm and your own imagination; clearly your belief in yourself and your mission is, without some higher warrant, unwarranted." Then the answer to the double doubt was so possible, simple, conclusive, "Command these stones to be made bread!" The temptation was great; had Christ lost faith in Himself, Christianity had never been. It was reasonable, too. Israel had been divinely fed while divinely led. What had been right to the people, need not be wrong to the Son, of God. And where supernatural power was supposed to exist, could it be wrong to test its reality in an act so holy and excellent as the preservation of an imperilled life? But the temptation, though formidable, was victoriously resisted. Christ did not take His life into His own hands, left it in the hands of God.

Now, what constituted this a temptation? where lay its evil? Suppose Christ had commanded the stones to become bread, what then? To Christ, considering the work He had to do, two things were necessary. He had to live His personal life (1) within the limits necessary to man, and (2) in perfect dependence on God. Had He transgressed either of these conditions He had ceased to be man's ideal Brother or God's ideal Son. Man cannot create; he lives by obeying Nature. He has to plough, to sow, to reap, to garner and winnow, to bruise and bake his grain, that he may eat and live. Now, had Christ by a direct miracle fed Himself, He had lifted Himself out of the circle and system of humanity, had annulled the very terms of the nature which made Him one with man. While His supernatural power was His own, it existed not for Himself, but for us. The moment He had stooped to save self He had become disqualified to save men. The ideal human life must be perfect in its dependence on God, absolute in its obedience. The ideal Son could not act as if He had no Father. And so His choice was not to be His own Providence, but to leave Himself to the Divine. He conquered by faith, and His first victory was like His last. The taunts He had to hear and bear on the cross—" He saved others, himself he cannot save;" "He trusted in God, let Him deliver him now, if He will have him"—were but a repetition of this earlier temptation; and then, as now, though the agony was deeper and the darkness more dense, He triumphed by giving Himself into the hands of the Father.

2. The Second Temptation.[1] Here, as before, the opening clause is hypothetical, and suggestive of the same double doubt; but it is proposed to remove it by an exactly opposite act. The first temptation required a miracle of independence; the second requires one of dependence. While that was sensuous, this is imaginative in its form. An act of absolute self-sufficiency was suggested through a subjective need and capacity; an act of absolute faith is suggested through the sublimity of an objective relation

[1] For reasons that need not be here stated, the order of Matthew is followed, rather than Luke's.

THE TEMPTATION OF CHRIST.

and effect. What could better exalt into a Divine and fearless ecstasy an imaginative soul, loving God too well to distrust Him, than the thought of a trust so boundless as to believe that the impalpable and yielding air would be made by His hands as safe as the solid earth ? or what could better lift into dauntless enthusiasm a mind anxious to regenerate sense-bound men than the vision of a descent into the crowd in the visible arms of Heaven, the manifest supernatural Messenger of the merciful God? The temptation was, on the one side, powerful to a spirit full of generous trust in God ; and, on the other, no less powerful to a spirit full of generous designs for man. And it came, too, clothed in the garb of a Divine oracle—" He shall give his angels charge concerning thee; and in their hands they shall bear thee up, lest at any time thou dash thy foot against a stone."

Now, what was the evil in this suggested act ? It was twofold, evil alike on the Godward and on the manward side. In the first aspect it meant that God should be forced to do for Him what He had before refused to do for Himself—make Him an object of supernatural care, exempted from obedience to natural law, a child of miracle, exceptional in His very physical relations to God and Nature. In the second aspect it meant that He was to be a Son of Wonder, clothed in marvels, living a life that struck the senses and dazzled the fancies of the poor vulgar crowd. In the one case it had been fatal to Himself, in the other to His mission. Had He been the Child of a visible Providence, which suspended for His sake every natural and human law, then He had ceased to be touched with a feeling of our infirmities, had never been made perfect through suffering, and so had never become, as " a merciful and faithful High Priest," a sublime object of faith and source of peace. Had He been encircled with wonders, heralded by marvels, then

He had led men by sense, not by conscience and reason, had reached them through their lowest and most vulgar, not through their highest and noblest, qualities; and so they could have owed to Him no birth from above, no real spiritual change. Special as were His relations to God, He did not presume on these, but, with Divine self-command, lived, though the supernatural Son, like the natural Child of the Eternal Father. His human life was as real as it was ideal; the Divine did not supersede the human, nor seek to transcend its limits, physical and spiritual. And His fidelity to our nature has been its most pre-eminent blessing. No man who knows the Spirit of Christ will presume either on the Providence or the mercy of God, because certain that these remain, even in their highest achievements, the dutiful servants of Divine Wisdom and Righteousness. He who came to show us the Father showed Him not as a visible Guardian, not as an arbitrary mechanical Providence, but as an invisible Presence about our spirits, about our ways, source of our holiest thoughts, our tenderest feelings, our wisest actions. The Only Begotten lived as one of many brethren, though as the only one conscious of His Sonship. And perhaps His self-sacrifice reached here its sublimest point. He would not, and He did not, tempt the Lord His God, but lived His beautiful and perfect life within the terms of the human, yet penetrated and possessed by the Divine.

3. *The Third Temptation.* Here the temptation seems eminently gross. Yet devil-worship can assume many forms, and some of these may be most refined. Worship is homage, and homage to a person, real or supposed, representative of certain principles, modes of action, and aims. What it here means seems evident enough. Jesus is recognized as seeking a kingdom, as intending, indeed, to found one. His aims are confessed

THE TEMPTATION OF CHRIST. 97

to be more than Jewish, not national, but universal, not an extension of Israel, but a comprehension of the world. It is known that His purpose is to be the Messiah, not of the Jews, but of man. The only question is as to the nature of His kinghood and kingdom. The kingdom here offered is one not of the spirit, but " of the world." And "world" here means not what it may be to the good, but what it is to the bad. It and its kingdoms may be won at once, will be if Jesus worships the devil, *i.e.*, makes evil His good, uses unholy means to accomplish His ends. It is as if the tempter had said, " Survey the world, and mark what succeeds. Away there in Italy lives and rules the Emperor of the world, a selfish sensual man, whose right is might. Over there in Cæsarea sits his red-handed, yet vacillating, Procurator. In your own Galilee a treacherous and lustful Herod reigns, its deputy lord. Up in Jerusalem are priests and scribes, great in things external, the fierce fanatics of formalism. Everywhere unholy men rule, unholy means prevail. Worldliness holds the world in fee. By it alone can you conquer. Use the means and the men of Cæsar, and your success will be swift and sure. Worship me, and the kingdoms of the world are thine."

The Temptation was subtly adapted to the mood and the moment, and was as evil as subtle. Bad means make bad ends. Good ends do not justify evil means; evil means deprave good ends. So a Messianic kingdom, instituted and established by worldliness, had been a worldly kingdom, no better than the coarse and sensuous Empire of Rome. And Jesus, while He felt the force, saw the evil of the temptation, and vanquished it by the truth on which His own spiritual and eternal city was to be founded. " Thou shalt worship the Lord thy God, and Him only shalt thou serve."

The three Temptations are thus as essentially related to

each other as to the spirit of Jesus. They are attempts to ruin the kingdom, the first through its King, the second through its God, the third through its means and agents. They are the successive scenes, or acts, of one great drama, where the actors are spiritual, the struggles and triumphs the same. And yet they describe a contest representative and universal. Jesus is here the representative Man, the Source and Head of the new humanity, the Founder of the kingdom that is to be. When He triumphs, it triumphs. When He is victorious, all are victorious that live in and by Him. And His victory, as it was for humanity, was by humanity. The supernatural energies that were in Him He did not use for Himself. In our nature, as in our name, He stood, fought, conquered. How perfectly, then, is He qualified to be at once our Saviour and Example! The heart that loves us is a heart that was once strained in a great battle, where the pain was its own and the victory ours. To Him, as He lives and reigns in love and might, we can come in sin and weakness, in joy and sorrow, certain that, as He " suffered, being tempted, He is able to succour them that are tempted."[1]

[1] Heb. ii. 18.

VI.

THE NEW TEACHER; THE KINGDOM OF HEAVEN.[1]

JESUS emerged from the desert to enter on His great career as the Preacher of "the kingdom of God." The season was the spring, with its bright heaven, its fresh sweet earth, its gladsome, soft, yet strengthening air, its limpid living water. And within as without all was springtime, the season of millionfold forces gladly and grandly creative, of sunlight now clear and blithesome, and now veiled with clouds that came only to break into fruitful showers. "Jesus returned in the power of the Spirit into Galilee," and Galilee felt and owned the Spirit and the power. In the homes of its peasantry and the hamlets of its fishermen, on the shores of its beautiful sea, in the towns and villages that stood on its banks and were mirrored in its waves, He preached His Gospel. Only His own Nazareth refused to hear Him.[2] Thither, indeed, He had gone, had entered the synagogue on the Sabbath, as His custom was, and had stood up to read. To Him the place was full of sacred associations. He had there, as boy and youth and man, listened for hours and days to the voice of God. Memories of visions more glorious than had come to Moses or Isaiah, of meditations that lifted time into eternity and filled man with God, of loved friends passed into silence and rest, of moments when the unseen

[1] Matt. iv. 17 ; Mark i. 14, 15 ; Luke iv. 14-32.
[2] Luke iv. 16-29.

opened to the eye and the unheard entered the soul, made the place to Him awful yet attractive as the gate of heaven to one who has approached with reverent feet and beheld in the distance the glories that dazzle mortal sight. But others had their associations as well as He, and theirs were not always as sacred as His. The synagogue was often the scene of strife. The conflict of opinion was not unknown there. Rival schools, sects, and teachers have never been slow to express their differences, and in the battle of words the Jew has shown pre-eminent skill. So the men of Nazareth had their personal rivalries and spites, and when One they knew, so far as the senses can know, rose, read, and applied to Himself the prophetic words, "The Spirit of the Lord is upon me, because He hath anointed me to preach the gospel to the poor," they received His gracious speech with incredulous wonder. But when He proceeded to speak with authority, to rebuke their unbelief, to quote against them their own proverbs, then they "were filled with wrath, rose up and thrust him out of the city." And He went His way, and found elsewhere men who heard gladly His words of power.

The strange thing about the new Teacher was not His having been untaught and a carpenter. The great creative spirits of Israel had never been the sons of a school. They were not made in the academy or the senate; their diploma came straight from Heaven, was the direct gift of the Almighty. Moses, the Lawgiver, was educated amid the sultry slopes of Horeb while tending the flocks of Jethro, his father-in-law. David, the typical theocratic king, the maker of the grandest Psalms, was taken from the sheepfold, "from following the ewes great with young." When the prophetic schools were worse than dumb, men like the herdsman of Tekoa, or the patient suffering son of Hilkiah, had become the true speakers for God. A man may be trained to be a scholar or thinker, statesman or mechanic, but not a prophet. That is a Divine vocation, and the calling must be of God, cannot be of man. And even when the vocation had ceased to come, and teaching was only professional drill in the letters of a dead past, the great man of the school might still be a son of the workshop or the field. The celebrated masters of the Talmud and the Targums were tradesmen and artizans, weavers, tent-makers, labourers. The rabbi was qualified rather than disqualified for his office by a handicraft. And so it was no strange thing in Israel that one hitherto known as a carpenter should stand forward a professed Teacher, a man learned in the law and the prophets.

But the strange thing was the new Teacher Himself. He stood distinguished from all the rabbis who had been, or then were, in Israel. Of the points that made Him pre-eminent and unique three may be here specified.

(1) The relation between His person and His word. The Teacher made the truth He taught. His teaching was His articulated person, His person His incorporated teaching. The divinity the one expressed the other embodied. He came to found a kingdom by manifesting His kinghood, by declaring Himself a King. The King was the centre round which the kingdom crystallized. His first words announced its advent; his last affirmed its reality, though a reality too sublimely ideal to be intelligible to the man of the world who knew enough to ask the question, "What is truth?" but not enough to wait for its answer. And the first word and the last were alike revelations of Himself; the truth He was incarnated, as it were, in speech, that it might live an ideal life on earth, while He lived a real and personal life in heaven.

(2) The consciousness He had of Himself and His truth; its authority and creative energy. He knew that He was true and His word true; was certain that, though He never wrote, only spoke, His words were imperishable

—would outlast heaven and earth. He was, at the first as at the last, at the last as at the first, certain of the reality of His words and claims, of their endurance and triumph. He was as calmly and consciously confident when He sat, pitied by Pilate, in the shadow of Calvary as when He went forth, approved by John, to preach, in His fresh and glorious manhood, "the gospel of the kingdom of God."

(3) His knowledge of His truth and mission was throughout perfect and self-consistent. His first word revealed His purpose, expressed His aim, embodied His grand idea. He did not learn by experience; He knew by Divine intuition what He had come to accomplish. His progress was not a series of tentative efforts, of mended mistakes, but an orderly movement to a consciously conceived end. "Had Christ at first a plan?" is a question which has often been discussed. "Plan" is a word too little ideal and spiritual, too mechanical and pragmatic, to be here appropriate. If we could use Idea in the Platonic sense, as a term denoting the archetypal image or pattern of things in the Divine reason, then I would say, Christ had at the beginning the Idea He meant to realize, knew the end toward which He and His were then and evermore to strive. And the evidence lives in the phrase which was the most frequent on His lips, "The kingdom of heaven." He who has penetrated its meaning knows what Christ came to do; he who has not done so has yet to know the Christ.

What, then, does the phrase "the kingdom of heaven" or "of God," mean? Now, it is not possible to explain it simply through the qualifying terms, "of heaven" or "of God;" we must first understand what the term they qualify signifies. "Kingdom" is the cardinal word, and it can be interpreted only through its cardinal idea, King. The notions of kinghood are very varied—differ in different nations, or even in the same nation in different ages. In England here the law is above the sovereign; *lex* is *rex*. The Queen is the greatest subject in these realms, has to be loyal to the superior royalty of the Constitution, our true lord paramount. The Roman Cæsar was an Imperator, the commander of an army become the monarch of many peoples, with his old military supremacy of person and will. Of the Greek kings the earlier were chiefs, leaders of men; but the later were tyrants, despots who had dared to usurp the inalienable rights of free men. In Israel the kinghood was theocratic; the king was consecrated by the priest and instructed by the prophet that he might administer the law and ordinances of the God who had given him the throne, and whose will he existed to enforce and obey. But this ideal had seldom been realized, had almost always been depraved; and the fond imagination of the people, despairing and sick of the oppressive present, had pictured a future in which an ideal king, the anointed of God, should come to reign in righteousness. Yet the good dreamed of was political rather than moral; exalted the Jew, but cast down the Gentile; magnified a nation, but did not ennoble man. Though it had been realized the perfect had not come.

Now these notions of kinghood hardly help us, save by way of contrast, to understand Christ's. Our ordinary ideas and experiences are here the worst possible interpreters. His sovereignty was not the creature, but the creator, of law; the kingdom did not make the king, but the king the kingdom. His will was not imperial—the transfigured and crowned might of the master of many legions—but moral, the expression of a self-vanquishing and victorious love. His authority did not lessen but enlarged the circle of human rights; made men awake to claims and qualities in their manhood they had never known before. He did not seek the sanction and seal of the priest, or the counsel and guidance of the prophet; but assumed His title and instituted His reign at the bidding of what seemed His own unauthorized will. And then He appeared without the attributes and actions, without the character and designs Israel had expected in its ideal king. He had no antipathy to Rome, but was willing to be a dutiful citizen of the Empire. He did not feel that His kinghood either denied or excluded Cæsar; that tribute either touched or tarnished His supremacy. Men said He was of David's line; but He never based His royalty on His descent. When they came to make Him a king, He fled from their hands. When they asked Him to exercise one of the oldest royal prerogatives and judge a cause, He refused. His whole attitude was a puzzle, a dark enigma, to His contemporaries; His claim a thing to be ridiculed. The superscription nailed above His cross was meant to be ironical. Pilate thought it mocked the Jews; the Jews thought it mocked Jesus. But the irony lived in its truth, which was bitter to him who wrote and those who read it, not to Him who bore it above His head.

Christ's great idea, then, is too much His own, has too little of the local and transitory, too much of the universal and eternal, to be interpreted through our notions of kinghood. If it is to be understood at all, it must be through His own varied and many-featured presentation. We have to note then, at the outset, that He has two formulæ for His great idea—" The kingdom of heaven," and " The kingdom of God." These are used with a slight difference of meaning, and each is best understood through its antithesis. " The kingdom of heaven " stands opposed to the kingdoms of earth, the great world-empires that lived and ruled by the strength of their armies. " The kingdom of God " has as its opposite the kingdom of evil, or Satan, the great empire of anarchy and darkness, creative misery and death to man. By the first antithesis Christ opposed His kingdom to the empires that were in means and ends, in principles and practice, bad. These had grown out of the cruel ambitions, the jealousies, and hatreds of men and states; had created war, with its inevitable offspring, bloodshed, famine, pestilence, the oppression which crushed the weak, and the tyranny which exalted the strong. But the kingdom from above was no empire of an overgrown state, no ambitious scheme of a ruthless conqueror, realized by merciless agents and means; but was the descent of a spiritual power, calm and ubiquitous as the sunlight, plastic, penetrative, pervasive as the crystal air, silently changing from ill to good, from chaos to order, both man and his world.

By the second antithesis Christ opposed His kingdom to the empire of evil, the dominion of sin in the individual and the race. Out of sin had come ruin to the single soul and the collective society. Evil had made man the enemy of man, the estranged and fearful child of God. But the kingdom of God was good, belonged to Him, came from Him, existed to promote His ends, to vanquish sin, and restore on earth an obedience that would make it happy and harmonious as heaven. So, though the phrases were Hebrew, the ideas were Christian. The old terms were transfigured and made radiant with a meaning high as heaven, vast as the universe, inexhaustible as eternity.

Were, then, the two phrases to be distinguished as to meaning, it might be thus : the one indicates the nature and character of the new kingdom, the other its source and end. But for the interpretation of the idea it is necessary to understand, not only the names that denote it, but also its more distinctive qualities, aspects, and relations. (1) It is present, an already existing reality, none the less real that it was unseen, undiscovered by the very men who professed to be looking for it.[1] (2) It is expansive, has an extensive and intensive growth, can have its dominion extended and its authority more perfectly recognized and obeyed.[2] Its real is also its potential being. While it has come, it is yet always coming; the idea exists, but its realization is a continuous process. (3) It does its work silently and unseen; grows without noise, like the seed in the ground, which swells, bursts, and becomes a tree great enough to lodge the birds of the air.[3] And its intensive is as silent as its expansive action. It penetrates and transforms the man who enters it. Its entrance into him is his entrance into it, his being born again, his becoming as a little child, the new citizen of a new state.[4] (4) It creates and requires righteousness in all its subjects. To seek it is to seek the righteousness of God.[5] Where righteousness is real the kingdom is realized. (5) It is the possession and reward of those who have certain spiritual qualities. "The poor in spirit," the "persecuted for righteousness' sake," the child-like and the simple are its possessors and heirs.[6] (6) It is without local or national character, can have subjects anywhere, has none for simply formal or hereditary reasons.[7] No man belongs to it simply because a Jew, or is excluded from it simply because a Gentile. (7) It is at once universal and individual, meant to be preached everywhere and to every one;[8] to comprehend the race by pervading all its units. And (8) the universal is to be an everlasting kingdom, to endure throughout all generations. Heaven and earth may perish, but it must for evermore endure.

We must now attempt to formulate the idea of the kingdom. It is in nature and character heavenly: comes

[1] Luke vi 20; xvii 20, 21, Matt xx. 1.
[2] Matt. vi. 10; xiii. 3–8, 19–23 [3] Ibid xiii 31–33.
[4] Matt. xviii 1–3, Luke xviii 17; John iii. 3–5
[5] Matt vi. 33; v. 19, 20. [6] Ibid v. 3, 10; xviii. 4.
[7] Matt. viii. 11; xxi. 31, Luke xiii. 29. [8] Matt. xxiv. 14.

by the will of God being done on earth as it is in heaven. It is in origin and aim Divine: proceeds from God that it may fulfil God's ends. Its being is real, but its ends are not yet realized, though the realization is in process. The process is silent and spiritual, and the end is the creation of righteousness in the individual and the race.

The idea includes, then, as an essential element, the notion of a reign, the reign of God in men, and through men over mankind. As such it must be, on the human side, inner, invisible. The nature of the king determines the character of the kingdom. Where authority is legal, it can employ legal processes and forms; where it is ethical and spiritual, it must be enforced through the conscience and obeyed by the spirit. An invisible and moral sovereign implies an invisible and moral reign. The unseen is not, indeed, the unknown God. He knows, but does not see, Himself. We can know though we cannot see Him: the heart can feel His presence, the conscience can confess His authority. And where it does so righteousness is born. Where He is known and obeyed He reigns, His kingdom is realized.

But a second element involved in the idea is that it is a reign by ideals, by truths believed and loved. The men who enter and live in the kingdom know God, believe the truths personalized in His Son. And so, with its sphere in the spirit and truth as its instrument of authority and expansion, it is in its proper nature ideal. It is neither an institution, nor capable of being embodied in one. It cannot be identified with the church. The two are radically dissimilar. $Ἐκκλησία$ does, $Βασιλεία$ does not, denote an institution or structure. The kingdom is "righteousness, peace, joy in the Holy Ghost,"[1] but the church is a community, a body, a building.[2] There may be many

[1] Rom xiv. 17.
[2] Gal. i. 2; 2 Cor. i. 1; Ephes i. 22, 23; Col. i 18; 1 Tim. iii. 15.

churches:[1] there is only one kingdon. The voluntary action of men can institute the former, but not the latter. The kingdom created the church, not the church the kingdom. The parables that explain and illustrate the one are inapplicable to the other. The $Βασιλεία$ was the most, the $Εκκλησία$ the least familiar idea of Christ. Of the first He never ceases to speak; of the second He speaks only twice;[2] and each time so as to indicate its structural or institutional character. The church and the kingdom may thus be more properly contrasted than compared. Only two points of contrast can be here noticed.

1. The church[3] has, the kingdom has not, a formal or organized being. The one must be a more or less elaborate organism, the other can only live a spiritual and unembodied life. A polity is as necessary to the voluntary society we call a church as to the involuntary society we call a nation. The ideals of church polity, realized or realizable, are many; but each has had, or may have, its counterpart in the state. There are, indeed, in each case but two great political types, though each may branch into very dissimilar forms. A state may be either monarchical or republican. If monarchical, it may be either autocratic or limited, imperial or constitutional. If republican, it may be either aristocratic or democratic—either a republic proper, where the authority is vested in representatives elected by the people; or a democracy proper, where the supreme authority is the people in council assembled. And the church, like the state, may be either a monarchy or a republic. If the monarchy be autocratic, it is, in

[1] Acts. ix. 31 ; xv 41 ; Rom. xvi 4, 16 ; 1 Cor. vii. 17.
[2] Matt. xvi. 18 , xviii 17.
[3] The term "church" has indeed both a universal and specific reference. But the idea in both cases is the same It always denotes an organized society There are obvious advantages connected with the use of the term in a generalized sense. It enables us to deal with the general notion.

ecclesiastical phraseology, a Papacy; if limited, an Episcopacy. If the republic be a representative aristocracy, it is Presbyterial; if democratic, Congregational. And so, while a polity is necessary to the church, it is not a polity of a particular type. The church creates the polity, not the polity the church. It has existed, can exist, under each specific form, just as France has been Legitimist, Orleanist, Imperialist, and Republican, and remained France still. Men may argue that the one polity is more, the others are less, perfect; but no man has any right to argue that any one is essential to the being of the Christian Church.

While, however, we can so describe and classify the polities of the church, we cannot attribute one to the kingdom. It is without a polity, properly so called. A πολιτεία implies both a πόλις and πολῖται, but a βασιλεία simply a βασιλεύς. The king creates the kingdom, but the citizens the state and its polity. And the king here is the eternal and invisible God, who seeks to establish on earth the reign of heaven.

2. Men can make and administer laws in the church, but not in the kingdom. The very name of the former implies its power to determine its own constitution, the terms of communion or citizenship, the rights and privileges it will grant to its members, the duties and services it will require from them. And this power the church has always exercised, often with a most rigorous will. It has formulated creeds, declaring one opinion orthodox, another heretical. It has framed laws and executed judgment on every bold transgressor. It judgments have been now righteous, now unrighteous, often pronounced against the evil, almost as often against the good. But in the kingdom of God the authority is God's, not man's; its laws are Divine, administered from heaven though obeyed on earth. Exclusion from the church need

not be exclusion from the kingdom. The excluded and excluding may be both within it. The man who seeks or loves God's righteousness lives within God's kingdom, even though the excommunicated or the unknown of the churches. The real is not always a conscious Christian. Men come from the east and west and sit down with Abraham in the kingdom of God. It has room enough for Anselm and Abelard, Pole and Parker, Milton and Rutherford, Baxter and Laud, Bunyan and Ken. Rival churchmen are not rivals in the Divine kingdom. Where man ceases to make and administer laws he must cease to anathematize his brother, and humbly begin to speak the praise of the God whose grace he enjoys, whose reign he confesses. There he lives like a little child, meekly learning to be the obedient vassal of the Eternal King.

But while the church and the kingdom thus differ, they are most intimately related. The relation is twofold. (1) The kingdom creates the church, but (2) the church exists for the sake of the kingdom. The ideals, the Divine and redemptive truths, which actualize the reign of God, create the men and purposes constitutive of the church. It could hardly be said to exist in Christ's day. While He speaks of the kingdom as present and real, He speaks of the church as something still future; not as building, but as to be built.[1] It begins to exist, after His ascension, with the first Christian community. Persons were necessary to its existence. It was a society, an association, of the like-minded. But minds are made alike by being persuaded to think alike, and the persuasion came of the truths that were embodied in Christ. He was the truth, the ideal, that made the kingdom impersonated. His very being created it; but the effective action of His truth was needed to create the church.

And the created was meant to serve the Creator; the

[1] Matt. xvi. 18. "Upon this rock I will build my church."

church was to promote the ends, to realize the ideals, of the kingdom. If the βασιλεία was steeped in Hebrew, the ἐκκλησία was penetrated with Greek, associations. Its sense is not to be etymologically explained; its use was too specific and well defined to admit of that. The ἐκκλησία was the assembly of the citizens—the citizen assembled to ordain or administer laws, to transact the business, maintain the being or secure the well-being of the state. And so the church exists for the kingdom—is, as it were, the society of the enfranchised organized to further the national weal. Within the one empire there may be many πόλεις, and each may have its own πολιτεία, at once determined and exercised by its own ἐκκλησία; but the cities, however variously constituted, are alike members of the state, united in a common devotion to imperial interests, often best promoting these by honourable attention to their own. So the great βασιλεία τοῦ θεοῦ is one, but its πόλεις, with their respective ἐκκλησίαι, are many. Yet the multitude does not exclude unity; cannot so long as loyalty to the kingdom and its ends is common to all. And without this loyalty the church loses its right to be. It is not in itself an end, but a means, and lives as it fulfils its purpose. Its purpose is to magnify its Creator, enlarge the kingdom, promote its extensive and intensive growth. Christ lives in the church, in and by it reigns that He may put all His enemies under His feet, and bring the time when the kingdom shall be delivered up to God, even the Father, that He may be all in all.

We have only space for a word on the Ideals of the kingdom, its great creative truths. These may be reduced to two: the paternity of God and the sonship of man. God is man-like; man is God-like. The first gives us, on the Divine side, the grace that can stoop to incarnation and sacrifice; the second gives us, on the human side, the nature that makes restoration both possible and desirable. And these were embodied in Christ. He was the manifested paternity of God; the realized sonship of man. In Him the highest truths as to God and man were personalized, made real and active, living and creative for earth. His very being made the kingdom; to be was for Him to be both the Truth and a King. And so, while He was king, the kingdom was God's; the reign of God through and by the Truth Christ both made and was.

The kingdom, then, Christ instituted was sublime and glorious enough. While it has only an ideal being, or being in the realm of the spirit, it is creative of the best and noblest realities on earth. It has made our churches, and inspired these to do every good work they have accomplished. It is the spring, too, of our philanthropies, our ambitions to be and to do good. While it can be embodied in no institution, it forms and animates every institution that promotes the common weal. The state feels it in all its higher legislation, aims, and endeavours. Art in all its branches pulses with an enthusiasm it creates, is charmed by visions it sends, and fascinated by ideals it raises, making our perfect seem imperfect still. It is, too, the one power creative of righteousness. It seeks the good of the race by seeking the good of all its individuals; blesses the mass through the units that compose it. The rewards of the kingdom are the virtues of the kingdom, the holiness that is happiness, the graces that adorn the saints of God. And it does its glorious work without ceasing, making earth more like heaven, man more like God. While it lives He reigns, and while He reigns man need fear no victory of evil, either over himself or his kind; may rest assured that the Divine Father who guides the world, will guide it, through its shadow as through its sunshine, to the calm and glory of an eternal day.

VII.

GALILEE, JUDÆA, SAMARIA.

THE preaching of the kingdom was a creative act; the word of Jesus instituted His reign. His simple and modest means stood in curious contrast to His extraordinary and sublime ends. His mission was to create a new society in the heart of the old, a new that was to reform the old by reforming its members. The man was allowed to live where he had lived before, within the old state and obedient to its laws; but he was to become a new man, the seed of a new society. The citizens were not to be changed through the state, but the state through the citizens. Ancient polities and institutions were not directly assailed and overturned, but the renewal of the spirits that create law and order was to make all things new. And this stupendous work was to be done by simple unadorned speech, the telling of a simple history by simple men. And Jesus believed that His end was attainable, and could be attained by His means. In this faith He became a Preacher, the Preacher of the kingdom; and His Word was creative in the very degree that it was tender and quiet. The Christ and the Baptist were, as Preachers, the antithesis of each other. John had roused the nation, had made the banks of the Jordan as populous as a city, had forced the proud and priestly as well as the simple and sinful to seek his baptism and confess their sins. But Jesus avoided crowds and commotion, stole as it were into obscurity, lived simply among simple people in a province remote from the city and temple of His race, only now and then, as at a Feast, emerging on the greater stage they supplied. Yet this quiet and unobtrusive work was soon perceived by friends and foes alike to be more radical and penetrative than John's, more destructive of the old and creative of the new. Action that at first seemed so obscure as to be wasted was proved by the result to be work too deep to be audible, too eternal to be visible, at the foundations of the new society, the City of God.

It seems curious, inconsistent, indeed, with the Messianic mission and claims, that Jesus should choose Galilee as the scene of His first and creative ministry. Jerusalem appeared its natural field. It was the city of David, the centre of the nation, the symbol of its unity, the home of its schools, the seat of its worship, the abode of its priesthood. Galilee was a despised province, "the circle of the Gentiles:" out of it arose no prophet, from it no Messiah could come. To belong to it, to live in it, was to allow as it were *a priori* disproof of His claims. There, too, appreciative spirits were few, an audience of the cultured impossible. To seek Galilee was like courting defeat, inviting the contempt of Judæa, surrounding Himself with men too dull-witted to understand His words or quicken and gladden His soul with the sympathy possible to men of trained and nimble minds. But the Wisdom that justifies her children justified the choice of Jesus, proved that it was, as He was, of God.

Judæa and Jerusalem had been the worst of all fields for the early ministry of Jesus. It had made conflict precede and accompany creation. There were serene depths in His own spirit which the conflict could not have disturbed, but it would have troubled and bewildered the simpler spirits He wished to form. Old societies have an immense power of repression, are easily moved to a jealousy that as easily glides into revenge. It had been ill had His

career ended ere it had well begun, had He gone to seek
His final sorrow and suffering instead of leaving them to
seek Him. Amid the peace His early obscurity afforded
He could meeten and mature His Spirit for the Passion
which was to be at once supreme sacrifice and supreme
glory. There, too, He could best form His society out of
men who combined the simplicity of childhood with the
strength of manhood. The men who incarnate the genius
of an ancient polity or state are brittle rather than malle-
able, tend so to break as to wound the hand that attempts
to fashion them into finer forms and for nobler uses. The
men who can be so made as to become makers are men
who unite the open sense and innocent wonder of the child
with the high faith and resolute will of the man. Official
or officious teachers are seldom made of teachable stuff.
The soul long fed on subtleties becomes too absorbed in
the distinctions to care for the truths and realities of life.
The priests and scribes of Jerusalem were too thoroughly
possessed by the old to be readily penetrated by the new.
The simple Galileans were not mismade, only unmade,
men, waiting but the coming of One who could breathe
into them the breath of life to rise up quick and quickening
spirits. Then, too, the influence of Jesus increased in intensity with the narrowing of the circle within which He
moved. The more extensive the stage the smaller His
power. He did not need to make many, but to make
thoroughly. The many only touched had done nothing,
but the few transformed could reform the world. His presence, where understood, was power. His person and
word stood in an exegetical relation to each other, were
mutually illustrative and explanatory. But to be so they
needed to be seen in their ideal relations, living together
in happy and beautiful unity, undisturbed by the presence
of jealous and disputatious Jews. And Galilee allowed
the ideal relations to be realized. While He waited for

the Passion that came towards Him with awful inevitable step, He made the meaning of Himself, His truth, and His mission penetrate and possess His simple-minded disciples. The obscure but great ministry of those days not only created the new society, but has been the regulative force in its history, as fruitful of the principles that have commanded as the Passion of the motives and emotions that have inspired the church. Its influence lives in our Synoptic Gospels. Its memory was so potent as to eclipse the ministry in Judæa, and a fourth and later Evangelist was needed to tell the story of those visits to Jerusalem that the authors of the earliest Christian *Memorabilia* had forgotten in their vivid recollection of the life lived and words spoken in Galilee.

His earliest ministry in Galilee may be said to have been private and tentative, a preliminary or prophetic ministry. It grew out of the Baptist's. John's preaching had sifted his hearers, had determined and revealed their spiritual affinities. The men of Jerusalem had soon withdrawn from him. What would not be absorbed into Judaism they could not tolerate, and so, while they began by accepting the baptism, they ended by rejecting the Baptist. He had a devil, as had every one too generous to be a Jew. But in the men from Galilee he had awakened a new spirit, a grand consciousness of human evil and Divine good. The spirit he had awakened he could not satisfy. It wanted more than he could give—the baptism of the Holy Ghost and of fire. And so an elect circle waited near John, held there by the Divine hunger of their spirits. And they soon found Him for whom they waited, Jesus of Nazareth, the Son of Joseph. There is no finer proof possible of the power and spirit that lived in the Baptist than the quality of the men he quickened, but could not satisfy. Peter and John, Andrew, Philip, and Nathanael, were not ordinary persons, were men of the high creative order. They were the atoms that, with all their spiritual affinities awakened but unsatisfied, only waited the coming of the Word to crystallize into the New Society. With them Jesus returned into Galilee, and "manifested forth His glory" as they could bear it. It was a period of home ministry; on His part a making known, on theirs a coming to know. The Fourth Evangelist allows us a glimpse into this period, shows us Jesus by His presence at a marriage making the heart of man glad and the home of man holy, creating the spirit at once of belief and obedience.[1] Cana was the scene of His first miracle, but it was a miracle of the home, not of the synagogue or the market-place. His ministry was only beginning, had not yet begun.

Christianity, like Christ, was educated in Galilee, but was born in Judæa. The new faith, as a new faith supersessive of the old, could have as its appropriate birthplace only Jerusalem. The Christ could proclaim His kinghood only in "the city of the great King." John was the one Evangelist who saw the meaning of the event, and recorded it. When "the Jews' passover was at hand, Jesus went up to Jerusalem."[2] There as a boy He had woke into consciousness of His mission; there as a man He was to inaugurate His reign. Feast and city, time and place, were alike significant. As the Greeks at Olympia, the Jews at Jerusalem realized their unity, lived as a people unified by a common faith and a common descent and history. Then, as now, Jews were everywhere—merchants and philosophers in Alexandria, scholars and teachers in Athens, ministers of virtue and vice, diplomatists, traders, servants, interpreters at Rome, colonists in Gaul and Spain, settlers in the towns of Syria, in the isles of Greece, in the valley of the Euphrates, beside the once hated streams of Babel. But the Jew had then what he has not

[1] John ii. 1-11.   [2] Ibid. ii 13.

now—national being, a city that incorporated and symbolized his religious, if not his political ideal. And so, though he forsook he did not forget Zion, looked with longing eyes to the city where God dwelt, which the deeds of his fathers, the songs of his faith, the words of his prophets, had so consecrated and glorified. And thus the scattered sons of Israel loved to come from far, and while they stood within Jerusalem, become for one blissful day oblivious of their mercenary and down-trodden present, by becoming conscious of their glorious past, and hopeful of a splendid future. No passover came without bringing troops of pilgrims yearning to see—

> The Holy City lift high her towers,
> And higher yet the glorious Temple **rear**
> Her pile, far off appearing like a mount
> Of alabaster, topped with golden spires.

The Temple was not simply the expression of the nation's faith, but the symbol of its spirit and epitome of its history. The one sanctuary had helped to create the one faith, had contributed in an almost equal degree to the spread of Hebraism and the growth of Judaism. It served the former well at first, but the latter most and last. The Temple may indeed be regarded as, while the creation of prophetic monotheism, the creator of Judaic sacerdotalism. If it did not form the priesthood, it greatly promoted the formation of a priestly caste; tended to decrease the spiritual by increasing the sensuous elements in Mosaism; to turn men's minds from thinking that God was best served by righteousness to thinking that He was best served by sacrifices and ceremonies. The Temple helped at once to fulfil and to defeat the prophetic ideal: to fulfil it by realizing the faith in one God, to defeat it by localizing Jehovah. The Deity of the Hebrew prophets was the one and universal God, but the God of the Jewish Temple was

GALILEE, JUDÆA, SAMARIA.

only a magnified and sublimed tribal deity. If there was only one God He must be the God of all men; but a God who could be worshipped only in one place and by one people remained *their* God. And this difference involved another: the universal was an ethical conception, the particular a sensuous and sacerdotal. To the prophets the supreme matter was God, and the obedience He demanded; but to the priesthood, worship conducted in proper form by proper persons. The conflict of these opposite and contradictory tendencies lasted through several centuries, and the Jewish Temple represented the victory of the second, a universal religion localized by a tribal and inflexible sacerdotalism.

We can understand, then, how the Temple might be to a mind like Christ's at once a pleasure and an offence. The symbolical significance might please, but its actual state would pain. It was a symbol of the highest spiritual realities, God's search after man, man's search after God; of the heroic struggles that had created the first monotheism, the mother of all the rest. But as a place it was the scene of a worship that had extinguished religion. The zeal for ritual was everywhere; men could not get to God for priests and sacrifices, were so beset by formal laws and ordinances that ethical obedience was impossible. Yet the most exacting ceremonialism is always most accommodating—exacts scrupulous observance of its rites, but supplies facile access to the means. The worshipper had no need to neglect any form, or omit any sacrifice; the instruments and articles of worship stood waiting to be purchased. If he wished to sacrifice, he had a choice of beasts—sheep, oxen, doves—could select according to his purpose or his means. If he came with the stamped money of Cæsar, he could exchange it for the unstamped sacred shekel, that nothing with any sign or image might be presented to God. He entered the Temple of his fathers through a market, where he bought the means of rightly approaching and worshipping their God.

Now, if we would understand Christ's mind and emotions in presence of this scene of praise through purchase, we must do it through His saying, "Make not My Father's house a house of exchange."[1] The phrase "My Father's house" expresses His ideal of the place and its purpose: it is where parent and child may meet each other, where the filial may commune with the paternal spirit, not alone, but in the home, amid its loved and trusted kin. The phrase "a house of exchange" expresses His idea of the actual scene, what made it so direct and painful a contradiction to His ideal. Honest merchandize He did not condemn. What He condemned was not simply the intrusion of merchandize into His "Father's house," but its attempt to regulate and express the relations between Father and child. It first depraved, and then destroyed, the filial spirit. It was fatal to the pure and delicate affection, the soft and gentle love, that made the home of God the best home of man. It was the corporate expression of the cardinal sin of Judaism, the reduction of man's worship of God to a service by acts formal and artificial, through instruments and articles sensuous, external, purchasable.

The cleansing of the Temple is an event that has been provocative of much criticism and discussion. Paulus, true to his not very rational naturalism, reduced it to what was little else than a popular tumult led by Jesus. Strauss, in his first *Leben*, explained it as a myth suggested by Malachi iii. 1-3. Bruno Bauer made merry over it as the evidently fictitious story of a free fight, in which, had it really occurred, Jesus would have been certain to find the dealers in sheep and doves and the money-changers more than a match for Him. But in

[1] John ii. 16.

truth the event is intrinsically one of the most probable. It had a sufficient reason, and was in no way inconsistent with the character of Jesus. Severity is but a form of gentleness—is gentleness become strenuous against the evil and injurious through its love of the good and the injured. A character incapable of indignation is destitute of righteousness, without the will to give adequate expression to its moral judgments. Here there was almost the worst possible perversion of the holiest things, an offence the conscience would condemn in the proportion to its purity. The emotions awakened in the mind of Christ by the conflict of the ideal and the real could not have been more strongly, and therefore more fitly, expressed. Then, too, the act was finally intelligible to a Hebrew, an act of splendid loyalty to his God. The man who was zealous for God could not allow His house or His name to be profaned. The prophet but asserted his inalienable right when he commanded worship to be reformed, the Temple to be purified. Christ is here but resurgent Hebraism declaring in brave and expressive acts the doom of apostate Judaism.

But there is another side to the matter, present to the mind alike of Christ and His Evangelist. The Jews ask, " What sign showest thou unto us, seeing that thou doest these things ? " They do not absolutely deny His right to do what He had done, they only demand His warrant, by what authority. Now the remarkable thing is the answer of Christ, " Destroy this temple, and in three days I will raise it up." This answer explains His act, shows it to have been to His own mind, as later to John's, symbolical. The Temple was the type of the ancient worship, embodied and represented Judaism. To destroy it was to abolish the system it represented. As it was the type of the old faith Christ was the type of the new. He was the true ideal temple — in Him God was manifested, through Him man found God. He was the tabernacle of God with men, the personalized Divine presence.[1] Here, then, were the false and the true, the sensuous and the spiritual, the depraved type and the perfect reality, facing each other; and Jesus says, " Destroy this temple—the whole ancient system as here incorporated and symbolized—and in three days I will create a new and permanent form for the eternal truth that had here a transitory type. The destruction is to be your act, not mine. I am not come to destroy the law and the prophets, but to fulfil them. My death may seem to you an expedient necessary to save the nation, but what you mean to save the nation will really destroy it. In three days I will make it evident that the Temple is superseded, that Judaism is doomed, the reign of the letter over and the reign of the spirit come. The holy city, the New Jerusalem, shall then come down from God, and its Temple shall be the Lord God Almighty and the Lamb."

The saying explains the prominence John gives to the incident. It was to his mind the inauguration of the new economy, the explicit claim on Christ's part to be the true temple of God, the heart of the new religion. The impression made on him by the scene and the saying seems to live in his awed and frequent references to the temple or tabernacle of God with men. And the claim appears to have impressed other minds almost as much as his. Two significant things he mentions ; first, that many believed on Christ; and next, that He did not commit Himself to them. The belief was sensuous rather than spiritual, due more to miracles seen than to truths understood. And in such faith Jesus did not confide. The men who gave it He did not receive into His own inner circle. Those who stood there must believe in Himself rather than His works. John happily illustrates

[1] John i. 14; *cf* Rev xxi. 3, 22.

both points by a person. Nicodemus was the type of a man who believed because of the miracles, and who was, however well-meaning, anything but a man to be trusted. He is indeed exceptional—the one Pharisee and ruler who honestly seeks to be instructed by Christ. But while he was discontented with the past, he cannot quite break with it. The prejudices of a life are hard to conquer, but the coarse yet subtle persecutions of society are still harder to bear. Nicodemus was stronger than the first, but weaker than the second; and Jesus speaks to him as one weak while strong, who believed the miracles but did not trust their Worker. The discourse was, while particular, universal, while addressed to the man, addressed to him as a representative of a class, in a sense of the race.

It is one of the notes and peculiarities of the Fourth Gospel that the reflections of the historian often so blend with the discourses of Christ that it is hardly possible to tell where the latter end and the former begin. It is so eminently here. The discourse of Christ ends most probably with Verse 15, and Verses 16-21 express the explicative thoughts of the Evangelist. Yet his mind has become so completely possessed with the Spirit of his Master, that his words are as the words of Christ. The commentary so finely harmonizes with the discourse as to make it into a more perfect whole, a discourse not simply to Nicodemus, but to the Christian ages. It may be necessary to exhibit the two sections in their relations to each other, and to the historical and ideal elements in the person of Christ.

The discourse proper falls into two parts: the first (Verses 3-8) explains the condition of entrance into the kingdom, and this condition at once explains the nature of the kingdom and is explained by it. The kingdom is a kingdom of the Spirit, and the birth into it is a spiritual birth, an effect whose cause is the ubiquitous, silently ever-operating Divine Spirit, whose historical symbol or expression is "the water" that purifies and renews. The second part (Verses 10–15) explains Christ's relation to the kingdom and to the men who seek it. If men enter it, it must be by faith in Himself—which is but the intellectual and personal side of the change that had been before described on its spiritual and social—but it must be absolute faith in Him as one who testifies of what He knows, as a Speaker who knows heaven as earth, and has descended that He might speak with the authority of one who had a celestial as well as a terrestrial presence. And He who requires such absolute faith can do so only as the creative spiritual centre of the world, the spiritual pole, as it were, of humanity, drawing all eyes and hearts towards Him, that He may illuminate all with His light and gladden with His love. The discourse thus speaks to the deepest needs of Nicodemus. He is but a seeker after the things of the senses. What he needs is a change of the spirit, entrance as a trustful child into a new society which he is too sensuous to perceive. And to enter, it is not miracles he must regard, it is their Worker. The Christian society is constituted by faith in Christ.

The commentary, again, falls, like the discourse, into two parts, the first being an explicit statement of truths implied or indicated in the discourse; the second, an exposition of the principles that govern the conflict of light and darkness, love and hate, which the gospel is written to pourtray. The former part (Verses 16–18) explains the ideal cause and design of Christ's historical appearance; the cause being God's love to the world, the design, most agreeable to the cause, "that the world through Him might be saved." The latter part (Verses 19–21) explains the real or historical results of His appear-

GALILEE, JUDÆA, SAMARIA.

ance; on the one side, men so loving the darkness as to hate and refuse the light; on the other, men so loving the light as to seek it that they may live, and be seen to live, in God. The two sections thus blend into a fine unity, constitute, when combined, a discourse which progresses from the idea of the kingdom and birth into it through the King to the causes and results of His historical appearance, the unequal though long protracted conflict of Divine love and human hate.

In this discourse and commentary it has been contended that there are ideas strange to the Synoptics and their Christ, peculiar to the Fourth Evangelist, late in origin, and unhistorical in character. The most foreign and offensive of these ideas is the second birth; but it is only a more radical and expressive formula for a most characteristic thought of the Synoptic Christ, entering into the kingdom by becoming a little child.[1] The Apostolical Epistles, too, prove that the idea had so penetrated early Christian thought [2] as to be explicable only as a creation of its common Creator. The idea expressed in the phrase "born of the Spirit" stands in fine harmony with John's prophecy, "He shall baptize you with the Holy Ghost," as with the later notion of baptism in its name.[3] The commentary, too, is as distinctive of John as the discourse of Jesus. "Only begotten" occurs in his characteristic sense.[4] Love and God, light and God, are associated as he likes to associate them [5]—the divinest qualities in God used to explain at once his antagonism to the ignorance and the evil of man, and his strenuous service of man's highest good.

[1] Matt xviii 3; Mark x. 15; Luke xviii 17.
[2] Titus iii. 5 , 1 Peter 1 3, 11 2 ; 1 Cor. iv. 15 ; Gal. iv. 29 ; Phil. 10 ; 1 John 11 29 , 111 9 ; v. 1, 4, 8.
[3] Matt. iii. 11 , John 1 33 , Matt. xxviii 19 , Acts i. 5 ; xi. 16.
[4] John 1. 14, 18 ; 1 John iv. 9
[5] John 1. 4, 5, 7–9 , 1 John 1. 5 ; iv. 8–10.

Jerusalem was not to be the scene of Christ's ministry. It was tried and rejected. Yet with a noble love and loyalty to the queenly city He lingered in her neighbourhood, speaking His truth, baptizing[1] men who came to confess their sins and be instructed. But He could not remain in Judæa; Pharisaic jealousy was too strong, threatened premature conflict. So He " departed again into Galilee," and He " must needs go through Samaria."[2] The necessity was not geographical, but ethical, was rooted in His nature and mission, was not caused by His place. The story of the Samaritan journey is symbolical. John tells it as an allegory, while a history. The two were to him, where Christ's action was concerned, identical—the real ever representing an ideal. Strauss regarded it as a myth suggested by the beautiful tale of the meeting of Jacob and Rachel at the well. The woman was the representative of an unclean people; the five husbands represented their five idols, and the sixth their illegitimate worship of Jehovah. Hengstenberg and Keim are here in curious agreement with Strauss, with these differences, that the former of course rejects the mythical theory, while the latter substitutes religions for idols. But the narrative is too finely and minutely historical to be an allegory in their sense, and their interpretation fails to explain its most significant touches. The cardinal point of their allegory is but a secondary incident in the story, and obtained by the sacrifice of its essential symbolism. For there is here a real enough symbolism, looking out from the double senses in the " water," " the well," " the mountain," " the harvest." What it is we may best discover through the feelings that must have been in the mind of Christ. When He retired from Judæa two thoughts must have possessed Him—the evil of the hateful formalism of the Jews, and the failure of His ministry

[1] John iii. 22; iv. 1, 2. [2] Ibid. iv. 3, 5.

in Jerusalem. Judaism had localized and concealed God; though a universal God, He could be found only at Jerusalem; though a righteous God, He could be worshipped only by sensuous forms and ceremonies. And these ideas of God stood in so radical antithesis to His that they had caused the failure of His mission, made the Jews not only disinclined to hear Him, but unable to understand the splendid significance of His words. But now this narrative supplies the contrast that at once illustrates and defines His truth and His mission. God is proved to be universal and ethical, capable of being worshipped anywhere, only to be worshipped in spirit and in truth. And the mission which establishes this truth is just in its spring-time, but it is a spring which not only had the promise of harvest, but is equal to it. Though Judæa is behind, the world is before; if the one is a proud and exclusive city, the other is a field ripe to the sickle.

It is strange that Christ should often speak His most remarkable words to the least remarkable persons. Here is a woman who for one splendid moment emerges from the unknown, stands as in a blaze of living light, and vanishes into the unknown again. But while she stands she is immortalized, the moment becomes an Eternal Now, in which Christ and she face each other for ever, He giving and she receiving truths the world can never allow to die. For the woman is a type, a particular that expresses an universal. She represents heathenism, the world waiting for the truths Christ was bringing. And what He gives to her He gives to the race; what she receives she receives for mankind. In that woman man lived, and in her became conscious of the truth—" God is a Spirit, and they that worship Him must worship in spirit and in truth."

The influence of Judæa lives in words like these. The " in spirit " is an assertion of the universal presence of

God everywhere in man, never in a temple or city, to be worshipped by mind, never as in a place. The "in truth" expresses the essential quality or element of worship, stands, as it were, opposed to "in form" or "in ritual." The worship that is everywhere possible must be always ethical; what is independent of place is dependent on spirit and truth.

But while the "in spirit" is in contrast with the "in Jerusalem" of Judaism, it is in essential agreement with "God is a Spirit." Where God is conceived as a Spirit, worship must be spiritual; where worship is sensuous, God is sensuously conceived. Worship is but the mutual speech of the Divine and the human; God is as active in it as man. And so it is only where He is rightly conceived that man can rightly worship. He could as little worship a God that was only cold eternity or silent speechless space as it could know or speak to him. And so Christ verifies and personalizes "spirit" by the term Father, seeks by creating a new consciousness of God to create a new attitude of the spirit towards Him. As His phrase "in truth" is in contrast with "in ceremonies" or "in sensuous forms," so it is in radical agreement with the idea expressed by "Father." Falsity in worship may be either in the object or in the subject: if the first, it is idolatry; if the second, it is hypocrisy. These, as commonly used, are opposites: heathenism is better than hypocrisy; honest faith in a false religion is better than false worship in a true. But they may really be so related as to be opposite sides of one thing. Man cannot offer false worship to a true God. Where the worship is false the God must be the same; the one falsifies the other. God is conceived and addressed, not as He is, but as the worshipper imagines Him to be. Hence Christ's aim was to create true worship by creating true knowledge of God. The Father deserved honour, the Son owed reverence.

Filial reverence was always beautiful and always honourable. It would not write a wrinkle on the brow that grows more beautiful with age, or touch with pain the heart loved for the love it had given. Filial honour grows with years. We become better sons and daughters the more the memory of those we first knew and loved

> Wins a glory from their being far,

and orbs into a rounded and mellow beauty we did not see while in their home. It is doubtful whether any daughter ever knew what her mother was or how she loved her till she herself had tasted the bliss and pain, the anxieties and joys, of motherhood. Possibly no son ever honoured his father as he could and should have honoured him till he had sons clustering round his own knees and sitting at his own table. So Christ seeks to create filial love by creating a conscious filial relation, certain that the reverence which flows from love would make " worship in spirit and in truth" a happy necessity, local and sensuous worship a sure impossibility. The idea of God which Judæa cast out and Samaria received was the idea creative of the true worship, everywhere possible, but possible only as ethical.

And for this faith, what hope? The Outcast of Jerusalem, the city of the one God, might well despond. Yet to Him comfort had come and largest hope. His own words to the woman, the woman's attitude to Himself and His truth, had evoked visions that became to Him, weary, as He was, as the very food of God. He saw the world standing all open in eye and soul to receive His truth, made by it reverent, obedient, holy; and His words told the vision that gladdened His soul: "Lift up your eyes, and look on the fields; for they are white already to harvest. And he that reapeth receiveth wages, and gathereth fruit unto life eternal: that both he that soweth and he that reapeth may rejoice together." [1]

[1] John iv. 35, 36.

VIII.

THE MASTER AND THE DISCIPLES.

THE fame of the things Jesus had done "at Jerusalem at the feast"[1] went before Him into Galilee, and He was welcomed for His works' sake. He avoided Nazareth—the Prophet was not as yet received in His own country[2]—and settled beside the lake of Gennesareth, near the homes of the men that formed the noblest legacy bequeathed to Him by John. There, beside the bright waters, in the shadow of the graceful palms, within sight of the cornfields and vineyards that sloped from the blue lake till they seemed to touch the blue sky, He breathed a purer air, enjoyed a happier life, looked upon wiser, because simpler, men than at Jerusalem. And these stiller and sweeter surroundings were but the conditions He needed to perform and perfect His great constructive work.

There are certain moments and scenes that profoundly touch the imagination. Abraham, his back to Chaldæa, his face to Canaan, setting out with his young and beautiful Sarah from the cradle of the great world-empires to seek a land where they could found an empire of the Spirit, become the progenitors of the people of the Book, who, while despised and hated as a nation, were yet to be, as the apostles and prophets of Jahveh, supreme legislators in religion; the first rude settlers building their huts on the hills beside the Tiber, tending their

[1] John iv 45. [2] Luke iv 24.

flocks, praying to their gods, spoiling their enemies, laying—in the blind and unconscious way common to men doing greater things than they dream of—the foundations of a city whose dominion was to be for centuries coextensive with civilization; Columbus leaving Europe, or standing on the deck of his ship watching the new world, with all its boundless hope and promise to the old, rising from below the horizon;—are scenes which mark so great moments in the life of man that the imagination feels equally awed and inspired in their presence. But the return of Jesus to Galilee was a moment that far transcended these alike in seeming insignificance and real immensity of issue. He entered it apparently a fugitive from Judæa, really the conscious Creator of the new yet eternal City of God. The society He was there to create was never to die; was to spread through every land as through all time; was to bind the ages in a wonderful harmony of spirit and purpose, man in a mystic brotherhood of faith and love. If we can conceive the marvellous vision of the future as open to the prescience of the Master, His soul may well have been cheered by the joy that was set before Him; while the men that were being, all unconsciously, fashioned into the agents of His great will, must have been to His mind a present rich in the rarest meanings, the grandest promises, a sort of new infant humanity, with all its infinite possibilities open to the eye of God, but concealed from its own innocent and dependent gaze.

We have been accustomed to associate the miraculous with action in the sphere of things physical, but a physical miracle is often only a marvel to the senses The distinctive miracles of Christ are spiritual. His living, penetrative, permanent power over man is like a standing miracle within the order known to our experience. There is nothing in history like the change

Jesus wrought in the Galileans He called into His society —unless, indeed, it be the similar changes He has been working ever since. Later, a proud Roman [1] and a cultured Greek [2] were to pour contempt on a religion whose Founder had been a crucified carpenter, whose earliest preachers had been wretched publicans, ignorant fishermen, itinerant tent-makers. But what they thought its shame, after and wiser ages were to think its glory. For the power to make the mean noble, the wretched happy, the ignorant more enlightened and beneficent than the wise, the wandering workman an unresting preacher of great and inspiring truths, is the divinest power that has yet been known to act within the region of the spirit. And this is the power Christ exercised while He lived, and has never since ceased to exercise. He elected men into His society, not as made, but that they might be made. The men He chose were only masses of latent capabilities, full of meaning to no eye but His, and to it the latent was more real and more precious than the patent. His selection, superficially regarded, might seem a studied offence to the authorities of His day; fundamentally regarded, it proves His pure and prescient wisdom. The world has not been inclined to seek its "mute inglorious Miltons" among its fishermen. As a class they are simple, superstitious, unintellectual, accustomed to exercise the senses rather than the reason. Publicans, too, have not been an admired class: the men that extorted money for a hated state have always been hated as personifying its worst vices. To select men from these classes for a great religious mission, looked like selecting the worst persons possible, the most disqualified for the work, the least able to command success. Yet from these classes Christ selected men that He pene-

[1] Tacitus, *Annal.*, xv 44
[2] Celsus, in Origen, *Contra Cels.*, lib. iii. cc. 44, 50, 52, 55.

trated, permeated, possessed with His spirit, in a personal, yet real, sense Christianized. They became vehicles of His influence, carried, as implanted, the life that lived in Him as original and innate. What He communicated to them they communicated to the race. They became in Christ's society the patriarchs of a new Israel, the founders of a new faith. Association with Him was a Divine education which qualified not only for citizenship in the kingdom of heaven, but also for creating citizens, the institution of the churches that were to extend and realize the reign of God. The marvel is, not that the fishermen of Galilee conquered the world, but that Jesus of Nazareth made them its conquerors. The wonder lies in the making of the men, not in their doings. The Inspirer is more extraordinary than the inspired, especially when they were men so little susceptible of His influence that He had to create the very capacity to receive His inspiration, with the consequent ability to realize His ends.

Now, this making of the men is what is here to be studied. It was, indeed, a process that continued throughout Christ's ministry; but the creative period was the period of intimate and tender association in Galilee, when the Master lived in humble and beautiful beneficence, and the disciples grew and rejoiced in His light. It was to His and their souls a time of fine and fruitful rest, of activities that played while they worked in the glad sunshine. The discourses belonging to it show a calm and almost joyous spirit, untouched as yet by the shadow of the cross. They do not speak of the decease to be accomplished at Jerusalem, are not concerned with controversy or conflict, do not gloomily forecast troubles to come. These qualities were to maik the discourses of later and darker times. Meanwhile all was sunny in His spirit and speech. Heaven was about Him, as within; His truth and wisdom were subduing His little society unto Himself. His words seem fragrant of the vineyard, the meadow, and the grove; full of the love that turns into glory the light of common day, the spirit that changes into music its most familiar sounds. His haunts were not the great cities, but the towns and villages that stood round the lake He loved, or the hills that overlooked the plains where, with the open and beautiful sky above and the fragrant fruitful earth around, He could speak to His disciples of their Father in heaven, of His care for all that lived and breathed, of the truths the soul could hear spoken by the lovely and modest lily, or sung by the soaring and singing bird. This quiet and beautiful time, when the Master lived with and for His disciples, was the time when He instituted His society by creating its creative citizens, the men that were to stand round the King.

The method of Christ was twofold: His great formative agencies were speech and fellowship. His words created a new world within and around His disciples, filled their minds with new thought, aims, ideals, hopes. We know how His speech has embodied and embalmed His truth, made God a new Being to man, made man a new being to God and to himself; but we can ill imagine the influence exercised by His living speech, by His words as interpreted by voice and eye, by the invisible soul that yet looked visibly out from every feature and sense. To hear His daily speech was not simply to receive His thoughts, but to share, as it were, the inmost life of His Spirit—to stand within the holy of holies, and listen to the soft yet awful voice telling the highest mysteries, speaking the last secrets of the Unknown. It was to the disciples a sudden elevation, a being lifted from a twilight more delusive than darkness to the sunlit, glory-crowned Mount of God—a revelation that must have dazzled the men who received it, had it not been subdued into softest yet purest light by the

THE MASTER AND THE DISCIPLES. 135

medium through which it streamed. His speech is, after eighteen centuries, exceeding wonderful to the world, and humanity still listens to it as one listens to a tale he cannot choose but hear, yet to the men who first heard it it was made finely intelligible by His person. To hear His speech was to enjoy His fellowship, and His fellowship created the sense that understood His speech. His words came to them explained by a living and articulate commentary; their edition was, as it were, illustrated, the illustrations being *tableaux vivants* composed from the acts, chaiacter, and conduct of the Speaker. The men might not understand the text, but they understood the illustrations; they might find the saying hard, but the commentary was entirely intelligible. Fellowship is the most potent of educative agencies, and its highest potency was realized in the society which knew by experience what spiritual forces were embodied in the Christ.

If, then, we are to understand Christ's method of educating His disciples or founding His society, it must be through His two great agencies—His Speech and Fellowship. His mode of using the first may be best seen in His Sermon on the Mount. Matthew and Luke both recognize it as essentially a discourse to the disciples.[1] To both Evangelists it is an inaugural sermon, but Matthew alone perceives its proper place and value, and reports it at length. In it Christ explains His conception of the kingdom, imparts His own mind to His disciples. It implied faith, but aimed at creating knowledge, and the obedience and sympathy knowledge alone can evoke. The discourse is in itself remarkable enough. It contains the most weighty, because the most weighed, words of Jesus; is His most deliberate deliverance—the set speech, as it were, fruit of forethought, for which He made rather than found occasion. The parables were for the most part oppoitune

[1] Matt v 2, Luke vi. 20.

words, drawn from Him by the suggestion or necessities of the moment, intended to rebuke, to warn, to encourage, or instruct particular men or classes. The sayings that pointed the moral of miracle or event, that expressed the joy or sorrow caused by incident or outlook; the answers called forth by disciples or seekers after truth or health, by Pharisee or Sadducee anxious to entangle Him in His talk, or by Pilate flinging out in a question that jested His heart-sick doubt—were, one and all, occasional, even where most divinely significant. But here Jesus does not wait to be found by event or inquiry: He stands forward to institute His kingdom by revealing its nature and proclaiming its laws. He speaks to the men He had chosen to be its first and creative citizens, that they might know His purpose and mission, know where they themselves stood, to what they had been called, and what they ought to become and to do.

We do not regard this sermon, then, especially as it exists in Matthew, as a mere agglomeration of disconnected and isolated sayings, or a patchwork made up of fragments from various forgotten discourses.[1] We believe that it is an unity, harmonious in all its parts, coherent throughout, progressing in the most rational order from beginning to end. We believe, too, that it has been set in its right place, that it is an inaugural sermon, delivered soon after the return to Galilee, bearing evidences of the recent visit to Jerusalem, expressly designed to make the consciousness of Christ an open secret to His disciples, His kingdom a reality to intellect and conscience. It is evidently an early discourse, expository, not apologetic—save, indeed, as regards one most significant point; and so belongs to a period while opposition was still future, before contradiction had assailed His doctrine, or hatred threatened or maligned His person. The one apologetic point is where

[1] Renan, *Les Évangiles*, p. 177.

THE MASTER AND THE DISCIPLES. 137

He declares He has "not come to destroy the law and the prophets."[1] His words imply that there were suspicions or charges on this matter, but the only thing that could occasion these belongs to His Judæan, not to His Galilean, ministry—His saying, "Destroy this temple."[2] Matthew[3] and Luke[4] significantly mention, just before reporting the sermon, that "there followed Him great multitudes from Jerusalem and Judæa:" and may not their presence in Galilee be best explained as the result of His presence at the feast and the interest it had caused? Then, too, the manner in which He describes and contrasts real and unreal worship seems to indicate an imagination vividly impressed by recent scenes, too freshly touched to be altogether calm; and the scenes that could so move could be witnessed only at Jerusalem. The sermon appears, too, to be subtly and variously related to the discourse to the Samaritan woman. They differ thus: the one is a discourse on worship, the other on obedience. Their subjects are, respectively, How ought God to be worshipped? and, How ought God to be served? But these differences are due to the accidents of time and audience, and must not be allowed to conceal their essential affinity. The attitude, as we may call it, of Christ's mind is the same in both cases: in the one He enjoins spiritual worship, in the other He inculcates spiritual obedience, each in contrast to its sensuous and formal opposite. The discourse exhibits the new and perfect as opposed to the old and imperfect worship; the sermon, the new and spiritual as opposed to the old outer and ceremonial law. As is the new worship, so is the new obedience; each is, and for the same reason, "in spirit" and "in truth." In the one case, as in the other, the Divine Paternity is the determinating idea; the worship and obedience must, to be real, be agreeable to the nature

[1] Matt. v. 17.
[2] John ii. 19.
[3] Matt. iv. 25.
[4] Luke vi. 17.

and character of the Father. Then, too, Christ's sense of the Divine sufficiency is the same in both cases. In the one He speaks of the harvest as present though distant, as so contained in spring that sower and reaper can rejoice together; in the other, He speaks of the happy faith that is satisfied with to-day, that can work in the present, certain that its fruits and the future are safe in the hands of God. Spiritual worship and spiritual obedience alike proceed from a spiritual and filial conception of God: where such a conception exists there is certain to be a faith victorious over sense.

These affinities seem to indicate that the Discourse in Samaria and the Sermon on the Mount stand in point of time near each other. Similar thoughts and associations seem to be active in the mind of the Speaker, His speech differing because place and purpose are different. If our infeence is right, it helps us not only to define the time of the sermon as soon after the return to Galilee, but also the better to describe its design. The disciples had been made to know His mission—that He had come to establish a kingdom, that His kingdom stood in antagonism to Judaism, the only theocratic system they knew: but what His kingdom was, its essential nature and laws, they did not know. Their faith was, in a sense, blind—a faith in Himself alone. Of the things He had come to do, and purposed doing, they knew nothing. But an ignorant trust was not to His mind; they must know His idea if they were ever to realize His ideal; must possess His thoughts if they were to be possessed of His Spirit and aims. The men who were to constitute His State could do so only as they understood its constitution and laws.

From this standpoint, let us attempt to interpret in rough outline this great sermon. The Introduction (Chap. v. 3-16) presents discipleship, or rather citizenship, under two great aspects: first, as regards its rewards and privileges—the Beatitudes (Verses 3-12); second, as regards its essential functions and duties (Verses 13-16). The Introduction is a glorious vestibule, altogether seemly and suitable to this new yet eternal palace of truth. The Beatitudes significantly stand first. The strength of the old law lay in its stern sanctions, but the strength of the new is to be its benedictions. Moses constrained to obedience by pronouncing the disobedient accursed, but Christ invites to loving loyalty by pronouncing the citizen of His kingdom blessed. This alone was a new thing in the world. Men were to be no more made religious by terror, but were to be won to righteousness by sweetly winsome hope and happiness. Obedience, as Jesus conceived it, could not proceed from fear; the obedience of fear was but disguised disobedience. The man that obeyed God through terror would have obeyed His opposite had he been still more terrible. But to Jesus obedience is love, a sweet and welcome necessity to a heart that knows God as its Father and itself as His child. And so religion is beatitude, love active and exercised; the kingdom which makes righteous makes blessed. And the blessedness is not uniform, all of one kind: it exists in many varieties, adapted to every degree of love, to every quality and condition of soul. The God who made men to differ creates for each man a happiness of his own, allows no loyal citizen to go empty away.

The Beatitudes fall into two great classes—those of resignation and those of hope, or blessings for those who learn obedience through suffering, and blessings for those whose obedience is active, though hated and persecuted, beneficence. To the first class belong the poor in spirit, the mourners, the meek, the men who hunger and thirst after righteousness; to the second class, the merciful, the pure in heart, the peacemakers, the persecuted for righteousness' sake. Each has his appropriate blessing. The poor in spirit, vacant of self, waiting for God, conscious of a poverty that only the Divine indwelling can change into wealth, feeling, like the wondrous beggar of *Meister Eckhart*, that they " would sooner be in hell and have God, than in heaven and not have Him," [1] are already citizens ; " theirs is the kingdom of heaven." The mourners, who feel the evil of sin and the sanctity of sorrow, who are, like the man of the " marred visage," " acquainted with grief," but only so as to be " made perfect through suffering," are " to be comforted," their " sorrow shall be turned into joy," transformed by the soft and silent comfort of God. The meek, conscious of human littleness and Divine greatness, sweetly reasonable with man, humbly reverent and obedient towards God, are to " inherit the earth : " their patience, the muffled gentleness of Divine strength, shall yet prevail over boisterous pride. The men who hunger and thirst after righteousness, who seek the living God, conscious that they were made for Him, are to be filled, are to be satisfied with the object of their desire and search. The merciful, generous to the fallen, gentle to the weak, gracious to the offender, are to " obtain mercy," are to be twice blessed ; blessed as givers and receivers of the grace that " droppeth as the gentle rain from heaven upon the place beneath." The pure in heart are, as light-ful, able to receive more light, to enjoy that beatitude which has been the hope and passion of the devout in every age, " to see God ; " because, being like Him, " they shall see Him as He is." The peacemakers, creating brotherhood, making our troubled earth the home of love, are to be " the children of God," like in spirit and in work to their Father in heaven. The persecuted for righteousness' sake are not to be vanquished by persecution, but to have the reward of the righteous—theirs is to be the final good, the kingdom of heaven. So, at length,

[1] Martensen's *Meister Eckart*, p. 107.

there is hope of happiness for man. It has ceased to be an outer, has been made an inner, good. The happy man is to make the happy world, not the happy world the happy man. The kingdom and its rewards are spiritual, "not meat and drink, but righteousness, peace, joy, in the Holy Ghost."[1]

The second section of the Introduction is intimately related to the first. The essential functions are, in a sort, the Beatitudes in their outward aspect—the men who are saintly exercising the influence inseparable from sainted men. The functions are not voluntary duties, are but the action of qualities already possessed. So the men who are "blessed" are "the salt of the earth"—preserve it; are "the light of the world"—guide and teach it. Conscious beatitude is necessary beneficence; to make a man good is to do good to man. Personal vice is social disintegration; the virtue of individuals is the strength of a nation. In the alleys and slums of our crowded cities cleanly families are sanitary powers, are not only witnesses for physical cleanliness, but prevent the circle they influence from falling complete victims to impurity. So in morals a good man is not simply a witness for virtue, but a means of repressing vice, of keeping alive in men a sense of duty, a consciousness of right, an ideal of the good and the true. "Ye are the salt of the earth." But the citizens of the kingdom are more than preservative, they are dynamical and directive forces. Their faith is a faith in progress, in a world governed by righteousness and love. They are never satisfied with the actual, must ever strive towards the ideal. They keep alive the knowledge of God, and all that God represents, both as to the present and future of the race, as to what is the worst evil and what the greatest good alike to the individual and the nation. "Ye are the light of the world." The sun, so long as it

[1] Rom. xiv. 17.

is a sun, cannot but shine; it is of its very essence to give light, and light is the mother of life. We are all the children of the sun. "Even so let your light shine before men, that they may see your good works, and glorify your Father which is in heaven."

The body of the discourse (Chap. v. 17-48, and Chap. vi.) is a discussion of the new law in its relations and contrasts to the old, and in its essential principles, duties, and aims. He begins by defining His relation to the old: "I am come not to destroy, but to fulfil." He is the end of the law, abolishes by fulfilling it, is at once its consummation and cessation. He is the end of prophecy; for Him it lived, to Him it pointed, in Him is fulfilled. The law and the prophets were (1) predictive, and (2) enactive and creative of righteousness, and in both senses they were fulfilled by Christ. The law was prophecy in act; prophecy was law articulated or proclaimed. Each affirmed in its own way, " God reigns in righteousness; man owes Him obedience; the Holy can only be worshipped by the good, cannot be worshipped by the evil as evil; they must approach Him by sacrifice, and sacrifice that involves renunciation of sin, the quest after clean hands and a pure heart." And what each thus declared, Christ fulfilled. He was humanity become holy, perfect before God. And in Him perfect holiness was perfect sacrifice. Every truth as to God and His righteousness, every duty, hope, and aspiration as to man embodied in the law, proclaimed by the prophets, was fulfilled by Christ. But the end of the old is the beginning of the new, the $\tau \acute{\epsilon} \lambda os$ is here an $\dot{a} \rho \chi \acute{\eta}$. Every function possessed and discharged by law and prophecy He possesses and discharges, realizing their essential end, carrying into grandest performance their every endeavour and dream. The righteousness they attempt to enact and create He causes to exist. He succeeds where they failed. The righteous man is dutiful towards men and reverent towards God ; righteousness is but right action as regards man and right worship as regards God. Legal righteousness, which ought to be distinguished from the righteousness of the law and the prophets, had, as exemplified in the scribes and Pharisees, become a gross caricature of the great reality. Jesus exhib ts His in contrast to legal righteousness, first, as regards murder (Verses 21-26) ; second, as regards adultery (Verses 27-30) ; third, as regards divorce (Verses 31, 32) ; fourth, as regards perjury, or rather the conditions and forms of veracity in soul and speech (Verses 33-37) ; fifth, as regards retaliation (Verses 38-42) ; sixth, as regards social feelings, sympathies, and antipathies. And then He finally expresses and enforces His grand ideal in the words, " Be perfect, as your heavenly Father is perfect." Duty done to man is God imitated. Obedience is imitation of God. The law of God is just His spoken character, His expressed righteousness. To do His will is to become as He is, like Him in character, righteous as He is righteous. God's perfection is not physical, but moral; and the moral is ever the imitable. Were Satan Almighty, he would not cease to be Satan, would be none the less, rather all the more, the evil opposite of God. Might can never make right—is great only as the arm of righteousness. To know all things were not to be perfect, for an infinite eye that saw misery unpitied were but the serene cruelty that is so cruel because so cold. To be everywhere at every moment were not to be perfect, for an omnipresence that had neither the will nor the hand to help were a presence of mockery and insult. The perfection of God is the sovereignty of His moral attributes—the rule they exercise over His physical, making His omnipotence strength clothed in gentleness, His omniscience the herald of swift-footed mercy, His omnipresence the ever-active body of reigning and restoring righteousness. And a perfection that is moral is a perfection that can be imitated. Man has been made in the image, that he may live after the mind of God. Our spirits bear His likeness that our characters may embody His righteousness. We are His sons that we may love as He loves, be good as He is good, perfect as He is perfect, strenuous in the spiritual service that alone can please and honour a spiritual God. Christ in creating the spirit of a son creates the desire to imitate God, to act as we think He would act did He live as we live under the conditions of space and time.

Christ then turns to the duties that are more specifically religious, and pursues the same method of contrast as regards three—alms (Chap. vi. 1-4), prayer (Verses 5-15), fasting (Verses 16-18). Almsgiving was a religious act, a reminiscence of the truth that mercy to man was the best service of God. Jesus in effect says, " Do it as unto God; let it be a matter between thee and God, done for Him, approved by Him; then the act will be good like His mercy, and do good like His love." Prayer, too, concerns God and the soul alone; must be not formal, but filial, speech; speech that as filial is full of reverence, the consciousness of dependence, a sense of the brotherhood in which man is bound, of common sonship to the common Father, with all the love and tenderness to earth and heaven it involves. Prayer is the communion with God of a Godlike mind; where there is antipathy to man there cannot be affinity or intercourse with God. Hence prayer and forgiveness are so related that the one is the necessary condition of the other: only a forgiving spirit can ask to be forgiven. " Fasting," too, is a private and personal matter, to be done to and with God alone; without meaning, as seen, with meaning only as it enables the soul to meet and speak in secret with God. But prayer, intensified by the meditation which fasting allows, becomes the mother of desire—God the supreme object, in whom alone our hearts can repose (Verses 19-21). The more man has of God the more he desires to possess: here possession but increases capacity and quickens desire. But where the heart is turned in desire towards God, there the light of God enters and abides (Verses 22, 23). And where light and love dwell, there perfect obedience and absolute trust ought to be (Verses 24-30). These can never be disjoined. There cannot be obedience without trust, or trust without obedience. The faith that is without care is expressed in unwearied activity, in a dutiful fulfilment of the little as well as great obligations of life and time. The man who thinks Providence exists simply to make up his lack of service, despises Providence. The fowls of the air are diligent and unresting workers; our heavenly Father feedeth them by means of their own unweariedly exercised activities. But man's energies ought to be employed about dutiful and necessary things, ought not to be exhausted in anxiety about the possible, probable, or contingent. Duty done, all is done that man need be concerned about; God will mind the rest. And so Christ turns to the practical inferences (Verses 31-34). Do not spend your energies on distrustful and enervating conjectures as to things sensuous. Seek the kingdom of God, become citizens there, realize righteousness, and then everything will be secured. The future can have nothing to alarm, no evil can happen that shall not be made a means of higher good. To trust in God is to believe that infinite righteousness can never allow the righteous to suffer any real or ultimate wrong.

With the sixth chapter the expository part of the sermon ends; what remains is but a series of exhortations and admonitions. Hurried as our glance through it has been, it has sufficed to show certain of the more distinctive qualities in Christ's conception of the kingdom, of man's duties to God and man. His conception was throughout spiritual, had no sensuous, legal, or sacerdotal element. His worship could be as little embodied or conducted in symbols as His God could be represented by a graven image. The obedience He required stood as remote from ritual or ceremonial observances as He did from Judaism. But how could a conception so elevated, so unlike the notions then common and traditional, be made intelligible to men so simple and uncultured as His disciples? Here the action of His other great educative agency came in. His fellowship made His sermon luminous, interpreted His words, filled out their hidden and inarticulate meanings. The only religion the disciples had hitherto known had been one of symbols and symbolical acts. As exhibited in its acknowledged representatives, it was altogether a most manifest and mensurable thing. To fast twice in the week was to be eminently pious. To be an ostensible giver of alms was to be benevolent. To utter formal prayers in frequented places was to be devout. To wear phylacteries was to be full of faith. To despise and avoid publicans, to hate and shun sinners, to dislike and stand apart from the Gentiles, were evidences of sure fidelity to the Eternal and His law. Symbols and symbolical acts, sensuous distinctions and deeds, constituted the religion that then claimed to be the alone true. But now let us observe how Jesus lived, and what immense educative value belongs to certain too little studied acts of His. He did not fast, but lived a sweet and winsome, and, even in spite of His sorrows, a cheerful social life. He did not give alms, though He helped the poor in ways that lifted their spirits while lightening their poverty. He never prayed openly in the chief places of concourse, where men could see and hear, but rather on the still mountain side when alone with the Father, or when surrounded by His loved and trusted band, He implored that He and they might be one. His short, swift petitions, the cries, wrung from Him in

THE MASTER AND THE DISCIPLES.

His agony, that seemed to pierce the silent heaven like the sob of a heart grief had broken, were personal, came straight from Him, and went straight to His Father. He wore no phylactery, knew and loved Scripture too well to use it as an idol or a charm. He associated with publicans and sinners, became their "Friend," so familiar with their society as to be charged with being "gluttonous and a winebibber." He did not abjure the Gentiles, passed through and taught in Samaria, visited and preached in the coasts of Tyre and Sidon. Now all this must have made Him a great puzzle to those who saw Him only from without. The ordinary signs and acts of religion were absent, and men who judged by these would think He had none, just as later heathenism thought Christianity atheism, because the Christians were without images and temples, and refused to worship any of the recognized gods. But what bewildered His enemies instructed and informed His disciples. They saw that His religion neither consisted in, nor existed by, things external; that these might bury or betray, but could not make or express it. Instead, it was a state of the spirit expressed or revealed in conduct; a love to God that was equal to any service, making obedience, however seemingly hard, spontaneous; a love to man equal to any sacrifice, able with a truly Divine freedom to give self for the life of the world. And so just as the meaning of His person and life became through fellowship dimly intelligible to the disciples, His words would become full of the significance that made them the last and most perfect revelation of God.

We here touch a great subject, the relation of the person and words of Christ to each other. These are indeed inseparable. The words are, as it were, the expressed essence of the person; the person, the cause or source of the words. But the person is the greater; the cause must ever transcend the effect, the thinker be more and mightier than His thoughts. Without Jesus, the teaching of Jesus had been comparatively impotent. If His sayings had fallen from heaven like the great Ephesian goddess, they had never made for man a new faith and a diviner religion. The truths His words embodied His person incarnated, and without the life lived the words preached had been but spoken into the air. This subtle essential relation of speaker and speech, experienced all along the Christian ages, was most deeply and resultfully experienced by the men Jesus found fishermen of Galilee, but made into apostles of a new faith, founders of the new and universal and absolute religion.

IX.

THE EARLIER MIRACLES.

MIRACLES, once regarded as the great bulwark of the Christian faith, are now regarded as its greatest burden. Here, perhaps more than anywhere else, can be seen the kind and degree of the changes worked by the modern spirit in our fundamental assumptions and general attitude of mind to nature and history. What was once made to prove the Divine origin and authority of our religion, has now to be shown to be in no way inimical to its truth or prejudicial to its claims. The older apologists used to argue, Christianity is made credible, proved to be supernatural and Divine, by its miracles; they are signs that the God who transcends and created nature thus and then instituted a perfect and authoritative religion. Now it is argued, Miracles are possible and may be credible; need not, therefore, stagger faith or start doubt; events that may occur ought to be believed, when attested by credible witnesses. Once it was common to magnify the offensiveness of the cross, that its early successes might be traced the more directly to its miracles; now it is common to allow its physical wonders to grow pale or be forgotten before its spiritual and ethical glories. Mind, once credulous, is now suspicious of marvels, and can more easily believe truths that speak to its reason than events that appeal to its senses.

The change thus indicated is remarkable and instructive —a change to be welcomed rather than deprecated. The early use of miracles was an abuse, an almost exact inversion of the truth. Events that were by their very nature sensuous and transitory were made proofs of a faith that is essentially transcendental and permanent. The proofs and the thing to be proved were rather radically opposed than rationally related. Truths which abide for ever, which were full of the light that penetrates the intellect and the sweetness that wins the heart, were made to derive, if not their reason, their authority from events that, appealing to the senses, could never authenticate or guarantee what was spiritual and eternal. Truth is above time; like God, it can never grow old or become local and irrelevant; but miracles have at best only an occasional value, become less significant and credible by distance, grow strange to the intellect as they grow remote from experience. The claims of truth on belief increase with time, but those of miracles decrease. The accidents of the birth perish or are forgotten, but the reality of the life is evident every moment in every movement of the living being.

As men conceived miracles in general, they also conceived their special or distinctive relation to Christ. They were made to prove that He possessed supernatural power, could exercise it directly, by a word or act of the will, without any intermediate or instrumental agency. He could anticipate the slow and normal action of natural forces and processes, as in changing water into wine; could control the fiercest of the elements, as in calming the storm; could create, as in multiplying the loaves and fishes; could undo accomplished deeds, not only repeal laws of nature, but cancel events that had happened from their universal and necessary operation, as in raising the dead. These were made to argue Deity, Divine power possessed by nature and exercised by right. But miracles thus became the guarantees of His real being, evidences of

His nature and mission. They were His credentials; He was to be believed, not for His own or His truth's sake, but for His works'. This made Him what He had expressly disclaimed being, a worker of signs, a doer of wonders, that brought the kingdom of heaven with observation, a cause of physical events that could never constrain to spiritual faith. But while the miracles reveal, they do not prove, the Christ. They may be necessary to our conception of Him, but it is in their moral rather than their physical aspect; as symbols expressing the quality and range of His activity, rather than as proofs demonstrating the constitution of His person or being. The axiom, We believe the miracles because we believe in Christ, We do not believe in Christ because we believe the miracles, is true when rightly understood. The power to work miracles could never prove its possessor to be a person so extraordinary as we conceive Christ to be; but Christ once conceived to be the extraordinary Person we believe Him to be, miracles become to Him both natural and necessary. They are the symbols of the reality He is, the appropriate expressions of the force He embodies. They complete the picture of the Divine goodness He manifests, show that its action in the physical is in essential harmony with its action in the moral sphere. The natural action of moral beings is moral action; the miracles of Christ are physical witnesses to His essential spirit and aims—therefore formally physical, but materially moral. They, as it were, personalize for us the moral action of God, show how He acts towards the miseries and weaknesses of His creatures, and thus become essential elements in the declaration of the Father made by the Only Begotten.

We do not intend, then, to attempt here a defence of miracles, but rather a discussion and exposition of their right relation to Christ. That relation, indeed, is the best apology for their truth, and the true vindication of their worth. It lifts them into a sphere where they become intelligible, rational, necessary, legitimate effects of an adequate cause. The objections that annihilate miracles annihilate Christ; what preserves His Person saves their being. In the region of thought and history where He becomes a reality, they too become real. His and their opponent lives and thinks on the plane of the natural, and His nature is very shallow and circumscribed. It is a nature whose order can be transcended as little by personalities as by events. Persons, indeed, are to Him but a series of events, determined in their sequence by a named or nameless necessity. Nature is but sentient man, man but perceived or remembered nature, determined in all his choices, as in his coming and going, by forces ever persistent, yet ever in process of premutation; no freer in his action than the falling stone, or the ebbing and flowing tide, or the rounded and rolling star. And this invariable order, though it be termed the order of nature, is but another name for the imperfectly understood or ill-interpreted experience of man, is what he has observed, the way of nature as revealed to his senses rather than as explicated by his reason. But if the question be lifted from nature into spirit, from the domain of necessity into that of freedom, from the sphere of events into that of personality, then it is radically changed. It is no longer a question as to whether the order of nature can be broken, but as to what a given personality is, and what its normal action must be. The acts of extraordinary persons are extraordinary, measured by the ordinary standard, but becoming and natural, measured by their own personality. If events happen according to the order of nature, acts done are in harmony with the nature of the actor. If persons are not the products of physical forces, it is but rational to think that their acts will conform to the power

THE EARLIER MIRACLES. 153

or nature they embody, rather than the order that did not produce them. Given, in short, the Person of Jesus, and it is more natural that He should than that He should not work miracles; they become the proper and spontaneous manifestations, the organic outcome or revelation, of His actual or realized being. Our supernatural was His natural; what we call His miracles were but the normal expressions of His energy, as nature is but the manifested activity of the immanent God.

Of course this position affirms that the Person of Christ is, in a sense, a stupendous miracle. The nature of the physicists could not have produced Him. He was, in relation to their laws and forces, transcendental, supernatural. To a supernatural person supernatural action is proper or native; where he seems most ordinary he is most extraordinary. Now, personality everywhere transcends nature, and only the universality of the transcendence hides its essentially supernatural character. What is realized in varying degrees in man was realized in the most pre-eminent degree in Christ. His transcendence is an historical fact. The forces unified in His person have proved themselves unique alike as to quality and kind. His place in history but illustrates and explicates His historical person, enables us to judge the energies that lived in Him through the power and influence He has exercised. In Him was life, and the life has been the light of men.

It is, however, certain to be argued, A miraculous person is no more possible, no more credible, than a miraculous event. While every person transcends nature in the narrower sense—that of the physicists—nature in the larger sense—that of the philosophers—is the common mother of all persons, the maker of all personalities. It were a small thing to say, We concede the point; it is the very point for which we contend. Nature in the larger sense is nature creative, not simply created; includes, does not exclude, the Divine energies. What nature, so understood, does, God does; and its products or achievements must be interpreted, not through our idea of nature, but through our idea of God. While the former cannot explain Christ, the latter can; measured by the first, He is a miracle, measured by the second, He is a natural and spontaneous product. Our notion of Christ's personality may contradict the idea of nature we owe to the physicist, but it is in harmony with our idea of God—nay, grows necessarily out of it. And the latter is here the determinating idea; while the effect may explicate the cause, the cause alone can explain the effect. So long as Christ is conceived in harmony with this all-determinating idea, our conception of Him has the same rational basis as our conception of the being and becoming of the universe.

A discussion as to the possibility or impossibility of miracles is meaningless, unless carried back to first principles. These principles are in the last resort philosophical, concern our notion of nature or God, and our notion of man. These notions, though distinguished, are subtly and inseparably connected. As we conceive God, we conceive man. Our conception of the universe is variously yet faithfully mirrored in our conception of the individual, of the personal and conscious mind. Yet it is convenient to distinguish the notions, and Spinoza and Hume may be respectively used to illustrate how the notion of God or nature, in the one case, and the notion of man, in the other, determines the question as to the possibility and credibility of miracles.

To Spinoza, God and nature were one and the same; its laws were His decrees; nothing was contingent in it, everything necessary, determined alike as to being and action by the necessity of the Divine nature. God was the one and only substance, extension and thought were His attributes, and everything existed and behaved in a manner absolutely determined by His nature or essence. The only Cause, alike in nature and spirit, was the immanent God, whose actions were always the necessary results of His perfections. Hence any contradiction of natural law was a contradiction of the Divine nature. To affirm that God had done anything against physical law was, as it were, to affirm that God had acted against His own essence. The fundamental conception was a rigorous Monism, and to a Monism, theistic or materialistic, miracles are not only impossible, but absurd. The objection of the pantheist and materialist to miracles is the same, only stated in different terms. Each recognizes but one force in the universe, necessary, mechanical, homogeneous in nature, uniform in action, revealed in the order disclosed to sense; and so each is obliged to deny anything that requires or presupposes an active or conscious will above, yet within, the material universe. But if their first principles are denied, their inferences cannot be received as valid. If nature is held to reveal a personal reason and an active will, it is but logical to conclude that the universe will be governed as reason and will alone can govern —in ways that are voluntary and for ends that are rational. These may imply or manifest the miraculous, but our miraculous is our God's natural—*i.e.*, is the obedience of the Divine will to the ends or purposes of the Divine reason. What seems to contradict nature as real need not contradict it as ideal, as the arena on which a God works in ways and for reasons worthy of a God. While He remains the supreme object of our faith and thought, it is but the highest reasonableness to interpret through Him the greatest personality in history, the most natural when conceived through God, the most miraculous when conceived through nature.

The distinctive point in Hume's position was the denial of the credibility rather than the possibility of miracles.

The point is characteristic, though his reasons were a curious blending of principles he owed to his scepticism with principles derived from the dogmaticism he subtly concealed in its later form. Hume's scepticism, logically developed, did not allow him to pronounce against the possibility of miracles, but required him to pronounce against their credibility. He had resolved man into a series of sensations, a succession, without any rational connection or order, of conscious sensuous states. Knowledge was made up of impressions and ideas, or lively and faint, perceived and remembered sensations. Its cause was thus external and unknown; our knowledge was made for us, not by us—formed by our experience, created by our circumstances or environment. What could not be resolved into a sensation could not be an object of knowledge; what transcended experience belonged, as neither an impression nor an idea, to a region absolutely inaccessible to mind. To such a psychology only one conclusion was possible—the inexperienced was the unknown, the incredible; and Hume might have pushed it much farther than he did, or rather than he dared to do. His principle was fatal, not simply to the belief in miracles, but to knowledge—was as destructive of science as of religion. If his psychology is denied, his logic is deprived of its premises. If we refuse to recognize man as a series of impressions and ideas, a succession of actual and remembered sensations, he loses the assumption that can alone lend plausibility and force to his argument. If mind creates experience rather than experience mind, the argument is reversed, the position turned. The only philosophy that can explain knowledge is the philosophy that seeks reason behind and before sensation. Thought is first, not last, is not a product of sensation, pure and simple, but the only power that can translate and transmute it into knowledge. But if so, if without the transcendental elements in knowledge the elements furnished by experience are impossible, Hume's elaborate proof of the incredibility of miracles is but a castle in the air, no more consistent than the structure of our dreams.[1]

We cannot, then, feel the force of logic that starts from premises we deny. We do not feel that they in any way touch our faith in the Person of Christ. He may be a stupendous miracle, but He is a miracle it became God to work. While God is to us what Jesus represented Him to be, we must always conceive the appearance of Christ as supremely agreeable to His nature.

We come, then, back to our position: the main thing in the matter of the miracles is to discuss and determine their relation to the Person of Christ. The mysterious conscious force we so name was one, but the unity was variously manifested, and always in the most extraordinary forms. His spirit was revealed, or, as it were, incarnated in four forms, speech and conduct, institutions and action. These are organically related to each other and to Him,

[1] Professor Huxley, in his interesting but somewhat sketchy monograph on Hume, characteristically gives up Hume's argument against the possibility of miracles, but maintains the validity of his argument against their credibility. By so doing he introduces at once consistency and strength into the position as he states it; but his statement carefully hides the radical impotence of the psychology on which Hume built. That psychology involved the most thorough-going scepticism, made knowledge, made science impossible, and impossible, too, proof of anything that had occurred, either as regards time or place, outside the particular individual experience. What resolves the individual into a succession of sensations that occur according to no actual or discoverable order and reason, dissolves the very ideas of nature and law, and makes it impossible that the experience of one can have any rational validity or truth to another. On this ground no science, because no knowledge, of nature is possible, and no proof of historical events, because no experience of the experience they describe. But these ultimate bearings of Hume's psychology it did not suit Professor Huxley to expound, involving, as they do, the downfall of many things he loves much better than miracles.

were rooted in the unity of His thought, expressed in their several manners His mind and aims. They are all alike remarkable in character, in their quality as works of the Spirit. His speech stands alone, constitutes an order by itself. There is no speech that can be compared with it, so simple, so transparent, so pre-eminent in power. His words could hardly have been fewer or mightier, have, indeed, behaved more like creative spirits ceaselessly multiplying themselves than like spoken words. His conduct, too, is unique, is our highest ethical ideal embodied. The religious genius He is confessed to have been is even more manifest in His conduct than in His speech. Love to God is more grandly illustrated by His life than enforced by His words; duty to man He more finely exemplifies than enjoins. Here He is incomparable, our one perfect Son of God and Brother of man. Then, His idea of a Divine society, a kingdom of God, is an idea extraordinary in its sublime and daring originality, and still more extraordinary in its realization. It was an absolutely new thought, a new ideal of the relations of God and man, realized at once in forms that created a new society, yet ever struggling towards realization in forms of greater perfectness. The Creator lives in His creation; the society of Christ is a permanent incarnation of His Spirit.

Now, the Person manifested in these three forms—in His speech, His conduct, and His kingdom—is a unique Person, characterized throughout by the rarest and most exceptional power. Were He as unique in action it would be but natural. The force He embodied could hardly be denied a physical expression. It was no more extraordinary to have miraculous power over nature than to have miraculous power over men. Miracles of sense are no more supernatural than miracles of spirit. To be the moral being He was, to live the life He lived, to die as He died, to achieve in man and society the changes He has

THE EARLIER MIRACLES.

achieved, is to have accomplished miracles infinitely greater in kind and quality than those of multiplying the loaves, walking on the sea, or even raising the dead. To be equal to the greater is certainly to be more than equal to the less. It cannot surprise us that the Creator of the speech, the conduct, and the kingdom of Christ should also be the Creator of health in the diseased and sight to the blind. It had rather surprised us had one whose position is so pre-eminent in man and history been feeble and commonplace in relation to nature and action.

It is impossible to separate miracles from the historical Christ: they are inextricably interwoven with the evangelical history. The words of Jesus often imply works that were held miraculous: no theory that allows veracity to the first can deny reality to the second. The older Rationalism, with its forced naturalistic explanations, became incurably absurd, died, indeed, of its exegetical absurdities. The mythical hypothesis was more scientific, but hardly more successful. It failed to explain why no miracles were attributed to the Baptist, why they were attributed to Jesus alone, why so integral parts of His history, so necessary to the picture of His historical appearance. Then, it had a still more radical fault. It made the New Testament miracles echoes or imitations of those recorded in the Old. Jesus was arrayed in the marvels that had been made to surround the prophets. What they had done He had to do, in order that in Him the prophecies and economies of the past might alike be fulfilled. But to this theory it was necessary that the miracles of Christ should exactly repeat and reflect those of the Old Testament; a difference in character and design was failure at a point where to fail was fatal. And here the failure was complete. The miracles of the Old Testament are mainly punitive, but those of Christ mainly remedial. The first express for the most part a retributive spirit, but the second are acts of benevolence. An attempt to persuade Jesus to work a miracle in the manner of the Old Testament evoked nothing but a reproof to the tempters.[1] His miracles express His will, show that He is gracious in word as in work. He is good, and does good. He is the enemy of disease, of pain and misery in all their forms. His speech is illustrated by His action, would be without it without its divinest meanings. Matthew, with wonderful insight, makes Christ's miraculous power express a vicarious and redemptive relation. He healed that He might fulfil the prophecy, "Himself took our infirmities and bare our sicknesses."[2] He came to redeem from disease as from sin, bore our sufferings that He might cure our sorrows. His action was like the incorporated or articulated will of God; showed it in its essential qualities active and exercised in relation to man. And this relation to the Divine Will lies at the root of His power over nature. His will is ethically so one with God's that the ethical becomes almost like physical identity. His Father works, and He works;[3] and His works are His Father's. This connection of absolute obedience to the Divine will with possession of Divine power helps us to estimate at once the ethical and evidential value of Christ's miracles. They are evidences of ethical perfection, of moral completeness. Nowhere does Pharisaic malice seem so malicious as when it attempts to trace His power to the devil, while His vindication of Himself is nowhere more victoriously complete.[4] The miracles, admitted by His enemies, are proved to express the will of God, and to reveal the ethical quality of His own spirit.

But this ethical quality is seen in repression as well as in exercise—perhaps even more in the former than in the latter. The miraculous action of Christ is distinguished

---

[1] Luke ix 54-56.   [2] Matt viii 16, 17.
[3] John v 17   [4] Matt xii 24-30, Mark iii. 22-27.

by what can only be called miraculous moderation. His abstention from the use of His power is even more remarkable than His exercise of it. Supernatural power is a dangerous thing to possess, an awful temptation. Few men could possess it without being depraved by the possession, without at least often using it unwisely. It is a power with which we should hardly be inclined to trust any man, and we should certainly regard its owner with the most unsleeping and jealous suspicion. But the extraordinary fact stands: the people believed Christ to possess it, and yet trusted Him, and He justified their trust. He was never untimely, extravagant, or ungracious in the exercise of His supernatural gifts. They were never used on His own behalf. He had power above Nature, but He lived under the laws and within the limits she sets for all her sons. He was often hungry and athirst, but He never fed Himself as He fed the multitudes on the hillside, or refreshed Himself as He refreshed the wedding guests at Cana in Galilee. He suffered, knew heart-break, pain, and death; but He never asked any sovereign might to lighten His sorrows, heal His wounds, or roll back the ebbing tide of life. Then, too, His power is never exercised for defensive or hostile purposes. His enemies acknowledge His miracles, yet do splendid, though unconscious, homage to His goodness by attributing them to the presence or help of infernal agencies, so confessing that He had a power more than human, but not the will to use it devilishly. His prayer on the cross explains and illustrates His conduct. What He asked His Father to do He was always doing—exercising mercy, forgiving men who did not know the sinfulness of their doings. He was thus, in what He abstained from doing, a witness to the Divine grace He incarnated, restraining anger and leaving evil men unharmed to life and time and possible penitence. And this repression becomes, in one aspect of it, sublimest self-abnegation, divinest sacrifice. A being so gifted with supernatural power did not need to suffer, to die, as Jesus did. His sufferings and death were voluntary, results of His own choice. As He willed to heal men, He willed to die for man. The motives that induced Him to work miracles moved Him to die. He exercised His power that He might save from suffering; He withheld it that He might save from sin And so to His disciples His final and crowning miracle was His acceptance of the cross, His submission to death. The act of repression was the exercise of the highest power, the power to lay down His life, to give Himself a ransom for many. Here men have found the wonder of the ages— " God commending His love to us, in that, while we were yet sinners, Christ died for us."

But the miracles stand in as intimate and indissoluble relations to the teaching and aims as to the character, or, as it were, historical ideal of the Christ. His words and works are as branches springing from the same root, twin bodies inspired by one spirit. Especially in the Galilean period—which is, too, pre-eminently the period of miracles —when He could order His life as He willed, when His path was not watched by the jealous hate of Pharisee and Sadducee, when the homes of the people were the scenes of His daily ministry, a fine harmony reigned between His speech and His actions, the first creating the light that cheered the spirit, the second creating the health that renewed the body. He conceived health to be as necessary to happiness as knowledge, and so He loved as well to make the diseased whole as to make the ignorant enlightened. The motives that moved Him to speak moved Him also to action, compassion in each case ruled His will.[1] The men that most profoundly touched His sympathies were the publicans and sinners on the one

[1] Matt. ix 35, 36; Mark i. 39-41.

THE EARLIER MIRACLES. 163

side, and the diseased and possessed on the other;[1] and as their sorrows drew Him to them His gracious and quickening sympathy drew them to Him. He had come to be the physician of the sick, to seek and save the lost. It had been said that the days of the Messiah were to be days of health as of happiness,[2] and He fulfilled the prophecy. The prophetic words He used to declare and define His mission[3] find an instructive echo in the words He used to describe His works, the signs which were to enable the Baptist to judge as to His character and claims.[4] In relieving suffering He was overcoming sin. His acts of healing were victories over the devil. By them He confirmed faith,[5] cast out Satan,[6] conquered evil, created peace, by creating one of its most essential conditions. His acts, like His words, contradicted tradition. He would not be silent to please the scribes or the schools, and He would not be prevented by an inflexible and inhuman law from lightening human sorrow. As He taught that the Sabbath was made for man, He healed on the Sabbath.[7] As He taught that humanity was greater than Judaism, that to be a man was to be a neighbour, owing the neighbourly duties of help and consolation to all men, He carried restoration and comfort to the alien as to the Jew.[8] If we interpret His works through His words, we can see how beautifully significant and ideal they were, the symbols of the Messiah and His age coming with hopeful and happy health to sick and wasted humanity.

These scattered and fragmentary paragraphs have not even pierced the surface of a great subject, but they may

[1] Matt ix 10-13; Mark i 32-34, ii 17.
[2] Isaiah lviii 8   [3] Luke iv. 17-19
[4] Matt ix 4-6
[5] Ibid. ix. 2, 29   [6] Ibid. xii. 22-29.
[7] Ibid xii 10-13; Mark ii. 27, John v 16.
[8] Matt viii 5-13, Mark vii. 24-30, Luke vii 2-10; x. 36, 37.

have indicated in a rough and hurried way the relation of the miracles to the mysterious and variously manifested personality we call the Christ. In conclusion, it may be enough to remark that, if we are right in our interpretation of this relation, it ought to shed some light on the once celebrated controversy as to the comparative value of the internal and external evidences. The miracles are no more external to the system of Jesus than His speech. Both are rooted in His personality, express His thought, reveal His spirit, manifest the inner and essential qualities of His heart and mind. Without either we should be without true and sufficient knowledge of His marvellous Person. His words exhibit the ideal, His works the real; the former explain Divine benevolence and human obedience, but the latter show Divine beneficence curing human misery, creating human happiness. What blossomed in the flower was contained in the seed; what was evolved in the history was involved in the Person of Christ. The sign to the sense is a symbol of the spirit, and miracles are but means by which the hidden and internal qualities of Christ become manifest and real to man.

X.

JESUS AND THE JEWS.

THERE are three things that at once characterize Jesus and His disciples, and distinguish them from the men who have founded the other great religions of the world. (1) What may be termed their secular and social sanity; (2) the calm religious temper and reasonable religious spirit in which they lived and acted; and (3) the entire absence of political character and motive in their words and works, methods and aims. Men deeply moved tend to become extravagant, the victims of passions so molten as to consume, or so liquefied as to quench, their common sense. When the motives that move are religious, come from the sudden and intense realization of the spiritual and eternal, the extravagance assumes one or both of two forms: either hatred of the world, its comforts, its wealth, its pursuits, whatever is every-day and present, attractive and loveable on earth and in time; or the passion after extraordinary relations, unnatural modes of intercourse with the unseen, ecstasies, visions, dreams, trance-like states that transcend nature, invade the awful presence of God, and snatch, as it were, from His hand mysteries beyond the grasp and hidden from the eye and ear of mortals. But in the spirit of Christ there lived a serene and radiant sanity. He loved the world, did not hate its wealth or its wisdom, or awaken fanaticism against the art that had beautified, or the thought that had dignified, or the treasures that enriched, earth and the life of men. And the

Spirit that lived in Himself He made to reign in the men and society He formed. The knowledge of God He communicated created relations with Him so sweet and peaceful that they needed no other and desired no more. His disciples were lifted to a higher plane than the one known to the men who crave after extravagant or ecstatic modes of speaking to God, or being spoken to by Him. And as was their knowledge, so was their temper and spirit. Christ created an enthusiasm too real to be noisy, too deep to be evanescent, too sober and sane in nature to be unwise in action. Their aims and methods were His because He had made His thoughts and spirit theirs; they lived for the kingdom of God, and did not concern themselves about the kingdom of man.

But while within the new society a fine process of assimilation to its Founder was going on, without it an opposite process was in active and ominous operation. Antagonism was being evolved, suspicion was growing into aversion, silent dislike into manifest and articulate hatred. Jesus was not like Judas, the Gaulonite, a theocratic zealot, a rebel against Rome, resolved to expel the foreigners and free Israel. He had not, like the Baptist, invaded the arena of politics, and attempted to become a teacher of courts and kings. And Rome did not feel as if it had a quarrel with one who had no quarrel with it ; or Herod, as if he must crush one whose path and purpose were too elevated to cross his. But the extraordinary thing is, that Christ's abstinence from politics helped to evoke a hatred that made the men who claimed to be the most pious and patriotic in Israel His absolute foes. While the Baptist had been full of strong stern words, had denounced scribes and Pharisees as a "viper's brood," worthy of "the wrath to come," they had yet gone to his baptism and been "baptized of him in the Jordan, confessing their sins." But though Christ had been gentle in spirit, soft and sweet

JESUS AND THE JEWS.

in speech, always and everywhere benevolent and beneficent, yet they had never stood in the circle of His disciples; had, instead, met Him with a hate so deep, that to be gratified it was willing to sink its hitherto deepest hatred. Now, why this difference of feeling, of attitude and action? Why did they applaud the John who filled the air with his poisoned epithets, and pierced them through with his sharp invectives, while they condemned and crucified Him who did not cry, nor cause His voice to be heard in the street, who did not break the bruised reed, nor quench the smoking flax? The question has interest enough to deserve an attempt at an answer.

It certainly does at first sight look strange that the opposition to Jesus should have originated with the Pharisees, and been by them conducted to the disastrous point where the tragic end became not only possible, but inevitable. They were the party of conviction, devoutly religious, splendidly patriotic. They were not like the Sadducees, —an aristocracy of blood and office—but a school or society penetrated and possessed by commanding religious beliefs. Their devotion to their theocratic national ideal was equal to almost any sacrifice, rose into a fanaticism that became now and then sublime. It were an insult, not simply to historical criticism, but to historical truth, to imagine that these men were in their opposition to Christ hypocritical, or in any way dishonest to their own convictions. They were even tragically honest—too terribly in earnest to be hypocritical. But this only makes their attitude and conduct the more strangely pathetic and instructive. It is indeed a most significant problem, How could men so enthusiastically loyal to a pure and lofty monotheism become so fanatically opposed to the spiritual truths and sub-sublime monotheistic beliefs that were personified in Jesus?

Geiger has said,[1] " Pharisaism is the principle of con-

[1] *Sadducaer und Pharisaer*, p. 35.

tinuous development," and Protestantism is only its "perfect reflected image." The first statement is, when properly qualified, finely true; the second, curiously incorrect. There is a development marked by the increasing authority of the letter over the spirit, and a development characterized by the increasing superiority and dominion of the spirit over the letter. The former is Pharisaism, the latter, Protestantism. There is nothing so unethical as an authoritative letter, nothing so moral as an awakened and regnant spirit. The one tends to make and keep man conscious of the morality embodied in his own nature, of the God who lives and speaks in his own conscience; but the other makes him the victim of arbitrary rules, that become with increasing authority increasingly minute, exercising a tyranny fatal to the faintest freedom. The continuous development of the letter is but the progressive enslavement of the spirit, with the consequent death of independent morality—*i.e.*, the reign of God through the conscience.

Now Pharisaism signified the authority and continuous growth of the letter. It believed that God was present and active in Judaism, that its unfolding was but the unfolding of His Will. It ascribed to the traditions of the Fathers, or the elders,[1] legal—*i.e.*, Divine—authority. The scribes and Pharisees sat in Moses' seat, and made laws as authoritative as His.[2] Moses was said to have received the law on Sinai and then committed it to Joshua, Joshua to the elders, the elders to the prophets, the prophets to the men of the Great Synagogue, who thus, as the makers of the oral, took their place beside the creators of the scriptural, law. And the oral became in reality more authoritative than the written. Rabbi Eleazer had said, "He who expounds the Scriptures in contradiction to

[1] Jos, *Antiqq.*, xiii. 16. 2. Matt xv. 2; Mark vii. 3.
[2] Matt xxiii 3. Jos, *Antiqq*, xiii. 10. 6, xviii. 1. 3.

tradition has no inheritance in the world to come;" and so the Mishna recognizes the voice of the interpreter as more authoritative than the voice of the interpreted. "It is a greater crime to teach against the words or ordinances of the scribes than against the Scriptures themselves."[1] Now a living and speaking letter is, in some respects, worse than one written and dead; is more absolute, can be less easily eluded, is more ubiquitous, can at once be more ruthlessly comprehensive in its grasp and more fatally minute in its details. Where the right of the individual reason to interpret the law is allowed, there may be liberty; where the right is denied, there must be bondage; escape is impossible; an infallible interpreter is an absolute authority. And under this authority the Pharisees stood, and their obedience was as fanatical as the authority was exacting. The Moses and prophets they knew were not those of history, but those of the schools. Their God was the God of oral tradition, infinitely concerned about legal minutiæ, not the God of the great spirits that had made the faith of Israel, infinitely concerned about righteousness and truth. They had faith enough, were believers of the most strenuous sort; but a faith is great, not by virtue of its subjective strength, but by virtue of its objective reality. The belief that the best thing God could do for the world was to create the traditions and institutions of Judaism, was a belief that could generate the fanaticism of the tribe, but could not inspire the enthusiasm of humanity.

We must now imagine Christ and the Pharisees face to face. They were like personalized antitheses, the Pharisees representing tradition, Christ the rights of the spirit inspired of God. The contradiction was absolute. It is ridiculous to say, with the latest historian of the sect,[2]

[1] Sanhedrin, xi. 3. Cf. Schurer, *Neutest. Zeitgeschichte*, p. 430.
[2] Cohen, *Les Pharisiens*, vol ii p. 29.

that "the antagonism existed only as to questions of conduct." The conduct of the Pharisees was but the natural and inevitable result of their beliefs. If their conduct was offensive to Christ, their beliefs were more offensive still. On their own principles their conduct was excellent; it was only when measured and tested by His that it became bad. And as He condemned their behaviour they condemned His, and for similar reasons. His embodied His spirit, His ethical and religious ideal; and men who held the ideal to be false could not admire the reality as beautiful The opposition as to conduct thus masked a deeper antagonism, one as to the nature and essence of religion, as to the law, as to the truth and character of God, His purposes and relations towards man. Their aim was to make their people the people of the law, every man throughout obedient to its every precept. The aim seemed great and noble; but in such matters everything depends on the nature of the law to be realized. Here it represented no high ideal, but only a multitude of juristical and ceremonial prescriptions. The cardinal duties were of course enforced—Moses had secured that—but the law that so lived and grew as to be a progressive revelation after a very curious sort, was a law of ritualistic acts and articles, a species of inspired or revealed casuistry. Moses had commanded the Sabbath day to be kept, but this finely general command had to be interpreted. It was declared that there were thirty-nine kinds of work prohibited, but each kind specified became in turn the subject of new discussions, distinctions, and prescriptions. It was, for example, pronounced sinful to tie or to loose a knot on the Sabbath. But there are many kinds of knots, and it was not always possible to be certain whether an exception might not be made in favour of some knot or knots of a special sort. So it was explained that if a knot could be

JESUS AND THE JEWS.

loosed with one hand it was not a sin to loose it; but a sailor's knot or a camel-driver's must not be touched.[1] Then the prescriptions related not simply to works forbidden on the Sabbath, but to acts or chances that involved only a possible profanation. The tailor was not to go out in the dusk with his needle, or the writer with his pen, lest he should forgetfully allow himself to do the same after the Sabbath had begun.[2] And these are but typical acts of legislation. An ideal constructed on such lines may be fanatically loved, but the love can as little ennoble the law as dignify the man.

We can but ill imagine how abhorrent to Christ must have been the notion that such laws were God's, and the obedience they created pleasing to Him. The strength of His love to the theocratic ideal can alone measure the greatness of His aversion to its miserable counterfeit. He condemned equally the conduct of the Pharisees and their perversions of the law, and found in their unveracious dealing with the Scriptures the secret and explanation of all their other unveracities. Their traditions transgressed the commandments of God.[3] Moses, like a wise lawgiver, certain that the family was the basis of society and the state, had made honour to parents the first and fundamental duty of man to man; but they had set the Rabbi above the Father, made the teacher of wisdom stand, as to His claims on obedience and service, above the parent,[4] and had instructed the people how, under the pretext of doing honour to God, they might neglect father and mother.[5] The most absolute slave of the letter is always the man who does it most violence. While he professes to be devoted to the law, he devises

[1] Schurer, *Neutest. Zeitgeschichte*, p. 485
[2] Ibid. p. 488
[3] Matt. xv. 3.
[4] Schurer, *Neutest. Zeitgeschichte*, p 442.
[5] Matt. xv. 6.

interpretations that annul its most distinctive precepts; and so the blamelessly faithful Pharisee was inwardly unfaithful and impure.[1] The one Christ drew, praying in the Temple,[2] was but a type of the man their beliefs tended to create, and was possibly so familiar and true that the sect could hardly understand the reason and righteousness of the judgment it was designed to express; might rather, in a bewildered away, regard it as a portrait they would have praised, had it not so evidently embodied its painter's disgust. Yet Christ's condemnation did not here reach its severest point. That point was reached only when He denounced their infidelity to their own laws, as well as to God's, so touching the last and most awful depth of the unveracity produced by the worship of the letter. It was the boast of the scribes that they loved the law, the truth and wisdom of the Fathers, too well to teach for fee or reward;[3] yet they "devoured widows' houses, and for a pretence made long prayers."[4] It was no wonder that Christ warned His disciples against "the leaven of the Pharisees,"[5] and declared to them, "Except your righteousness shall exceed the righteousness of the scribes and Pharisees, ye shall in no case enter into the kingdom of heaven."[6]

The antagonism of Christ and the Pharisees was thus essential and radical. It was so sharp and direct that they could not regard Him otherwise than with mingled amazement and horror. It appeared a most impious thing to deny and deride tradition, the more so that the denial rested on a conception of God and His Word that contradicted the conception of those schools whose voice had

---

[1] Luke xi. 39.   [2] Ibid. xviii. 9–14.
[3] Gfrorer, *Das Jahrhundert des Heils*, vol. ii. pp. 156-60. Schurer, *Neutest. Zeitgeschichte*, p. 443.
[4] Mark xii. 40; Luke xx 47
[5] Matt. xvi. 6, Mark viii. 15   Luke xii. 1   [6] Matt. v 20.

been to them for generations as the voice of God. They never imagined that He could be right, or they wrong. How could they, when they believed that they possessed this absolute and exclusive inspiration of God ? They could not pause to examine His claims or meaning—that had implied the possibility of His truth and their error. There was only one thing possible—an antagonism of action and feeling as sharp and bitter as the antagonism of thought and speech. His gentle spirit, His beautiful character, His winsome ways and words, might make opposition a sore thing to their souls; but the more the cruel inconsistency of love and duty, of the things wished with the thing that must be done, was felt, the more would their conduct become the Pharisaic counterpart of the higher heroism. They could not allow their Judaism to perish, and it was better that they should ruin Christ than that He should ruin it. How the antagonism of idea became an antagonism of act is what we have now to study, that we may the better understand the gathering of the forces that were so soon to break at Jerusalem, and in the cross.

We have, then, to imagine Jesus living and teaching in Galilee. In Jerusalem the jealousies and suspicions that had been awakened by His deeds and words at the feast had not been soothed to sleep. His career in Galilee was watched, His sayings duly reported and considered. The conflict He had shunned rather than courted was forced on Him, penetrated into His happy and beneficent seclusion. In the crowds that assembled to hear Him, dark and disputatious faces began to appear. His fame drew those who suspected and disliked, as well as those who loved and trusted. The enthusiasm was still in flood, but save in the innermost circle it was an enthusiasm of the sense rather than of the spirit. The possessed of devils had been dispossessed, the palsied strengthened, the lepers cleansed, the blind restored to sight. Jesus, weary of miracles and the curious crowds that followed Him, their souls in their eyes, had returned to Capernaum. Soon the house was filled, the door besieged, and Jesus seized the meet moment to speak the words of truth. While He preached, friends came bearing a man "sick of the palsy," but finding the crowd too great to get near Jesus, mounted on the roof, and let the man down into the house. It is possible that some relation may have existed between the man's physical and His spiritual state. Or it is possible that Jesus was sick of the physical, and wished to escape into the spiritual sphere, by working a moral where He had been expected to work only a bodily change. Whatever the reason, it is certain that His word to the man was, not, "Be whole," but, " Son, thy sins be forgiven thee." Into this saying was condensed the whole question of His claims. It asserted by implication His idea of the new kingdom, His right to be the king, His power to exercise the highest kingly functions. It was so interpreted by certain scribes who were present, and who by gesture or otherwise showed their denial of his claims. He blasphemed — forgiveness was the prerogative of God. Christ's answer was characteristic, one of act rather than word. The Pharisee believed that miracles were of God —a sign from heaven, a proof of its inspiration and authority. So Jesus, calling in the one proof they admitted and did not dare to deny, said to the sick man, "Arise, and take up thy bed." Yet there is no insult a man resolved not to be convinced so much resents as an argument he cannot answer. It only confirms his antagonism by intensifying his hate. The scribes might have forgiven the blasphemy; the miracle that proved it sober truth they could not forgive.

The conflict thus commenced **must** proceed. The

JESUS AND THE JEWS.

offensiveness of Jesus to the Pharisees grew daily. His society was to them a standing affront. He was preaching the Messianic kingdom, yet daring to associate with "publicans and sinners." It was an open outrage against their theocratic and religious idea. Their kingdom of heaven was a kingdom of the Jews, its laws those Mosaic and traditional laws they so fanatically loved, yet so finely contrived to elude and disobey. Within the land and over the people sacred to Jahveh no alien could righteously rule. He was their only lawful sovereign. For a Gentile to exercise regal authority in Judæa was for Him to usurp the place and functions of God; for a Jew to become a minister or agent of His rule, was treason against the Most High. And this was what the publican had become. He farmed and raised the taxes of Cæsar, not only so acknowledged the authority of the Gentile as to deny the authority of Jahveh, but also extorted from his brethren the tributes and taxes that were the signs of their bondage. And so the Pharisee as a patriot hated the publican as a traitor, while as a son of Abraham and the law he hated him still more as false to his faith and his God. And so the publican became an out-caste in Israel, detested and shunned as only the out-caste can be. Isolation made him reckless, exacting, insolent. Excommunication he answered by extortion, and the more extortionate he grew, the deeper became the religious hate, the higher the barrier which excluded him from the society and worship of Israel. Yet, though the exclusion made him worse, it could not disinherit him; he remained a child of Abraham, with the instincts that had made his people the people of God living in him neither silent nor dumb. But they craved in vain, their yearning but nourished the despair which he only can feel who has so broken caste as to have destroyed all hope of restoration or return. And so the publicans were the pre-eminent sinners of Judaism, the hating and hated, at once apostates and traitors.

And Jesus invited these men into His kingdom—nay, made one an apostle, a minister and chosen friend. The act was grandly declarative, proved that Christ's was a spiritual theocracy, indifferent to accidental or civil distinctions, alive to the spiritual possibilities or realities in men. But it was a mortal offence to the Pharisees. It contradicted their strongest convictions, crossed their most cherished prejudices, mocked their deepest and most righteous hatreds. It must have been with an altogether indescribable horror that they saw One whose special mission it was to preach the kingdom of heaven opening it to "publicans and sinners." Hence came many conflicts. The first thing that shocked them into speech was the call of Matthew, and the subsequent feast in his house. Christ's answer to the question, "Why eateth your Master with publicans and sinners?" "They that are whole need not a physician, but they that are sick,"[1] expressed His mission as He understood it, showed the essential contrast of His idea to theirs. But they were too possessed with their own to comprehend His idea. They knew the force of a stinging epithet, and named Him "the Friend of publicans and sinners." But their scorn could not break Him from His friendship, only wrung from Him some of His noblest words. Of these, two are pictures of the Pharisee, presenting him as he is before God and towards man. In the one he is made to appear as an elder brother,[2] who conceives himself to have been ever obedient; entitled, therefore, to everything his father has to give, free to feel angry and wronged when a younger brother, who has been a prodigal, returns home penitent and is received with joy. The image is

[1] Matt ix 10–13, Mark ii. 14–17, Luke v. 27–32.
[2] Luke xv. 25–32.

most moving, eloquent, real. He is pictured as "in the field," no idler, a toiler, indeed earning his very inheritance. Then he comes from the field and hears in the house "musick and dancing." The sound of joy creates in him the suspicion of wrong; but he is not above suspecting his father, and does not believe that even in *his* house gladness can be quite innocent. When he hears the cause of the joy—"what these things mean"—he is angry, and will not go in. He has no sense of brotherhood, no love for the lost that can kindle into joy over the found. He is altogether absorbed in himself and in what is due to him. So when the father entreats him to enter, the answer is characteristic. "Lo! these many years do I serve thee, neither transgressed I at any time thy commandments, and yet thou never gavest me a kid that I might make merry with my friends." There it was, unrequited toil, unrewarded obedience, the very gifts of God below the merits of the man. Then, too, it is a curious obedience, can co-exist with its opposite. He is, while proclaiming his obedience, disobedient; refuses to obey God while declaring that he never at any time transgressed His commandments. The obedience he fancied he gave to God was really given to his own passions and prejudices. He was pious and contented only so long as his will was a law to God. In him dislike to his brother became distrust of his father, and in his mind to receive the one he hated was to cast away himself. The Pharisee could not allow the God who loved the publican to love him, could not condescend to be received by a Messiah who received sinners.

The other picture is presented in the parable of the Pharisee and the Publican.[1] Consciousness of virtue lives alike in the attitude and prayer of the Pharisee. He has nothing to ask from God; he possesses everything that is

[1] Luke xviii. 9-14.

worth having. His prayer is a thanksgiving for his own perfection, which is made the more complete by contrast with the men about him, and especially the publican before him. He is not like other men—an extortioner, or unjust, or an adulterer, or even like the publican yonder; he fasts twice in the week, and give tithes of all he possesses. The self-complacency, so finely flavoured by a comprehensive uncharitableness, is inimitable. He is good—the rest of mankind bad. He thanks God he is so good that he may, in a euphemistic way, thank himself. When he comes to the list of his positive virtues, the catalogue is remarkable and significant. He fasts and gives tithes—these are his pre-eminent virtues, and in them his glory and his condemnation alike live. But the publican stands afar off, ashamed to stand amongst godly and devout men, conscious of sin, guilty and humble before God, with no prayer but the short sharp cry, "God be merciful to me the sinner." Christ's moral is—the Publican is justified rather than the Pharisee: in the one there was the semblance of religion, in the other the reality. God accepts penitence, but rejects sacerdotal arrogance; and the acceptance of God authorizes and vindicates acceptance by His Christ. The man who so worships has a right to the kingdom which God recognizes and ratifies; and where He does so, what matters the contradiction of the Pharisee?

But these points of conflict only prepared the way for others. The controversy had to advance from Christ's personal claims and authority, from the nature and constituents of His kingdom, to His and its relation to the old Law. If there was anything sacred in Judaism, it was the Sabbath; the most awful sanctities and sanctions hedged it round. It seemed essential to their monotheism, necessary alike to their faith and worship. It stood to them indissolubly connected with the origin of the world

JESUS AND THE JEWS. 179

and of their nation. The Creator had rested on the seventh day, and the Jahveh who had delivered their fathers from Egypt required the Sabbath to be sacred to Him. They were bound to observe it by reasons alike religious and political; it was the symbol and seal of their right to be the people of God, possessed of the law He instituted that they might obey. But the day of rest they had made toilsome through sacerdotal observances and minute legal regulations. The Sabbath of Jahveh had been lost in the Sabbath of the scribes. The greatest of the prophets had declared that He could not endure their "new moons and sabbaths;"[1] but the scribes proved mightier than the prophet, and their day of tyrannical prescriptions and observances was identified with God's. Against this idolatry of the Sabbath Christ protested in the most direct and practical way. He walked through the cornfields, and allowed His disciples to pluck the ears of corn.[2] He healed,[3] and in one case made the man He healed carry the bed on which he had before lain.[4] The scandal was great: such profanity had not been seen in Israel. Christ's answers were most significant, each covering the whole question alike of His truth and His relation to the law. In the first case His justification of Himself was elaborate and full. (1) The act was not unprecedented. (*a*) David had done a so-called profane thing and was blameless—supreme need was to him perfect justification. And (*b*) the priests in the temple profane the Sabbath: what is proper for the priests is not wrong for the people. (2) Their notion of the Sabbath was fatal to all true worship. Mercy was the best service man could render to God—better than sacrifice. (3) They failed to understand the true end or function of the Sabbath. It was for man; man was not made for it.

[1] Isa 1. 14.
[2] Matt xii. 1-9; Mark. ii. 23.
[3] Matt xii. 10-13; Luke xiii 10
[4] John v. 10.

Laws that turned it into a burden, destroyed it; where the service of God was made toil, man could not rest. (4) The Son of Man was Lord of the Sabbath—had the right to order it for man's good, to institute or modify it so as to serve his true weal. In the second case Christ but illustrated His own principles. If man needed help, he had the right to it. If the sick could then be healed, they ought to be healed; the act was worthy of the day. In the third case He added a great principle to His previous justification—it was God-like to do good on the Sabbath. God's rest is activity, not idleness. He has everywhere and always been working, and where He works man need not fear to do the same. The action of God nobly vindicates the action of His Son.

The antagonism was thus progressive, advanced from the personal claims of Jesus to the truth and rights of the new King and His kingdom as against the law of the Scribes and the Schools. And so Jesus was to the Pharisee a contradiction that became ever deeper and more exasperating. But while His words and conduct became daily more offensive, His acts grew ever more remarkable. In ordinary circumstances it would have been easy to trace His sayings to the inspiration of the devil: but the circumstances were not ordinary. His antagonism to Satan was as direct and apparent as His antagonism to them. He was miraculously successful in casting out devils. His power over them could not be denied. He was thus a cruel paradox to the Scribes and Pharisees. His words were like lies, but His acts were like the evidences of victorious truth. He was in speech like one who blasphemed, but in action like the very Messiah. They perceived in their blind way that speech and action must have a common root; both must be alike false or alike true. The cruel dilemma thus presented only deepened their exasperation. They resented the acts as an insult, a reflection on their veracity. They had either to abandon their hostile attitude, or frame a theory of the acts that would not only justify, but demand it. Consistently enough they chose the latter. The acts were as evil as the speech; the Actor, like the Speaker, was in league with Satan. They said, "He casts out devils by Beelzebub."[1] He is but an embodied falsehood, speaking lies, working a lie, professing to cast out Satan, that He may the better serve him. But the charge was as unwise as unveracious. The answer was easy: "If Satan cast out Satan, how shall his kingdom stand? If he work against himself, how can his works serve him? Then, if I cast out devils by Beelzebub, by whom do your disciples cast them out? By Beelzebub too? Let them be your judges."[2]

The cycle was completed; fanatical resistance to the light had become fanatical denial of its existence. It was little wonder that Jesus met the deputation from Jerusalem with the question, "Why do ye transgress the commandment of God by your tradition? . . . Ye hypocrites! well did Esaias prophesy of you, saying, This people draweth nigh unto Me with their lips; but their heart is far from Me."[3] "O ye hypocrites! ye can discern the face of the sky, but can ye not discern the sign of the times?"[4]

[1] Matt. xii. 24.
[2] Ibid. xii. 25-27.
[3] Ibid. xv. 3, 7, 8.
[4] Ibid. xvi. 3.

XI.

THE LATER TEACHING.

LOOKED at on the surface, the conflict of Jesus with the Jews seems but an ignoble waste of the noblest Being earth has known. And in many respects it was what it seemed. The antagonists of Christ were poor enough, especially when compared with Him. Shallow, selfish, short-sighted men; bigots in creed and in conduct; capable of no sin disapproved by tradition, incapable of any virtue unenjoined by it; too respectable to be publicans and sinners; at once too ungenerous to forgive sins against their own order, and too blind to see sins within it—they remain for all time our most perfect types of fierce and inflexible devotion to a worship instituted and administered by man, but of relentless and unbending antagonism to religion as the service of God in spirit and in truth. And to think of our holy and beautiful Christ, His heart the home of a love that enfolded the world, His spirit the stainless and truthful mirror of the Eternal, His mouth dropping with every word pearls of divinest wisdom—to think of Him hated and wasted by these men, is to think, as it were, of the crown of God, with all its stars, dimmed, corroded, dissolved by mists bred in dismal swamps formed by the decayed life of ancient worlds. The conflict of evil with good is inevitable; we dare not mourn it, dare only welcome it as the hard but necessary way to peace and perfection. But as the issues are immense, we expect the struggle to be manifestly immense also. If the Prince of

THE LATER TEACHING. 183

God stands forth to fight, we cannot but wish it to be with a God-like adversary, and not with men who hold tradition to be as sacred as the law and temple of their God.

But the ignoble was all on one side; on the other was a magnanimity that only became the more magnanimous in the struggle with the little and the mean. As the darkness deepened round the Hero's path His heroism shone the brighter; as the conflict thickened His strength became calmer, mightier, more manifest. His consciousness grew more exalted as His way grew more troubled. The shadows that fell upon His spirit were pierced and penetrated and made translucent by the light which streamed from within. And the change in His spirit was marked by a correspondent change in His teaching. He became sadder, was in speech as in soul more the Man of Sorrows, despised and rejected of men; less the exalted servant of God coming in beauty over the mountains and through the valleys to publish peace. The contradiction of sinners was the prophecy of Calvary. The iron had entered His soul, and His heart was bearing its cross. The springtime was passed; autumn with its falling leaves and withered flowers had come. Cities, once zealous, were cold; crowds, once ardent, were suspicious; enemies, once soft-spoken and fearful, were harsh and arrogant. But just when men were falsest and feeblest He was truest to Himself. His person came into the foreground; He Himself became the great theme of His discourses. He proclaimed Himself to be greater than David or Solomon, as the last and greatest of the prophets, as above the law, as superior to the temple, as the revealer of God. He declared Himself to be the Bread of Life, the Life of the World, the Light of the World. The impending suffering He glorified; the death that was coming so surely He interpreted into a sacrifice of universal efficacy and eternal worth. The gathering clouds left His soul clear. His confidence in His cause and triumph seemed to grow in calmness and rise in strength as the storm increased. His spirit had depths storms could not reach, heights they could not disturb. The fierce wind may vex the surface of the ocean till its waves look like loose and rolling mountains, but down fathoms deep the waters lie placid as the lake smiling in the summer sun. The clouds may darken the sky, and speak to us of tempest and thunder and gloom; but away above, on the everlasting hills, eternal calm and soft sunshine are making radiant sleep. So while human passions were darkening Christ's path, and human enmities were preparing the doom that was to be His glory, sweet peace sat like the blessed angel of God within His spirit, and filled it with celestial light and joy.

The conflict of Jesus with the Jews was thus fruitful of the most opposite results. While without Him it created an atmosphere of doubt, suspicion, and estrangement, within Him it marked the rise of a clearer and more certain consciousness of His nature and mission. The antagonism of the Pharisees affected the people. They could hardly imagine that the men who had been to their fathers and were to themselves like the incarnated wisdom of the past could be altogether wrong. Names, too, especially when coined in the schools, are moral forces of a very powerful order, and so to be called " the friend of publicans and sinners," " a speaker of blasphemies," " a Sabbath breaker," a child and agent of " Beelzebub," was to be enveloped in a set of associations that only the deepest knowledge and truest love could pierce and disperse. Then other influences came to the help of the custom that almost compels the led to follow the leaders. Jesus was too true to the Divine ideal He embodied to gratify the wishes or fulfil the hopes of the men who thought to make Him an idol. The idol of the crowd must not transcend it; if he does, the passion that prompted to worship passes into the fury that pants to destroy. To be hailed by a people that did not understand Him, must have been to Jesus but as the prelusive murmur of a cry that was to end in the shout, "Crucify Him!"

Most significantly the first word of doubt and disappointment comes from the Baptist. The man who had proclaimed Jesus as the Christ was also the man who sent to ask, "Art thou he who should come, or do we look for another?"[1] The question was that of a man not disillusioned, but doubtful, expectant, wishful, yet afraid that the hope which grew dearer and intenser in his solitude might prove to be false. He saw much in Jesus to justify it, His preaching, His call, His power to move and inspire the people; but he also saw much to condemn it, in His obscurity, His refusal to exercise political power, His love of seclusion and Galilee, His dislike of publicity and Jerusalem. The Baptist, as a prophet, could admire the great Preacher; but, as an ascetic, could only doubt the claims and authority of one who was reputed to be "gluttonous and a wine-bibber." So the conflict of doubt and desire, fear and hope, urged him to make the touching appeal to Jesus, to which Jesus so finely answered—"Go and show John those things which ye do hear and see: the blind receive their sight, and the lame walk, the lepers are cleansed, and the deaf hear, the dead are raised up, and the poor have the gospel preached to them."[2]

But the people did not halt and hesitate like John. More governed by impulse, less possessed by an exalted and spiritual faith, they took an ungratified wish for an unfulfilled hope. They did not feel, like the Baptist, the Divine beauty that lived even in the blurred image of Jesus presented to him by curious report, but they hastily con-

[1] Matt xi 3. [2] Ibid xi. 4, 5.

cluded that He who was not a Messiah in their sense could be no Messiah at all. So when Jesus returned to the cities where His mightiest works had been done, He found coldness: they refused repentance, and He announced judgment.[1] But even while the pain of desertion was freshest and most bitter, the consciousness of Divine Sonship was deepest and most real, and He knew Himself as the Son who knew the Father, whom the Father knew, the Revealer of His word and will to the world.[2]

Now here we find the root and source of the peculiarities that distinguish Christ's later teaching. It is more personal than the earlier, more concerned with the claims and meaning of His person, the reason of His coming, the authority of His words, and purpose of His work. In the very degree men turned from Him the face of the Father turned to Him, and so His filial consciousness became fuller, clearer, more intense. The two things, the growth of isolation and antagonism on the one hand, and the growth of this fuller consciousness of His person and work on the other, are variously indicated in the Gospels. The attempt had evidently been made to excite the jealousy and fear of Herod, to rouse him to action by representing Jesus as a dangerous political character, plotting and teaching treason.[3] The death of John was premonitory; and Jesus interpreted it as meaning that the man who did not spare the Baptist would, when his passions were roused, as little spare Him.[4] And so with an unfriendly people and a jealous ruler, prone to swift and cruel deeds, Galilee became to Him an uncongenial home; and He "departed into the coasts of Tyre and Sidon."[5] It was in those days of wandering and desertion, when He had come into the region of Cæsarea Philippi, that He asked His disciples, "Whom do men say that I, the Son of man,

[1] Matt. xi 20-24. [3] Luke xiii. 31. [5] Matt. xv. 21.
[2] Ibid. xi. 25-27. [4] Matt. xiv 1, 2, 13.

am ? "[1] The answer showed the conflict of opinion, and elicited the further question—" But whom say ye that I am ? " Peter's answer—significant of what his most esoteric teaching had been, " Thou art the Christ, the Son of the living God "—was hailed and ratified by the singular and suggestive words, "Blessed art thou, Simon Bar-jona. for flesh and blood hath not revealed it unto thee, but My Father which is in heaven." This remarkable response not only recognized and proclaimed the reality of His Christhood and Sonship, and faith in them as the necessary condition alike of discipleship and beatitude, but also ascribed the faith expressed in the confession to the special inspiration of God. The more perfectly the consciousness of His disciples reflected His own, the more certain was He that His Father was in them as in Him, that human apostasy only contributed to the reality of His Divine work. But while antagonism developed in Himself and His disciples this higher consciousness, it also made the dark and dread forms of the future stand out before His eye. " From that time forth He began to show " to the men who had confessed that He was " the Christ, the Son of the living God," " how that He must go unto Jerusalem, and suffer many things of the elders and chief priests and scribes, and be killed, and be raised again the third day."[2] The shadow of the cross never lifted from His soul; it saddened His spirit and deepened the meaning of His speech. His words became, as they had never been before, expository of Himself, of His relation to God and man, to death and life. And so the later is unlike the earlier teaching. He speaks less like a King proclaiming His kingdom, enforcing obedience, creating in man the sense of benevolent order and beneficent law, than like a Redeemer who redeems by death, a Deliverer who delivers by the sacrifice of Himself. And so within the apparent

[1] Matt. xvi. 13.   [2] Ibid. xvi. 21.

history He helps us to see a real Divine presence and purpose. While priests and rulers were to their own infamy and disaster plotting His death, He was preparing to make it the symbol of His truth, of His might to save.

Now here we have the point of view from which we must try to interpret His teaching as a transcript or explication of His own consciousness. His speech is the incarnation of His spirit, the mirror of His thought. His person is reflected in His words; the worth of the one explains the worth of the other.

His words do not expound a theology—they institute a religion. This is their essential and distinctive characteristic. In the Acts and the Epistles we have a theology: the disciples explain the mission and sayings of their Master, especially in their relation to the mind and will of God, and to the state and destinies of men. But the Gospels simply record the words which reveal the consciousness of Jesus, which helps us, as it were, to stand within His spirit and know the Person who created our religion as He knew Himself. And it is because His words stand in this relation to His Person that they are so creative. It is of far greater importance that we know what Jesus thought of Himself than that we know what Paul thought of Him; what the Son knew of the Father is of diviner worth to the world than what the disciples thought concerning Him. Religion precedes theology; every theology runs back into a religion, and every spiritual religion into a creative personality; and so the Person and words of Jesus underlie alike the religion of Christ and the discourses and discussions of His apostles. It is more possible to interpret the theology through the religion than the religion through the theology. Paul is inexplicable without Christ, but Christ is not unintelligible without Paul. The disciple explains the Master only after the Master has explained the disciple.

We can hardly approach the words of Christ without reverence. As we study them we almost feel as if we were overhearing His speech, or looking into His spirit, or watching the ebb and flow of emotion on His wondrous face. Theologians of a certain school have almost resented the attempt to present Christ the Teacher, as if it were better for Christian thought to be busied with His work than with His words. But what without His teaching would His Person and death signify? Are they not mutually necessary, reciprocally explicative? Would not His teaching be aimless without His death? Does not His death grow luminous only as He Himself is made its interpreter? His words have been a sort of infinite wonder to the world, a kind of Divine heart and conscience to it. They are but few; we can read in an hour all of His thought that survives in the forms human art has created to clothe and immortalize the human spirit. Nor was He careful to preserve them, wrote no word, commanded no word to be written; spoke, as it were, into the listening air the words it was to hear and preserve for all time. And the speech thus spoken into the air has been like a sweet and subtle Divine essence in the heart of humanity. If we imagine a handful of sweet spices cast into the ocean subduing its salt and brackish bitterness, and making it for evermore pleasant to the taste; or a handful of fragrance thrown into the air spreading and penetrating till it filled the atmosphere of every land, and made it healing and grateful as the breath of Paradise;— we may have an imperfect physical analogy of what Christ's words have been, and what His teaching has done for the thought and spirit of man. Had the words of any other great teacher perished; had the wisdom of Socrates, or the science of Aristotle, or the eloquence of Cicero, or the poetry of Æschylus or Sophocles been lost, our world had still been little different from what it is to-day. But had the words of Christ vanished into silence, passed into the great halls of oblivion, or had they never been spoken, our world had been quite other than it is, and been far from as wise and good as it is now. So great and infinite in value have been those teachings, in quantity smallest of fragments, in quality greatest and most priceless of the treasures that have enriched the world.

In proceeding to details, we had better start with Christ's teaching as regards Himself. Here our first duty must be to interpret the two descriptive titles, "Son of man" and "Son of God."

1. "Son of man." This title is in the New Testament significantly enough used, with one exception, by Christ alone. The exception occurs in the speech of Stephen, in the very last words he is allowed to utter. "Behold," he cries, "I see the heavens opened, and the Son of man standing on the right hand of God."[1] The position is remarkable and significant, expresses dignity, dominion, authority. And these are ideas that are usually associated with the title, and that it was manifestly intended to connote. Thus it is said, the Father "hath given Him authority to execute judgment, because He is the Son of man."[2] In one of the great eschatological discourses we read, "As the lightning cometh out of the east, and shineth even unto the west, so shall also the coming of the Son of man be;" and He is to be seen "coming in the clouds of heaven, with power and great glory."[3] The pre-eminent dignity the title is meant to express is evident from the text where it first occurs: "The foxes have holes, and the birds of the air have nests; but the Son of man hath not where to lay His head."[4] The force of the passage lies evidently in the contrast of right with fact, of ideal position with real experience. These usages place us on the line along

[1] Acts vii. 56.
[2] John v. 27.
[3] Matt. xxiv. 27, 30.
[4] Ibid. viii. 20.

which the explanation must be sought. The title belongs to one who possesses authority, and can execute judgment and first appears in the later prophetic literature. Daniel says,[1] "I saw in the night visions, and, behold, one like the Son of man came with the clouds of heaven." The vision is one of a cycle in which symbolical expression has been given to the essential characters of the great empires of the past and present. The symbols employed were beasts: the first, a lion with eagle's wings; the second, a bear, with ribs riven from a side in its teeth; the third, a leopard, four-winged, four-headed; the fourth, a mythical beast, "dreadful and terrible and strong exceedingly." The empires thus symbolized are brutal, based on mere fierce strength. When their dominion ceases, the one "like the Son of man" comes in the clouds of heaven; "and there was given Him dominion, and glory, and a kingdom, that all people, nations, and languages should serve Him."[2] The meaning is evident: the symbols of the old empires were beasts, but the symbol of the new Divine kingdom is "the Son of man." Its character was humanity, as theirs was inhumanity; it is personified in gentle and forethoughtful reason, as they were personified in cruel and selfish force. "The Son of man" institutes a kingdom that carries out the purposes of God as to man, and realizes in humanity His reign.

The title thus emphasizes the humanity of Him who bears it, but a humanity that accomplishes a Divine work, creates and controls a society which is so finely human because so entirely a realization of the thought or mind of God as to man. Schleiermacher rightly said: "Christ would not have adopted this title had He not been conscious of a complete participation in human nature. But His use of it would have been meaningless had He not had a right to it which other men could not possess. And conse-

[1] Dan. vii 13. [2] Ibid vii 14.

quently the meaning was a pregnant one, marking the distinctive differences between Him and other men."[1] These differences show the powers and prerogatives that belonged to the title, and the duties they involved. "The Son of man" is the bond between earth and heaven, belongs in an equal degree to both; He is the medium through which God reaches man and man reaches God.[2] As the One who unites and unifies earth and heaven, He is the Source of the Divine life in man, is the Light that creates, the Bread that maintains, life in the world.[3] As the Creator of the new society, the Founder of the Divine kingdom, He has the right to repeal whatever impedes its progress, to modify or adapt to its service[4] old institutions like the Sabbath. He must, too, exercise rule, see that His citizens are worthy of His city.[5] If to exercise authority be His right, to obey is man's duty; and confession becomes the subjects of the King.[6] But these powers and prerogatives are rooted in sacrifice. Without death, without resurrection, "the Son of man" cannot fulfil His mission, carry through His Divine work.[7] He suffers that He may save; by death He gives His life a ransom for the many.[8]

The title, so often and so emphatically used, enables us to see what Christ conceived Himself to be, and where He believed Himself to stand: He affirmed that He possessed our common human nature: He was a "*Son*." But He also affirmed His pre-eminence—"*the* Son of *man*." Other persons had been, or were, sons of individual men, members of particular families or nations; but Jesus, as "*the* Son of man," was no man's son, was the child of humanity; be-

---

[1] Schleiermacher, *Glaubenslehre*, ii. 91, 3rd edition.
[2] John i. 51; iii 13, vi. 62, viii. 28.   [5] Matt. xiii 41.
[3] Ibid. vi. 53   [6] Ibid. xvi. 13.
[4] Matt. xii. 8.   [7] Ibid xvii. 9, 12, 22, 23; xx. 18.
[8] Ibid. xviii. 11; Mark xiv 21-25.

longed to no age, but to all ages; to no family or people, but to mankind. He is, as the Divine Ideal realized, universal and everlasting, an individual who is, in a sense, humanity.

The title is, in a manner, translated and interpreted by Paul in the phrases, "the last Adam," "the second Man."[1] Adam failed to become what God intended him to be, was only a "living soul," did not become "a life-giving spirit." His sons were also failures, and earth, though built to be the home of humanity, had never seen humanity realized. But Christ came and realized it, appeared as the vital form of the Divine idea, the articulated image of the Divine dream. And so the "last Adam" was greater than the first, "a quickening spirit," able to vivify those that were as good as dead. Humanity was like a colossal aloe, growing slowly through many centuries, throwing out many an abortive bud, but blossoming at length into "the second Man," who remains its for ever fragrant and imperishable flower.

2. The "Son of God." This title was less common on the lips of Christ, but was frequent with the apostles, with whom it assumes a peculiar meaning, especially when qualified by μονογενής and ἴδιος. As used by Christ, it occurs only in the Fourth Gospel, and expresses not simply a figurative, but an essential filial, relation to God. The Jews so understand it, and charge Him with blasphemy for daring to use it.[2] One passage in the first Synoptic[3] shows that the use was no peculiarity of the Johannean Christ. The ideas it connotes are finely expressed in the great filial confession recorded by Matthew: "No man knoweth the Son, but the Father; neither knoweth any man the Father, save the Son, and he to whomsoever the Son will reveal Him."[4] The mutual

[1] 1 Cor xv. 45, 47.
[2] John xix 7.
[3] Matt xxvii 43.
[4] Ibid xi. 27.

knowledge is absolute: Father and Son know each other as they alone can who never were but face to face and heart to heart. The knowledge the Son possesses of the Father He possesses that He may communicate; He knows God that He may make Him known. Where His knowledge is received, His spirit is born; to know the Father as the Son knows Him, is to love as the Son loves. In this filial confession the High Priest's prayer is anticipated; the world that does not know the Father is to be brought to the knowledge of Him through the Son.[1] And here we can see the truths that meet and blend in the titles. "The Son of God," through His essential relation to the Father, is the vehicle of true and absolute knowledge concerning Him; "the Son of man," through His essential relation with humanity, is the medium of its living union with God. The first title denotes Christ as God's mediator with man, the second denotes Him as man's mediator with God.

Christ's common use of the one title and rare use of the other was a custom beautifully true to His nature. It shows how intensely His conciousness had realized His affinity with man, how He wished men to feel His and their community of nature. It was by His humanity that He hoped to lift and save men. The sense of our kinship with God through Christ is our regeneration.

It was a peculiar and transcendent consciousness that could be expressed in the titles "Son of God" and "Son of man;" and He who so conceived Himself showed He had a mission worthy of His transcendent Personality. Very early He had declared His judicial authority and functions, asserted and exercised His right to forgive sins, advanced His claim to the faith and homage of Israel.[2] But these general statements could not satisfy His consciousness: truth required Him to become more specific and personal.

[1] John xvii. 25, 26. [2] Matt. vii 23, ix 1-8, x 5, ff, xi. 19-24.

While He is the least self-conscious of teachers, He is of all teachers the most conscious of Himself; while the least egotistical, the most concerned with His own Person. He conceived His person to be a supreme necessity to the world : He is the Saviour of the lost; He is the Shepherd, now giving His life for the sheep, now returning with the rescued lamb in His arms. The death that is to come to Him by wicked hands cannot defeat His mission, can only help to fulfil it ; it is to mark the culmination of His sacrifice : it is to be the condition and symbol of victory. The theme of Christ's later teaching was Christ, and there is no finer witness to His truth than this: while His teaching is concerned with Himself it is never selfish, remains infinitely remote from egoism, is penetrated by the sublimest universalism. To speak of Himself is the highest boon He can confer on the race, for the words that unfolded the consciousness of His Divine Sonship are the only words that have been able to create a conscious Divine Sonship in the race.

Round this centre the varied elements of His teaching beautifully crystallize. Out of His twofold relation, to God and man, springs what He has to say of both. The Son who is in the bosom of the Father declares Him, shows Him mindful of sinful man, seeking him, receiving him with a weeping joy that makes all heaven glad. The "Son of man" reveals man to himself, shows the transcendent worth of the soul He loves to save, makes man conscious of the infinite possibilities of good within him, of the Divine affinities that sleep in His nature. The Person that manifests the Divine and the human in beautiful and holy unity, fitly shows how God and man can sweetly meet, and rejoice in each other with exceeding great joy. He who is, as it were, our virtues incorporated is the fit teacher of duty, a voice gentle where most authoritative, making its most imperative commands as sweet as reasonable. And so person and word combine to bring round the fulfilment of His grand prayer: " That they may be all one; as Thou, Father, art in me, and I in Thee, that they also may be one in us: that the world may believe that Thou hast sent me." [1]

[1] John xvii. 21.

XII.

THE LATER MIRACLES.

THE thought and action of Christ so lived in harmony that neither could move without the other; the progress of one was the progress of both. Hence the very qualities that distinguish His later from His earlier teaching distinguish His later from His earlier works. In the very degree that the former becomes, in the region of the spirit, transcendental, expressive of a higher consciousness and diviner claims, the latter become, in the region of nature, the more extraordinary revelations of the Son of God that had been realized in the Son of man. We may name the earlier the less, the later the greater, miracles; but we attach to these terms ideas almost the very opposite of those the Evangelists would have attached. We measure the greatness of a miracle by the degree in which it departs from the order of nature, but the Evangelists by the degree in which it manifested the nature and mind of Christ. To them it was not the contra-natural that surprised, but the manifested Christ that satisfied. The action became Him, and in the becoming action the Actor showed His essential character, declared His native and inherent qualities.

The Evangelists, then, did not look at the miracles through our ideas of nature, but through their own idea of Christ; and only where their idea is accepted as reasonable can their history be regarded as veracious. Our physicists say, the same law that moulds a dewdrop rounds a world. The law that brings a stone to the earth binds the planets to their spheres. In the processes of nature there is no great and no little. Force is one, everywhere changing, everywhere conserved, its action illustrated and its strength expressed in the minutest as in the mightiest physical phenomena. As the physicists conceive force in nature, the Evangelists conceived energy in Christ. To the one as to the other, to create life was as easy as to ripen the grape or form the leaf. The subdued fever and the stilled storm, the healed paralytic and the revived Lazarus, were each equally possible to the power immanent in Christ; they were marvellous, not as departures from the order of nature, but as revelations of the nature He possessed. And so the Evangelical narratives are distinguished by a historical sobriety of form in marked contrast to their extraordinary contents, utterly unlike the humorous gravity, the conscious innocence of exaggeration or incongruity, that looks so naively out of our ancient nursery or mythical tales. Our Gospels, while they describe miracles, are, as it were, without the atmosphere of the miraculous, and narrate events that they feel to be in fullest harmony with the wondrous Person they pourtray. Pascal said,[1] "Jesus Christ speaks the greatest things so simply, that it seems as if He had never thought upon them." That spontaneous unpremeditated speech was His glory, proof that His words reflected a consciousness which knew no struggle, that His being and truth were so transparent to Himself that His claims were but as fruits of nature, His words like fragrances flung into the air by His spirit as it blushed into perfect flower. And the simplicity which distinguishes the Master's speech marks the disciples' history; and for the same reason—each is conscious that the extraordinary and miraculous is to the Person concerned but the ordinary and normal. Their

[1] *Pensées et Lettres*, ii. 319 (Faugère).

faith in Christ made them insensible to the impossibilities of the physicist, and the narratives reflect alike in matter and manner the faith of their authors.

But their way of looking at events through their idea of Christ gives to the Evangelists not only a fine simplicity and realism of narrative—the more remarkable that their history is simply the most extraordinary ever written or believed by man; but also a fine consistency in their presentation of Jesus, a consistency the more striking and significant that it seems on their part unconscious and undesigned. His thought and action did not simply move in harmony; each seemed in its successive phases but a transcript of the other. The more He asserts in His teaching His personal pre-eminence, the more do His acts seem to declare it. As His speech became more egoistic, therefore more theological, without becoming any less ethical, His acts became declarative of a personality transcendent alike as regards nature and man. The ethical import of parables like the Prodigal Son, the Rich Man and Lazarus, and the Good Samaritan, is as exalted and pure as that of the Sermon on the Mount; but the theological import of the former is greater, marked by deeper insight into the character and aims of God, into the spirit and destinies of man. The discourse to Nicodemus is much more elementary than the great Johannean discourses to the disciples, speaks less of the Son's essential relation to the Father, or His organic connection with man. There are no indications in it of truths like this: "I and the Father are one;" "He that hath seen Me hath seen the Father;" or this, "I am the vine, ye are the branches;" or this, "If I go not away, the Comforter will not come unto you; but if I depart, I will send Him unto you."[1] In the later teaching of Christ His Person is thus made to become

[1] John x. 30 ; xiv 9 ; xv. 1 ; xvi. 7.

explicative of God, redemptive of man, and creative of peaceful and happy relations between the two. And these changes are reflected in His acts. The miracle at Cana is concerned with the elements, as it were, of the world; but the miracle at Bethany with the most awful mysteries of life, the saddest and most sacred secrets of the spirit. While at first He is only one who can " heal the sick of divers diseases," later He is one whom " even the wind and sea obey."[1] While His first hearers were not so much astonished at Himself as at His doctrine, He appeared later to the men who knew Him best as one "transfigured, and His face did shine as the sun, and His raiment was white as the light."[2] The power He possessed seemed to grow by exercise; His last was His greatest miracle, His greatest words were His last. No sayings so divinely become Christ as the sayings on the cross; no act so finely illustrates His mind and mission as the raising of Lazarus. Action and speech were in lovely and significant harmony. He went to death from a victory over the grave. His right to lay down His life was proved by His power to raise from the dead; the prayer for the men that crucified Him is explained by the quickening word that had changed death into life. And so in Christ doctrine and deed confirm each other; if by the one He predicted the death, by the other He explained the resurrection that was to be accomplished at Jerusalem.

These qualities of the Evangelical narratives as records of so-called miraculous events—so finely natural and immiraculous in tone, so finely consistent and harmonious, almost without consciousness or design, in their conception and literary presentation of Christ—suggest a line of thought supplementary to one we have already pursued.[3]

[1] Mark i. 24; iv 41. [2] Luke iv 32; Matt. vii 28; xvii. 2.
[3] *Supra*, 149, ff.

THE LATER MIRACLES.

The miracles were then discussed in their relation to the person of Christ; now they are to be discussed in relation to the Evangelical history. The former discussion rose out of the earlier miracles, the first manifestations of the supernatural in Christ; the present is directly concerned with the later miracles, the most extraordinary and least credible in nature. Yet these are the very events that the Evangelists relate so simply that it seems as if they thought nothing could be more natural than their occurrence, yet so subtly, that they are harmoniously woven into the very texture of the narrative, and essentially incorporated with its substance. And the qualities are indissolubly associated. It is because they conceive miracles as so natural to Christ, that they present them with an art so simple yet so perfect, so unconscious yet so complete.

Now it will best accord with our design not to allow the discussion to range over the whole field, and so it had better be confined to the very definite issues raised by a single typical case. The most typical case, fullest at once of critical difficulties and of the comfort that comes of the highest Christian truth, is the raising of Lazarus. It is the greatest of Christ's miracles: to know this is to know all. There is none harder to believe; none that, believed, is so rich in meaning, so glorious in its assurance to faith and in its promise to hope. The truths embedded in it, and embalmed by it, are many and cardinal. It expresses with wonderful force the tender grace, the holy human sympathy, of Christ. His love for man is made eminently intense and personal by His love for Martha and Mary and Lazarus. His place in the home is made inmost and secure by faith in the gentle Presence that dwelt with the sisters of Bethany, a Presence that seems to consecrate the family, and make it the seat and sanctuary of Divine influences. When, too, the soul sits dumb and desolate in "the shadow feared of man," peace and comfort come from the voice of Him who once spoke a dead friend into life; or when sorrow has come to the spirit like a hot wind, which dries its moisture and burns up its fruits and flowers, banishing at once the rain of heaven and the dew of earth, then those tears Divine Manhood once wept at the grave of the man He loved fall on the arid soil, and moisten it into soft humanity again. Then, too, Christian hope might wither and die, were it not for the words that, while they might as words of a friend cheer the sisters, nothing less than a miracle could verify or transmute into words of truth for the world. We love our dead; we love even their very dust. We love the memories that endear the past and the hopes that gladden the future; making us, in the very moment when the longing born of love is mightiest, feel "the touch of the vanished hand," and hear "the sound of the voice that is still." And the faith which created these hopes owes in a large measure its being to the words spoken and the deed done at the grave of Lazarus. The words, "I am the resurrection and the life," have created the angel of hope that watches the sleep of the Christian dead, and makes it to the living radiant with peace and immortality. Were they to cease to be Christ's, should we not feel as if a stream of dismal paganism had been turned against our sun, and clothed it in clouds? And if they stand alone, they as good as cease to be His; the words without the miracle become but an impertinent or idle vaunt, a promise that all nature and all history have combined to deny and disappoint. Only lips that could speak creative words could say with truth, "Whosoever liveth and believeth in me shall never die."

But the very eminence of its spiritual significance makes the difficulties that beset it graver and weightier. What is finely reasonable as a symbolical narrative be- comes, when studied as a sober historical record, amazing

THE LATER MIRACLES.

and incredible. A miracle of healing is comparatively explicable; it may result from the subtle co-operation of two imaginations and two wills: but a miracle like this is an act of creation, an event not only outside all experience, but contrary to it. Then, too, the evidence for it seems slender, altogether inadequate. It is peculiar to the Fourth Gospel; the Synoptists know nothing of it. On the supposition that it occurred, their silence seems inexplicable. It is exactly the sort of event they would have loved to describe: it exalts Christ and degrades His enemies; it is the victorious proof of His claims and their infamy. It is most remarkable that three men, the nearest, too, to the time and place, should omit all mention of what is certainly Christ's most extraordinary achievement, whilst a fourth and more distant historian describes it in so full and realistic detail. When the matter is so stated, it does seem as if the difficulties must vanquish belief, and reasonable faith be pronounced impossible.

But now let us look at the matter from the side of the Evangelical history, especially with the view of discovering how it is affected by the denial of the miracle, whether it become more or less consistent and comprehensible, more or less coherent and credible. Let us see, then, how any of the several forms of denial compatible with historical criticism would affect the narrative that more directly concerns us.

There is the theory favoured by the older Rationalism, that the fancied miracle was due to a series of happy accidents and coincidences; that the death had been apparent, not real; that the cool atmosphere of the tomb and the piercing accents of a loved voice had combined to awake Lazarus from his death-like sleep; that the agitation of Jesus was due to the appearance of the revived corpse, but, presence of mind overmastering fear, the summons, "Lazarus, come forth!" had as its result the emergence of the supposed dead man. This interpretation was intended, while denying the reality of the miracle, to preserve the historical truth of the narrative. But how did it succeed? The miracle is introduced by a history, which must be negatived if the natural explanation is to stand. Jesus said, " Our friend Lazarus is fallen asleep, but I go that I may awake him out of his sleep."[1] And this clear pre-intimation of purpose and prophecy of the event are at once emphasized by the words, "Lazarus is dead; and I am glad for your sakes that I was not there, to the intent ye may believe."[2] Then the words of Jesus to Martha are significant, "Thy brother shall rise again,"[3] especially in the light of His answer at the grave to her remonstrance about the removal of the stone, " Saidst I not unto thee, that, if thou wouldest believe, thou shouldest see the glory of God?"[4] These sayings were immovable stones of stumbling to the theory that maintained the reality of the event, but denied the truth of the miracle, for the accident of the end could not explain the expressed design of the beginning. The historical truth of both was impossible. If the event was accidental, the sayings must be false; if the sayings were true, the event could not be accidental. But the theory, granting as probable all its violent improbabilities, was even in more radical contradiction to the narrative. It failed to explain the conduct of Jesus. Why did He go to the grave? Why did He desire to see the buried Lazarus? A dead body was a hateful thing to the Jew; to touch it was to be defiled. If Jesus was above the prejudices of His own countrymen, He must still more have been above the morbid curiosity of ours. It would be hard to imagine anything more un-Christ-like than the desire to see the wasted dead, or to look into an offensive " charnel cave." The criticism that must assume such a

[1] John xi. 11.
[2] Ibid. xi. 14, 15.
[3] Ibid xi. 23.
[4] Ibid xi. 40.

desire stands convicted of incapacity to understand the Person it would reach and pourtray.

Has the mythical theory, then, which was more merciless to Rationalism than even to orthodoxy, been more successful? Strauss explained this and the similar Evangelical miracles as due to the early Christian imagination, unconsciously creative, clothing Jesus in the supernatural attributes and actions of Elijah and Elisha, the most wonderful of the Old Testament prophets.[1] With the philosophical bases and critical assumptions of the mythical hypothesis we have here no concern, but only with the question whether the explanation it offered be compatible with this narrative in particular or the Evangelical history in general. The first thing that strikes us, as affecting both points, is—it does seem strange that the finest creation of the mythical imagination, working under conditions essentially Jewish, and with materials derived from the Old Testament, should be found in the Fourth Gospel. It is marked throughout by almost fierce Judaic antipathies, and its want of a Hebrew atmosphere and colouring has been held one of its most distinctive characteristics. But the purest and most original work of Hellenistic speculation does not seem the proper soil for the purest and most original product of the Judæo-Christian phantasy. The one position is the negation of the other. The theory would have required our narrative to appear in Matthew, and can only regard it as misplaced in John, without being able to give any reason why it has been so misplaced. Then the narrative is wonderfully sober, vivid, and truthful in feature and detail—far too much so to be the work of an unconsciously creative imagination, which, being essentially exaggerative, never sees its objects as they stand revealed by the clear light of nature to a clear and searching eye. If the central event is mythical, the incidents

[1] *Leben Jesu,* § 100.

that surround it must show the action, the tool-marks, as it were, of the mythical faculty. But do they? The topographical accuracy is remarkable,[1] and still more so the minute and delicate way in which peculiarities of character are indicated,[2] the circumstantial and careful attention to unimportant yet most significant details relative to the persons, their relations, their history, their feelings, hopes, and actions, as influenced now by custom and now by personal reasons, sorrow, concern, or love.[3] This is not the way in which the mythical imagination goes to work: its creations are on a large scale, thrown off with a fine contempt for those delicacies of light and shade that in real life so subtly cross and blend. And when we analyze the narrative, we find it too full of tender and moving humanity to be a creation of the idea. "Now Jesus loved Martha, and her sister, and Lazarus."[4] The dropping out of Mary's name is a most significant touch, as if the stronger had absorbed the softer sister, or been to her a sort of mother or head. Then, their love to Christ is finely indicated in the message,[5] which expresses a trust that knows no hesitancy or fear. The conversation, too, of Jesus and His disciples is finely in keeping with their respective characters: they afraid to go into Judæa, He afraid only of the darkness, resolved to walk in the light, even though it should lead straight down into the valley of death.[6]

But the most perfect scene is the successive interviews with the sisters. Each is true to her character as we know it from Luke.[7] Martha—strong, self-possessed, not so absorbed in grief or in the formal comforts custom offered as to be blind or indifferent to what was going on

[1] John xi. 18.
[2] Ibid xi 16, 20, 28, 29, 32. *Cf* 21, 39.
[3] Ibid. xi. 1, 2, 5, 8, 19, 28-31, 33, 38.
[4] John xi. 5.
[5] Ibid. xi. 3.
[6] Ibid. xi 8-10.
[7] Luke x. 38-42.

around—is the first to hear that Jesus has come; and, with a heart equally divided between love and care for the living and sorrow for the dead, she goes out to meet Him. Mary, contemplative, emotional, a genuine mystic, so filled with her great sorrow as to be passive in its hands, sits still in the house. Martha, erect, calm while regretful, goes with quiet thoughtfulness softly out to meet Him. Mary, broken and bowed down, is suddenly, when she hears Jesus has come, filled by a new emotion, and driven, as it were, by an irresistible impulse, "she rose up hastily, and went out," and on reaching Jesus, "fell down at His feet." The myth-making faculty does not work in this delicate, yet most gentle and human, way. It is possessed by the love of the miraculous, lives in the region of sensuous exaggeration, where the finer qualities of the spirit are lost, and only the vulgar marvels of the senses live and flourish. Here we have a true "sanctuary of sorrow," with all its sorrowful elements born of man, all its sacred and comforting influences born of God.

But if the mythical theory was too violent and improbable, too little historical, too purely *a priori*, what of the theory that succeeded and superseded it, the theory which the Tubingen school, and especially its most distinguished representatives, Baur and Zeller, developed and applied to our narrative?[1] Baur thought the narrative was an artistic rearrangement of materials found in the Synoptists, especially Luke; its motive being determined by the dogmatic aim or purpose of the Gospel. It is, as it were, an acted parable, designed to illustrate the words, "I am the resurrection and the life." As Christ by healing the blind

[1] Zeller was the first to hit upon the ingenious application and illustration of the tendency theory above described *Theologische Jahrbucher*, 1842, pp 89, ff. Baur followed on the same line in the celebrated essay, *Ueber die Composition und den Character des Johan Evangeliums*, Theol. *Jahrbb*, 1844, pp 126-146, 408-411. Also his *Kritische Untersuchungen*, pp 248, ff

appeared as the Light of the world, so by raising the dead
He appeared as its Life. The narrative was but a symbol
or sensuous form for this truth. The materials used were
borrowed from Luke, the widow's son of Nain, the scene
between Martha and Mary, and the parable of the Rich
Man and Lazarus, where the wish was so devoutly expressed that Lazarus might be raised from the dead, in
order to instruct the living.[1] There was, indeed, no point
that more finely exercised the ingenious critics of Tubingen
than this, showing how John had so skilfully manipulated
a parable of Luke as to transform it into a history illustrative of the power of faith against the absolute unbelief
of the Jews. But their endeavours mainly proved their
own surpassing ingenuity. The parable and the history
are alike in this—each has a Lazarus, and in each he dies:
in every other respect they are fundamentally different.[2]
The parable shows how the rewards and penalties of the
future redress the wrongs of the present; but the history
regards only the present, and has no eye for the future.
In the parable the return from death is pronounced impossible; but the history brings Lazarus out from the very
bosom of death. The parable strongly emphasizes the
poverty of Lazarus; but in the history he lives in comfort,
if not in affluence. The moral of the parable is, " They
will not be persuaded, though one rose from the dead ;"[3]
but the history says, " Many of the Jews who had seen the
things Jesus did, believed on Him."[4] The Tubingen derivation of the narrative from the parable was thus possible
only by emphasizing two superficial resemblances, and
forgetting many radical differences. If Baur declared that
the Lazarus of the history presupposes the parable of Lazarus, Hengstenberg affirmed that the parable of Lazarus
presupposes the Lazarus of history; and each had about

[1] Luke vii 12 ; x 38-42, xvi 19-31.
[2] Hase, *Geschichte Jesu,* p 513
[3] Luke xvi. 31.
[4] John xi 45.

equal authority for his dictum, uttered the conceit of a vagrant fancy, not the sober judgment of criticism.

The Tubingen criticism was, indeed, here as thoroughly unscientific as unsound. It was often curiously unfaithful to its own philosophical principles—instead of regarding history as the manifestation and explication of the ideal, imagining that where the ideal began the real or historical ceased; that where persons like Martha, Mary, and Lazarus were made to exhibit or illustrate the power embodied in Christ, they could not really have lived. Yet when we find the sisters mentioned in Luke reappearing in John, with their respective characters so subtly and perfectly preserved in new and most tragic relations, it is a proof, not of literary invention working with borrowed materials, but of historian supplementing historian, the two halves of a broken ring joining to form a whole.[1] Then, too, if our narrative is to be interpreted as a conscious literary creation, meant to typify Christ, the incarnate Logos, as the Life victorious over death, how are sayings and acts that positively contradict this design to be explained?[2] He would be but a clumsy artist who allowed such incompatible elements to steal into his picture; but clumsy fiction is no fiction: it invites the detection and exposure that are its death. As nature, John's art is here inimitable; as art or invention, it is poor indeed.

But now we come to another and still more extraordinary explanation, without doubt the most unworthy ever proposed by a scholar and critic of reputation. M. Renan sees that an event little less marvellous than a miracle is needed to explain the enthusiasm of love and hate which at once glorified and embittered the death of Jesus. So he conjectures that[3] " something really happened at Bethany which was looked upon as a resurrection." In

[1] Hase, *Geschichte Jesu*, p 514   [2] John xi 4, 33, 37, 41.
[3] *Vie de Jésus*, chap xxiii

the heavy and impure atmosphere of Jerusalem the conscience of Jesus lost something of its original purity, and He was no longer either Himself or His own master. In the act which was desired the family of Bethany were led to take part. "Faith knows no other law than the interest of that which it believes to be true." Obedient to this comprehensive principle, " Lazarus caused himself to be wrapped in bandages as if dead, and shut up in the tomb of his family;" and when Jesus came and ordered the stone to be removed, " Lazarus came forth in his bandages, his head covered with a winding-sheet." The old Rationalism was sanity to the new Romanticism. It implies a moral obtuseness one may wonder at but cannot reason with. Lack of insight into the character of Jesus and the motives that inspired the early Christian society may lead to strange results, but it can hardly be either cured or corrected by hostile argument.

The narrative, then, does not seem rationally interpretable on any theory that negatives the miracle. But it is one thing to say, These theories are false, and quite another thing to say, The miracle is true. This is a point that does not simply concern the interpreter; it concerns the historical critic as well. From his side we are confronted with two questions—one as to the silence of the Synoptists, another as to the silence of the witnesses at the trial. If a miracle so extraordinary had really been performed, could the Synoptists have passed it over in silence? or could the trial, a few days later, of the Person who worked it have been conducted and concluded without any reference or allusion to what must have overborne and outweighed all oral testimony, however adverse? Are these two points capable of reasonable explanation? or must they be allowed seriously to affect the authenticity and credibility of the narrative?

Let us, as the most serious and significant, consider first

the silence of the Synoptists. And here it is necessary to observe that the silence is not peculiar to one narrative, does not affect it alone, but everything which John records as having been done and spoken in and about Jerusalem prior to the Passion. The difficulties connected with the silence must therefore be borne, not by our history alone, but by the Gospel as a whole; and, of course, the degree in which their pressure can be distributed over the whole is the measure of the relief given to each individual part. If the silence had been here, and nowhere else, it might have been ominous; but as it is, within the limits specified, general, it must be explicable through the essential character of the Fourth in contrast to the Synoptic Gospels, not through the peculiar nature of our special narrative. The Synoptists are, in a sense, not three, but one. They have a common source, and, it may be said, common materials. Then, their history is Galilean; alike as to scope and contents it is defined by the kind of ministry there exercised. When they come to Jerusalem it is to tell the story of the Passion; and, for them, its shadow is so deep that it eclipses and conceals all besides. The Galilean history is a unity, a circle which an incident like the miracle at Bethany would have broken. It is noteworthy that Luke's fragmentary notice of Martha and Mary says nothing as to their home, only that Jesus "entered into a certain village."[1] The incident could find a place in his history only as unlocalized. While their silence is thus not only explicable, but, in a sense, inevitable, it is significant that they make Bethany the home of Jesus while at Jerusalem,[2] and the point whence He starts on His triumphal entry.[3] Certainly He must have found there kind hearts; and there, too, the people must have found a cause of wonder and enthusiasm.

[1] Luke x. 38.   [2] Matt xxi 17; Mark xi. 11, 12.
[3] Ibid. xi. 1-11, Luke xix 29, ff.

But the speech of the Fourth is as capable of explanation as the silence of the Synoptic Gospels. John is as much concerned with the Judæan as the Synoptists with the Galilean ministry, and for reasons that touch the essential character of His Gospel. His history is ideal, without ceasing to be historical. The ideal that receives more sensuous expression in the New Jerusalem of the Apocalypse, receives subtler expression in the history that is so tragically localized in and round the Old Jerusalem, the city of the Jews, the enemies while the descendants of the ancient people of God. The city He had consecrated, but they depraved, was the appropriate scene of the last fell conflict between their guilt and His victorious grace. And John describes the various acts in that great drama, from the first ominous word to the tragic climax. Without his Gospel the death of Christ would, even on its simply historical side, remain to us a riddle — a mere wanton and unprovoked crime. With his Gospel, we can see the hostile forces gathering, and mark their inevitable march. The Synoptists show us the Master educating His disciples, founding His society, instituting His kingdom; but John shows us Christ in conflict with the Jews—how He came to His own, but His own refused to receive Him—with the consequent struggle between His light and their darkness, culminating on their part in the Cross, on His in the Resurrection.

And the history is written to exhibit this tragic struggle in its several successive stages. The miracles are so presented as at once to define and deepen it, as to show their influence on the progress of the dread story. The earliest miracles excite a wonder that almost becomes faith.[1] For a moment belief and unbelief seem alike possible; but the moment is of the briefest, only one "man of the Pharisees" seeking Jesus, the others holding aloof in disdainful neg-

[1] John ii. 23, iii. 2.

lect. The miracle at the pool of Bethesda shows the neglect developed into hostility; the Jews "persecute" Jesus, and "seek to slay Him."[1] The cure of the man born blind deepens the exasperation; Healer and healed are alike hated, and the "disciples" of Moses ominously pronounce "this man a sinner."[2] The raising of Lazarus forms the tragic climax: what most manifests Christ's power most provokes the Jews' anger; the very event that best proves His Divine energy ripens their guilty purpose.[3] The miracle forces the persons in the Divine drama to declare themselves, and face each other as absolute foes— so manifests the divinity in Christ as to compel the Jews either into submission or into fatal collision. The Nemesis that follows the guilty choice drives them on the latter: the Man is to die really on account of the miracle, or, rather, what it signified as to Him and threatened as to them, but ostensibly "for the people"—*i.e.*, His death is necessary to the maintenance of their religious ascendancy, but is to be demanded for political reasons. Our narrative is thus an integral part of the tragedy unfolded in the Fourth Gospel—is indeed at once a culminating and a turning point—the point where the hostility of the past culminates, and where the crime of the Cross begins. The speech of John was thus as inevitable as the silence of the Synoptists is explicable. Without the miracle His history had wanted its key; with it their history had wanted its unity—the unity it owed to its moving within the limits of the Galilean ministry, the geographical term denoting also a distinct intellectual, moral, and social sphere.

Our discussion of the first question, the silence of the Synoptists over against the speech of John, has brought us to the point from which we can best approach the second question, the silence of the witnesses at the trial.

[1] John v. 16. [2] Ibid. ix. 16, 24, 28, 29, 34.
[3] Ibid. xi. 47-53.

The reason is obvious; John subtly makes Caiaphas indicate it.[1] Jesus is to be a religious victim disguised as a political offender. Rome, tolerant to the religions of her subject peoples, would not judge in matters of faith.[2] To charge Jesus with an offence against Moses had simply been to release Him; their one chance was to convict Him of a political crime. To this point their energies were directed; so their charge was, "We found this person perverting the nation, and forbidding to give tribute to Cæsar, saying that He Himself is Christ the king."[3] The Synoptists and John are here thoroughly agreed. The priests and rulers translated the Hebrew theocratic into the Roman political idea, and urged the death of Jesus because He had claimed to be "the King of the Jews," which they denied, confessing that they had no king but Cæsar.[4] But John alone shows us the framing of the charge and the reasons for it—the craft that made the least political of teachers a sacrifice by clothing Him in the sins of the most tumultuous and rebellious of peoples; "It is expedient for us that one man should die for the people, and that the whole nation perish not." But this scheme required a carefully arranged trial, with well-selected witnesses. They must be theirs, not Christ's—speaking not to what He was, but to what He was needed to be. So there could only be suppression of whatever could make for His Divine mission and character, and bold suggestion of whatever could make out political speech and designs.

But it is not enough to show that objections urged against the truth of our narrative turn into evidences and claims on its behalf; we must also show that it is necessary to the subsequent Evangelical history. As it grew

[1] John xi. 49, 50. [2] Acts xviii. 15. [3] Luke xxiii. 2.
[4] Matt xxvii 11, 29, 37 ; Mark xv. 2, 12, 26 ; Luke xxiii. 38 ; John xviii. 33, 35, 37 , xix. 12, 14, 15.

THE LATER MIRACLES. 215

out of what preceded, what succeeds grows out of it. This is a point which M. Renan has well perceived. He says, "If we reject this event as imaginary, all the edifice of the last week in the life of Jesus, to which our Gospel gives so much solidity, crumbles at one blow." This is all the more serious that the Fourth Gospel from this point "contains an amount of minute information infinitely superior to that of the Synoptists."[1] But the relation our narrative bears to the Johannean history is less significant than its relation to the Synoptical. One side of this relation has been seen—that touching the trial; now we may note another. The triumphal entry is a very remarkable, and, as it stands in the Synoptists, an unexplained incident. The enthusiasm of the people seems to be without any real or adequate cause. The wonder that Jesus had at first awakened had long since died, and He had been living sadly with "His own" under the shadow of the Cross. Why this sudden outburst of an admiration and enthusiasm that mocked even the joyous homage of His early ministry? Why did the people in these last dark days do as they had never done in His first bright ones— hail Him as the Messiah, the King coming in the name of the Lord? In seeking an answer, we must note the point from which Jesus approaches the city, Bethany. In Bethany He finds a home; His fame seems associated with it. As He comes from it towards Jerusalem, the multitude flows out to meet Him, breaking, as it sweeps round His little band, into the glad shout, "Blessed be the King that cometh in the name of the Lord: peace in heaven, and glory in the highest!"[2] The event that explained the anger and guilty resolution of the priests will also explain the enthusiasm of the people—will explain, too, their sudden recoil into the fierce and pitiless passion which demanded the Cross and mocked the Crucified.

[1] *Vie de Jésus*, p. 514.   [2] Luke xix. 38.

Disappointed enthusiasm is dangerously akin to furious hate. The greater the act that kindled the enthusiasm, the harder it is to satisfy its demands. The men who had been stirred to admiration by a miracle would be certain to crave miracles, and the craving ungratified would leave them, first suspicious, then discontented, then angry. Where enthusiasm was for the power rather than the person of Christ, His behaviour in Jerusalem could only disappoint and provoke. When the men who had hailed Him as Christ the King saw that He did no miracle, but quietly submitted to indignities, capture, mockery, they felt like men who had been deceived into acts of undeserved honour, and, turning against Him revengeful, they broke into the cry, "Crucify Him, crucify Him!" Thus our miracle explains the enthusiasm at once of their homage and their hate, shows how the people that welcomed Him into the city could also be the people that followed Him along the way of sorrow with the scornful cry, "He saved others; Himself He cannot save."

Into the rich and most varied spiritual meanings of our narrative it is not possible to enter. It is a Divine allegory, full of the most sublime and consolatory truths; and to attempt to unfold these would be to attempt to reach the deepest treasures of our faith. Two living poets have, each in his own way, used this narrative. Tennyson seizes its influence on Mary, and imagines the sister satisfied in the possession of her brother, and restful in the presence of Christ.

> Her eyes are homes of silent prayer,
>   Nor other thought her mind admits,
>   But he was dead, and there he sits,
> And He that brought him back is there.
>
> Then one deep love doth supersede
>   All other, when her ardent gaze
>   Roves from the living brother's face,
> And rests upon the Life indeed.

THE LATER MIRACLES.

> All subtle thought, all curious fears,
>   Borne down by gladness so complete,
>   She bows, she bathes the Saviour's feet
> With costly spikenard and with tears.

Browning, stronger, more masterful, has, with rare imaginative insight, gone to the heart of the matter, and presented us with a picture of Lazarus as he may have lived and must have spoken. Karshish, the Arab physician, meets him, and feels—

> The man had something in the look of him—

awed, convinced, credulous in the presence of his story, unable to disbelieve it, yet ashamed of his belief. Browning has nothing finer than the analysis of Karshish as he tells the story he has heard from Lazarus.

> This man so cured regards the Curer, then,
> As—God forgive me !—who but God Himself,
> Creator and Sustainer of the world,
> That came and dwelt in flesh on it awhile !
> —Sayeth that such an one was born and lived,
> Taught, heal'd the sick, broke bread at his own house,
> Then died, with Lazarus by, for aught I know,
> And yet was . . . what I said, nor choose repeat,
> And must have so avouch'd Himself, in fact,
> In hearing of this very Lazarus,
> Who saith—but why all this of what he saith?
> Why write of trivial matters, things of price
> Calling at every moment for remark?
> I noticed on the margin of a pool
> Blue flowering borage, the Aleppo sort
> Aboundeth, very nitrous !   It is strange !

Yet the tale fascinates him ; its wonderful truth has filled his imagination, and melts him into admiration and awe.

> The very God ! Think, Abib   dost thou think?
> So, the All-Great were the All-loving too—
> So, through the thunder comes a human voice
>   Saying, "O heart I made, a heart beats here !
> Face, my hands fashion'd, see it in myself !

> Thou hast no power, nor may'st conceive of mine,
> But love I gave thee, with myself to love,
> And thou must love me who hast died for thee."

And there, for Lazarus and for all ages, lies the inmost truth of the miracle.

XIII.

JERICHO AND JERUSALEM.

THE mission to Bethany had been one of danger and of mercy: of danger to Jesus, of mercy to the sisters who had loved and lost. In their home sorrow had been turned into joy; their brother lived and their Friend was present.

> From every house the neighbours met,
> The streets were fill'd with joyful sound,
> A solemn gladness even crown'd
> The purple brows of Olivet.

But over in Jerusalem another spirit reigned. Into the city the strange news had been carried. Through the bazaars and the market-place, from gate to gate, and home to home, into the temple and the schools the whisper ran, "Behold, a man raised up by Christ!" The common people heard it gladly, and said, "Lo, a sign from heaven; the Son of David has come; He will break the yoke of the oppressor, and we shall be free." Tumult was in the air, and the priests knew it; a great spiritual act by a great spiritual Person had blown the slumbering political desires of the multitude into flame, and the scribes felt the glowing heat underfoot. The Pharisees were anti-Roman, loved to foster in Israel dislike of the alien and devotion to the hopes and ideals proper to the people of God; but they could only fear and oppose a movement that might end in saluting Jesus of Nazareth as the Christ. The Sadducees were tolerant to Rome, knew, feared, obeyed her, and dreaded nothing so much as the revolt that might rouse her unpitying wrath. So the ancient rivals, united by common hate for hateful ends, met to plot. No man comprehended the situation better than Caiaphas, high-priest that fateful year; and he, cynically, though diplomatically enough, formulated the need of the hour—"It is expedient that one man die for the people, and that the whole nation perish not."[1] What he meant was this: "We are on the eve of disaster; the enthusiasm of the people for this Galilean will carry them into revolt, unless we strike it through the heart by bringing Him to death." The Sanhedrin understood the priest, complimented his astuteness by adopting his policy and working out his scheme. They did not mean to be bad, only patriotic, and so obedient to the maxim, "Salus populi suprema est lex." It was in this heroic spirit that the ancient enemies, who so cordially despised each other, made their covenant, and as new but dear friends assumed their parts in what was to be a drama at once more infamous and more glorious than they knew. Their parts, indeed, were to be different, the priests the more active, the Pharisees the more passive, the evolution into practice of the priestly policy being not at all to the Pharisaic mind, the thing done in fear of Rome being done by the help and arm of Rome. And had they been able to foresee the result, they would have disliked the policy the more. Their expedient was both to succeed and fail. The one man was to die for the people, but the nation was to perish. The eternal righteousness that restrains the wrath of man, and even forces it to praise Him, was to turn their selfish expedient into a Divine Sacrifice, which, while it saved man, was only to help the more surely to throw their proud city under the iron heel and devouring torch of Rome. So in the wisdom of God does a soul of

[1] John xi. 49, 50

good issue from things evil to do the will alike of His mercy and justice.

But Christ knew that, though His hour was at hand, it was not yet come. The Prophet was not to perish out of Jerusalem, or in it, save at His own time. So He withdrew "into a country near to the wilderness, into a city called Ephraim,"[1] and there waited the coming of the feast that was to mark the moment of His sacrifice. When the roads were thronged with pilgrims from Greece and Egypt, from Italy and Gaul, from Spain and Syria, He, too, turned His face to the holy city, and began His great march to brief bitter death and eternal glorious power. For the time He had become an enigma to His disciples. They could not understand His sorrow, especially as they were still living in the sunshine of His greatest miracle. In His supreme moments society was impossible to Christ. He lived in an atmosphere where human sympathy had to sleep or die, and the human voice to speak unheard. The grief of God is too deep for the thought of man. He who embodied the first could only be a riddle to the second. Life by death, salvation by sacrifice, were truths lying outside the horizon of the spirits then around Christ. The feeling that made Peter rebuke Jesus at the first mention of His sufferings was common, was, too, finely natural.[2] Why should He speak of suffering and death? What need had He who had raised Lazarus to die? So His words seemed mysterious, enigmatical, created shadows of the mind all the deeper because of the recent sunshine. Like men puzzled, they became bewildered, dubious, suspicious, feeling as if they were threatened by evils they had no right to anticipate. Mark, after his manner, gives us a glance of real and living insight into the sacred circle just at the moment the pilgrimage of sorrow began: "And they were

[1] John xi. 54.   [2] Matt xvi. 22.

in the way going up to Jerusalem; and Jesus went before them: and they were amazed; and as they followed, they were afraid."[1] With their expectations unfulfilled, without the experience that could act as interpreter or guide, perplexed by hearing prophecy contradict miracle, and seeing miracle contradict prophecy, they grew bewildered, astonished, doubtful, fell out of fellowship with their Master, and left Him to begin His high and glorious way alone. The shadow that rested on His Spirit so awed and "amazed" theirs that they could not walk by His side, or listen with quick, interpretive sympathy to His speech, could only follow after, full of uneasy fears, with thoughts they could speak to each other, but not to Him. Yet though they were reluctant learners, the suffering that was to make Him perfect was teaching them. He could not leave them in the pleasant illusions their fancies had woven out of their own desires and His great deeds. To do so had been worse cruelty, had made the awakening an awakening to sorrow that could never have blossomed into joy. And so He turns ever to them with His unwelcome speech of suffering, death, and resurrection,[2] leaving time to be His interpreter. The process was painful, but from it almost all were to come forth purified; one alone was to issue dark in soul, angry in spirit, prepared for worst and darkest deeds, yet with goodness enough in Him to be remorseful, and pass hence to His own place, not a seared and conscienceless ruffian, but an anguished and self-despising man, who had by fell experiment made the dreadful discovery that to no man is evil so bad as to the evil-doer.

The miracle at Bethany was thus a centre whence had issued the most conflicting influences; and we must watch their operation in the various circles, friendly, indifferent, inimical, that surround Jesus. Within His own

[1] Mark x. 32.   [2] Ibid. x. 32-34.

society it created the high hopes that listened amazed, incredulous to His prophetic words. The disciples found it more agreeable to believe the eye than the ear : on the act they could place their own interpretation, which was so much happier than any meaning they could get out of His speech. The miracle was a prophecy in act, signifying that the hour of His power was at hand. In its light certain former words of His were re-read and made by their quickened imaginations to speak the thing they wished. The Palingeresia,[1] in their sense, was as good as here; the twelve thrones as good as set, and they seated judging the twelve tribes of Israel. How heedless the new ambitions were of the new prophecies an event significantly shows. He had hardly ceased speaking of the betrayal and death, when Salome, with her sons, came to Him, saying, " Grant that these my two sons may sit, the one on Thy right hand, the other on Thy left, in Thy kingdom."[2] The nearest to Him were yet far from Him; even love was too blind to divine the truth; and so in His answer there seems to live the infinite sadness of a spirit not understood, where understanding is life : " Ye know not what ye ask. Are ye able to drink of the cup that I shall drink of, and to be baptized with the baptism that I am baptized with ? " Their answer is a tragic revelation of ignorance, and the vain courage that is born of it : " We are able." They did not dream of Gethsemane and the cross, but of the chalice of victory, the baptism that consecrated the throne and purified for judgment. For these they were " able "—qualified for the highest seats, offices, acts in the kingdom. Men who think themselves equal to rule are often found unequal to obedience ; and so this conscious ability for the throne was soon to be proved inability to serve in suffering and obey in sacrifice. They did not know that men must suffer with Christ before they

[1] Matt. xix 28-30. [2] Ibid xx. 21.

could reign with Him; and, in their ignorance, they wished to reign before they had been perfected. And the truth He stated: they *were* to drink of His cup, and be baptized with His baptism; His agony and cross were to be theirs; in Him and with Him they were to suffer. Fellowship with Him in life involved fellowship with Him in death, and as the joy of the first had been, the sorrow of the second would be. But the seat on His right hand or His left was not an absolute or arbitrary, but a conditional, gift; it was reserved for those "for whom it is prepared of my Father." The reward was to the worthiest; proximity was to depend on affinity. His must suffer with Him, if they were to "be glorified together."[1] But His words were as yet a parable whose meaning they could not read; the cross, with the mingled agonies and joys that followed it, was needed to teach them. The brothers, puzzled, turned to face the disciples; the disciples, angry, turned to rebuke the brothers; all confused, bewildered to listen to the words, "Whosoever will be chief among you, let him be your servant; even as the Son of man came not to be ministered unto, but to minister, and to give His life a ransom for the many."[2] A generation later, one of the men who stood there as in a dream, with a deed of highest power in his memory, visions of judicial glory in his imagination, words of sorrow and death in his ears, was to be a prisoner in Patmos "for the Word of God, and for the testimony of Jesus Christ."[3] There, with the blue Ægean all round him, he was still to feel as in the presence of the Son of man, hearing Him speak with a voice like the sound of the multitudinous waves ever breaking in music on the beach. There, too, he was to dream of "dominion and glory," of a heaven that ruled earth, and a Christ that made men "kings and priests

[1] Rom. viii. 17.   [2] Matt xx. 27, 28.   [3] Rev. i. 9.

unto God and His Father."[1] But there he had no vain vision of a throne to him who had first claimed it. His visions were now of "a multitude no man could number" "before the throne and before the Lamb." And he does not ask, as of old, for a place, but simply rejoices to hear, "These are they which came out of great tribulation, and have washed their robes and made them white in the blood of the Lamb."[2] He knows now what he knew not then: to drink Christ's cup and to share His baptism is to live and reign with Him.

So Jesus begins to go up to Jerusalem with the vision of the cross standing out clear before His own soul, while the disciples dream of His kingship and their own coming authority. The pilgrimage that was now beginning was to be His last—a strange contrast to His first. Then He was a boy, full of great wonder, of large questions, of dim foreshadowings of what was to be; now He is a man, who has realized the ideal of humanity the ages behind had been straining after and the ages before were to worship; a man, who has lived His high, holy, lonely life, and is going forward to the death which is to finish the work His Father gave Him to do. Then He was an object of beauty and delight; the nature within Him rejoiced, and nature without whispered to Him her divinest secrets; now He is like a root out of the dry ground, without the beauty that awakens desire, "a man of sorrows, and acquainted with grief." Then man turned to Him his best and most amiable side, as man ever does to a child; parents were trustful, neighbours kindly, the very doctors of the temple gentle, admiring, fond, won by the winsomeness of the glorious boy; now that His physical is sublimed into spiritual loveliness, they can see in Him nothing to admire; leave Him so unloved that He feels more homeless than the fox that, when hunted, can hide in the earth, or

[1] Rev. xx 1–6. [2] Ibid. vii. 14.

the bird that can sit and sing to its brooding mate. And His homelessness was now becoming loneliness; the men that had known Him were ceasing to know, dreaming dreams that made them unconscious of the realities that awed His spirit. Earth has its changes for every man, but to whom did it change as to Thee, O Thou Lamb of God? Heaven was about Thy infancy; may we not say, hell was about Thy manhood? In Thy cradle Thou didst hear the song of the heavenly host; but on the cross Thou wert to hear the hoarse and angry cries of men who mocked Thy sufferings and demanded Thy death.

Yet when the pilgrimage began it seemed a triumphal procession. The spirit that lived in the disciples possessed the multitude, and the fame of this great miracle clothed Him to their eyes in the attributes of the expected Messiah. So we see Him approaching Jericho, on His way from Ephraim to Jerusalem, the centre of a wondering crowd.[1] Though He still bears the name "Jesus of Nazareth," it is used as if big with latent significance. Curiosity is on tiptoe, and reigns over rich and poor alike. As He enters, a blind beggar invokes His aid. The multitude, vain of their wonder, wished to silence him; the person they marvelled at must be above hearing a blind man's prayer. But the "Son of David" heard and healed, and the people, gratified while surprised, only the more "gave praise unto God." As He passes through Jericho the crowd thickens, and a rich publican, determined to see Jesus, but unable to do it for the crowd, climbs up into a sycamore tree. He was a very different man from Bartimæus; notice of him was a far more serious thing. The publican was always an offence to the Jew. He was the symbol of bondage, of Gentile conquest and tyranny. He was worse than an outcast; he was one who had sold himself to the alien as an agent of his

[1] Luke xviii. 35, 36.

robbery and oppression. He was a son of Abraham who had not only dishonoured his father, but was helping the heathen to woik his death and shame. And to love such a son, nay to recognize his sonship, was to sin against the father and all the hopes represented by his name. But the most hated of the hated race was the rich publican, whose wealth had grown by extortion, who had with unpitying hand robbed the widow and made the orphan destitute. And Zaccheus was a man of this type, an object of horror to the pious and hate to all. It was the right and religious thing to pity and help the beggar, and to despise and avoid the publican. Yet the Jesus who came clothed in fiesh glory from His work on Bartimæus suddenly pauses, looks at Zaccheus, invites him to descend and receive Him into his house. The people saw and heard with amazement which deepened into anger; the new horror eclipsed the old admiration, and displeasure silenced praise. Yet the act was one that expressed the Actor's mind, especially in its contrast with the minds about Him, far more forcibly than the most forcible speech. It was symbolical, signified that He had come not to work miracles, but to change men; not to dazzle and delight the curious, but "to seek and save the lost." The men around Him were saying, "Here is our Messiah; His deeds show Him to be the power of God. He is on His way to Jerusalem to establish and proclaim His empiie, to fulfil our law, to make the Jew the conqueror of the world and the king of man." And He to their evident, though unexpressed, thoughts made answer, "I am come to do, not your will, but my Father's, to be no political, but a spiritual King, to be not the tool of the priest and the scribe, but the Saviour of the fallen and outcast. And look how simply, yet thoroughly, My spiritual work can be done. You have had your will with Zaccheus, hated him, despised him, dealt **wit** 1 him as with a heathen and an alien, and he has answered your hatred with extortion, your anathemas with oppression, your censures with heavier exactions. But see how potent are gentle words and gracious acts; under them the bad publican becomes the good Hebrew, dutiful to Israel and obedient to the law of love, giving half his goods to feed the poor, and restoring fourfold what he had wrongfully obtained." Yet the results only aggravated the offence. To fanaticism good done in ways that displease it is no better than evil, or rather is worse, inasmuch as fatal to its exclusive claims to be right. So Jesus, to get at the root of the matter, strikes at the source of their false hopes, the thought "that the kingdom of God should immediately appear."[1] He would not go to Jerusalem as their Messiah, to be in their sense the Christ. The Jews had been citizens of the Divine kingdom, servants of the King. Their duty was to develop its resources, guard His interests, and extend His authority. Some had done so. Lawgivers and prophets had splendidly served the ideals and ends of the kingdom of God; but one, the one, too, in possession, had not. He, the living Jew, had bound the eternal truth in His napkin of legal maxims and ceremonies, and buried it in the soil of rabbinical and sacerdotal formalism. He feared God as "an austere man" feared to use his trust, and so buried it, cast it out of his spirit into the earth that it might suffer and waste there unused! And Jesus declines to be judged by this faithless servant, claims rather to judge and condemn him; refuses to be measured by his acts and ideas, asserts rather His right to take from him the treasure he had so abused. The Jew had thrown away his splendid opportunity, and now he was to lose it. His infidelity to his trust had, as its punishment, his inability to understand the Christ of God, and now he was to be to the ages the grand illustration of the truth,

[1] Luke xix. 11.

"To him that hath shall be given, and from him that hath not, even that he hath shall be taken away from him."[1]

Six days before the passover the pilgrims reached Bethany, and there paused. Wonder still lived in the village. Love still dwelt in the home of Lazarus. Into it Jesus entered, and there He was consecrated, anointed the Divine Sacrifice which should abolish the old faith and create the new. Love has often a sweet unconscious wisdom, and in its humblest ministries meanings may lie so great as to be visible to the eye of God alone. And here its kinship with the saintliest stood confessed. In these closing hours nothing seems so tragic as the blindness of the disciples, and the clear open vision of the Master as to the doom that was to be. They were full of hope in a soon to be manifested glory, He full of prophetic agony as to the death to be endured. Like those who knew His power and believed in its impending final victory, Lazarus and his sisters thought only of a glad welcome to their Friend. The hour was all sunshine; the fast-falling shadow was unseen and unfeared. So His coming was celebrated by a supper, and he who had known the gloom of the grave tasted the deepest joy of his life. But Mary's love, too deep for speech, too great for tears, as if she felt within the joy the cold heart of sorrow, stole, while Martha waited, behind Jesus, and anointed His feet "with ointment of spikenard very costly."[2] And then, as the fragrance filled the room, strange things became manifest. The feeling that had long slumbered in one breast broke into speech. "Why this waste?" cried Judas. "Why was not this ointment sold for three hundred pence, and given to the poor?"[3] But the unholy avarice which dared to clothe itself in the form of sacred charity was rebuked by the sad voice

[1] Luke xix. 26.   [2] John xii. 3.   [3] Ibid. xii. 5.

which revealed the heart sad by the realized presence of death: "Let her alone; against the day of my burying hath she kept this."

The words of Judas were characteristic—the familiar words of his kind the world over. A work of what seems splendid improvidence may be greater than what seems a work of needed beneficence. Some men cry out against waste when what they mean is some loss to their sordid selves. If the money that bought the "ointment of spikenard" had been "given to the poor" it would have done them little good; but, used as it was, it became the condition of an act which has filled the world with its fragrance, and enriched our poverty with one of the loveliest deeds of devotion. In Mary and Judas two opposite spirits live: in the one, a love to Christ that seeks to live for Him; in the other, a love to self that means to use rather than serve Him. For Mary to give, for Judas to receive, was to be blessed. To the one, Christ's suffering was a welcome opportunity for service; to the other, a detested occasion of weakness, an inexplicable and disastrous moment of failure. Mary is an ideal disciple, one with love great enough to transform Jesus of Nazareth into the Christ of Christianity; Judas is the type of the disciple by accident, seeking by association with Christ personal advantage rather than assimilation to Him. And the results of the discipleship were to be tragically unlike: a growing joy to Mary, a growing misery to Judas. In the society of Jesus she found a congenial home, but he an irritating and hateful element. As his nature and Christ's developed alongside each other, their dissimilarities and antipathies must have become ever more pronounced. The man must slowly have come to feel himself an alien; and as the truth dawned upon him, he would be first bewildered, then wretched, feeling like Satan among the sons of God, only without the serene cynicism that could sneer at eternal goodness in its very presence and to its very face; or rather, like an evil spirit, moody and melancholy, who had strayed into a circle of angels, where the contrast of their light and his darkness deepens his misery tenfold. A man that so feels is near to despair, and may do the deed of the desperate. When the last hope perishes, the desperation that seeks revenge and begets remorse is sure to come. For Judas the moment is at hand. If Jerusalem does not reveal Jesus as the Messiah, he will forswear Him, forsake His society, destroy himself, and be over and done with the profitless misery that is now paralyzing spirit and spoiling life. So within the chosen circle devotion waited to be perfected by suffering, and disappointment to be avenged by treason.

On the next day Jesus entered Jerusalem. The part of the pilgrim band that had gone forward carried into the city the news of His coming, and the people, all enthusiasm for the "Son of David," the Man who had raised the dead, prepared for Him a fitting welcome. Those who had passed the night at Bethany joined the circle that surrounded the Master, partook of its spirit, and shared its hopes. As they ascended Olivet, feeling as if they had in their midst the sent of God, the salvation of Israel, they were joined by pilgrims hastening to the feast, and on the summit they were met by the multitudes who had sallied from the city to meet the advancing Christ. The enthusiasm grew as the crowd increased; clothes were spread, palm-branches scattered in His path, and as each fresh stream blended with the river, the shout rose, " Hosannah! Blessed is the King of Israel that cometh in the name of the Lord."[1] That might have seemed the proudest moment in the life of Jesus, the moment when the homage of man was most spontaneous and most real; but in truth it was one of the saddest. The enthusiasm only deepened

[1] John xii. 13.

His solitude, made it more awful to His spirit, while throwing upon the coming events a more tragic colouring. Their praise was pain, for what they praised was the idol of their own imaginations, not the Christ who was coming to suffer and to die. In the midst of their joy He rode possessed of the vivid consciousness that the discovery of the truth would change their jubilant cry of welcome into the delirious shout of passion and revenge. So, as they swept round the shoulder of the hill, and the city burst upon His view, turreted, temple-crowned, lying white and radiant in the glorious sunlight, hallowed by a thousand sacred memories, darkened by a thousand sins, the pathos of the place and the moment, the then and the to be, the ideal and the actual, the men and the city as they seemed and as they were, was more than His heart could bear, and He wept, saying, " If thou hadst known, at least in this thy day, the things which belong unto thy peace! but now they are hid from thine eyes."[1]

Once within the city, the great drama began to unfold its successive acts. Jesus asserted His authority as the Christ by purging the temple and teaching in it.[2] The enthusiasm of the people paralyzed the priests and the Sanhedrin.[3] They could not as yet use popular passion against Him, and so they cautiously assailed Himself, seeking to involve Him in conflict with the multitude, or with Rome, or with Moses. Their first point was to question His authority. Whence had He it? Who gave it?[4] He replied by subtly revealing the purpose of their question and their consequent inability to judge His truth: " The baptism of John, whence was it? from heaven or of men?" If they said, "From heaven," they condemned their own unbelief; if "Of men," they broke with the people—a dangerous thing while they were moved with Messianic en-

[1] Luke xix. 42.
[2] Ibid. xix. 45–47.
[3] Ibid xix. 47, 48, Mark xi. 18.
[4] Luke xx 1, 2. Mark xi. 25, 26.

thusiasm and inspired by Messianic hopes. So they could only plead ignorance. But how could men too ignorant to judge of the Baptist's claims judge as to the Christ's? The next point was political—an attempt to find occasion for "delivering Him into the power and authority of the governor."[1] The men chosen for this work were, significantly enough, "Pharisees and Herodians."[2] The Pharisees were a religious, the Herodians a political, party. The former were the exponents and representatives of the ancient theocratic ideal; the latter, the adherents of the house of Herod. The Pharisees hated the alien, believed that there could be no true king in Israel, unless he came of the family of David; the Herodians served and upheld the kinghood of the alien, the brood of the cruel and abhorred Idumean. The Pharisees stood in absolute antagonism to Rome. To them its sovereignty was the worst bondage, the dominion of the heathen over the people of God; but the Herodians accepted, diplomatically at least, the authority that had placed the sons of Herod in their respective kingdoms or tetrarchies. Now these parties, thus radically opposed, combined against Jesus, submitting this question, "Is it lawful to give tribute to Cæsar?"[3] On this point they were divided. The Pharisees held it wrong, but the Herodians held it right, at least as a matter of political expediency. Hence they would, with fine innocence, submit their difference to His arbitrament. But the innocence masked a deep design. If He said, "It is lawful," He would offend the people and the strongest and noblest national beliefs and hopes; if He said, "It is not lawful," He would come into collision with Rome, the power that, with equal ease and equal coldness, crushed its least and its greatest opponent, and then passed serenely on. But it is not in the nature of wisdom to play into the hands of cunning.

[1] Luke xx. 20. [2] Mark xii. 13. [3] Luke xx. 22; Mark xii. 14.

He said, "Show me a denarius," and asked, "Whose is the image and superscription?" "Cæsar's." "Then the coin is his—minted, issued by him, used, circulated by you. It is a coin by his act, is, too, regarded and treated by you as money, and therefore the question is none. The use of Cæsar's money is tribute to Cæsar. Render to him his, and to God God's."

But though the Pharisees were vanquished, the Sadducees were, if not of a subtler, of an astuter race. They had been educated in a fine contempt for vulgar superstitions, the traditions and doctrines for which the Pharisees were so zealous. They did not believe in development or a continuous revelation. God had spoken to Moses, but had been silent ever since. The law had embodied His will; what was not law was of man, not of God. And so they were exceedingly zealous for Moses, and exceedingly jealous of "the traditions of the fathers." They had hitherto left the conflict with Jesus to the Pharisees, rather pleased that their rivals should be so beset and bewildered; but now that Caiaphas had declared His death to be necessary, they would confront and overpower Him with the authority of their Lawgiver. They selected their point carefully. Jesus had explicitly affirmed His belief in a future state,[1] and the Pharisees were here weak, for they believed in it as firmly as He. But the Sadducees were strong; they did not find the belief in Moses; found it, indeed, conspicuously absent and explicitly disproved. So they elaborated their most conclusive argument, and presented it thus: "Master, Moses wrote unto us, If any man's brother die, having a wife, and he die without children, that his brother should take his wife, and raise up seed unto his brother. There were therefore seven brethren; and the first took a wife, and died without children. And the second took her to wife, and he died childless. And the

---

[1] Luke xvi 19-31.

third took her; and in like manner the seven also; and they left no children, and died. Last of all the woman died also. Therefore in the resurrection whose wife of them is she? for seven had her to wife."[1] The case was a splendid one for discussion in the schools, excellent for the exercise of subtle wits. If there is a future state where all these husbands are alive, and this poor over-married woman alive also, " whose wife shall she be? Come now, good Master, tell us." They did not raise the question whether immortal relations must be adjusted to provisional arrangements; they took for granted that a temporary and barbarous expedient was an eternal law. Yet their own hearts might have answered their question. We may imagine in the company that came to Jesus a young Sadducee, with the wistful sadness in the eyes that can be seen only where the light that has gladdened life has been extinguished. He has known the joy of posses-sion and the agony of loss. A gentle womanly presence had once made his manhood beautiful, his home happy, his life rich with sweet and soothing grace. But just when his joy was deepest, hateful death had come, and left him sitting dumb in the shadow of a great affliction. The first desolation is past, but only that a level and cheerless melancholy might come, which forces ever to his lips the cry,

> O for the touch of a vanished hand
> And the sound of a voice that is still!

Yet no hand is stretched through the darkness, no voice an-swers out of the eternal silence: and he can only mourn,

> The tender grace of a day that is dead
> Will never come back to me.

But had such an one been in the company, would not the longing, the strong desire, that could almost create the belief in immortality, born of necessity and the very nature

[1] Luke xx. 28–33.

of his own spirit, have made him loathe the cruel frivolity of the case supposed, with its primitive and provisional law, and listen for words that might shed upon his own sorrow the consolation of a great hope? And if he had been there, he would not have been disappointed. Jesus lifted the question into a region far above the heaven of the Sadducean spirit. They erred through ignorance.[1] He recognized no sanctity, no universal and eternal validity, in the law of a semi-civilized people. In the resurrection men were not governed by the law of Moses; they were "as the angels of God." Their natures determined their relations, affinities created society. And the Highest was the regulative nature. The living God involved the life of those that lived to Him. Men who lived in communion with Him became as needful to Him as He was to them. And this truth was expressed in the ancient saying, "I am the God of Abraham, Isaac, and Jacob." He could not be their God unless He was a real Being to them; they could not be real beings to Him unless they still lived. To be the God of them, He must be a God to them; and He could be a God only to living persons, not to silent memories or empty names.

Jesus thus found immortality at the very heart of the Mosaic law, involved in the distinctive name of God, Jahveh, the living, the creative. The Sadducees erred because they did not know God. If they had rightly conceived Him, they had strongly believed in the immortal being of man. The man who is made in the image of God is made to be as God, and be like Him for ever. The thought embodied in His answer was so new and strange to the Sadducees that it was almost like an answer in an unknown tongue. They were silenced, bewildered, and humiliated before the multitude, who "were astonished at His doctrine."[2]

[1] Matt xxii 29.   [2] Ibid xxii 33.

And so His enemies could not so involve Him either with the people, or with Cæsar, or with Moses, as to carry through their expedient. But what they failed to do His own revelation of Himself accomplished. The revelation was double, by antipathy and by sympathy, the one showing what He was not—to the Jews; the other showing what He was—to His disciples. As regards the first, it was made both by action and speech. He acted like the Man of sorrows, not like the victorious Messiah. There is nothing more marvellous, even in the Gospels, than the self-repression of Jesus in His latest hours. He was in every respect a contrast and contradiction to the Messiah of tradition, and He emphasized, as it were, the points of difference. The homage of ignorance was to Him only latent aversion, and He could not allow His true nature to remain unknown. And so, the more He revealed Himself, the cooler grew their enthusiasm; the less He fulfilled their expectations, the more dubious, suspicious, watchful for offence they became. And what they wanted they found in His words. His discourses in Jerusalem predicted the overthrow, not the triumph, of Judaism, denounced the hypocrisy that reigned in high places, praised the piety that lived in poverty and seclusion.[1] The city, the temple, the worship, the very people were to perish, and only a remnant was to be saved. False Christs were to rise, be welcomed, believed, followed; confusion was to grow into anarchy, and anarchy to end in death.[2] This was strange language for one who claimed to be the Christ to use in Jerusalem, and respecting the Jews. History was to prove it true; but meanwhile it was held worse than the worst falsehood. But while He was becoming to the people as an enemy by telling them the truth, He was privily drawing His disciples round Him, opening to them

[1] Matt xxiii. 13, ff., Luke xxi. 1-4.
[2] Luke xxi 5-24, Matt xxiv 3-31.

the inmost secrets of His spirit, the deepest mysteries of His truth. They heard, but were slow of heart to believe. Yet in speaking to the men that were, He spoke to the men that were to be: and words not understood then became in later days words of spirit and life. What estranged the heart of Jerusalem was to draw the heart of the world ; and the wisdom of Christ was to be justified to all after ages by the events which proved that His antagonism to Judaism was the sublimest service to man.

XIV.

GETHSEMANE.

In the dark eventide before the final agony the souls of the disciples were clothed in darkness, but the soul of the Master walked in light. They were as men that dreamed; He was as the one wakeful being in a world of dreamful sleepers, and His wakefulness was more than the world's sleep. Their talk seems like the cheery and heedless prattle of a child at the knees of a man whose heart grief has cloven in twain, or like the babbling of a summer brook under a sky dark with thunder-gloom and gathering storm. Yet as to the Master these figures are impertinent. The sorrow that filled His soul did not quench His sympathy; the clouds that enfolded His spirit did not shut from those who had clustered round Him the sunshine of His love. If they live with touching, almost tragic, unconsciousness of the fate He sees approaching with inevitable step and awful form, He, living at the same moment, as it were, in the present and in the future, with suffering in idea translated into utmost reality, thinks of His thoughtless disciples, and with forward-looking care seeks to arm them against the evil day. And so here emerges one of His divinest qualities, illustrated in action at every moment of His closing sufferings. Sorrow is often selfish, loves to be indulged, to sit blind and deaf to the world and duty, ministered unto, but not ministering. But here is suffering, the greatest ever known, the deepest, intensest that ever strained a heart, yet He who bears it, and is being borne by it to death, broods over His unsuspecting children, thinks of their agony when His shall have reached its climax and done its work, thinks of their misery when He is laid, the smitten Shepherd, in the tomb of Joseph, and they, the scattered flock, shall have fled every man to his own. Were there nothing else, this sublime thoughtfulness, this conquest of the sorrow that conquered not Him, but His life, would speak Him in a real sense Divine.

It is, then, in His last sorrows that Christ seems most Christly. "Though He were a Son, yet learned He obedience by the things which He suffered," and through His sufferings He was "made perfect" as "the Captain of our salvation."[1] His sorrows have been the great interpreter of Christ to man; in them lie the source and secret of His power. They have in a real sense redeemed man, and were, in a sense no less real, universal, doing for the race what the discipline of suffering is designed to do for the individual. The German who, while a modern, had a genius at once most classical and pagan, has introduced us to "the sanctuary of sorrow." But the "sanctuary" he conceived was little else than the outer court of the temple—his hand had never touched the veil, his foot had never crossed the threshold of the holy of holies. As there is a path the eagle's eye has not seen, so there is a "Divine depth of sorrow" which the clear but cold eye of Goethe never descried. Its *poetic* depths his cultured thought had sounded; its *religious* were to him unknown, even unsuspected He heard in it "the still, sad music of humanity," but not the voice of God. Yet without that voice the music is but discord. If only through sorrow the deepest things in a man can be educed, so only through it can the deepest truths in God and the universe be seen. A tear is a telescope which reveals to the eye that can use it a heaven, otherwise concealed, of starlit galaxies and shining

[1] Heb. v. 8 ; ii. 10.

GETHSEMANE.

suns. God is never so personal and real to man as when, in the darkness of some great sorrow, the soul stretches out "lame hands of faith," gropes till it grasps His right hand, and is by it led up into the light. And the height to which He leads us is a sun-gilded mount of vision, far above the clouds and storms of earth, where the soul can rest as in the lap of God, hearing the songs of peace and hope the angels in Paradise sing.

> As angels in some brighter dreams,
>   Call to the soul when man doth sleep;
> So some strange thoughts transcend our wonted themes,
>   And into glory peep.

And the sorrow of Christ has had as beneficial a mission for humanity as personal sorrow for the individual. It has so revealed God to man, and so bound man to God, as to be his salvation.

The history of the Passion, which is to us the greatest of all histories, is what we must now attempt to understand. At the outset we must note the time, the Thursday evening, by Roman reckoning the 13th of the month, but by Jewish the 14th, the day beginning for the Jew with sunset. The morrow is the great day of the preparation, and the day after the great day of the feast. The days that have passed since the triumphal entry have been full of change. The people have been disappointed, and a disappointed mob is a dangerous thing, prepared to break or burn the idol it can always make, but that cannot always fulfil its maker's intentions. The Jesus it had hailed as the Christ had proved not its Christ, and to be not its Christ was to be as good as none. The rulers knew the people, read the meaning of their disappointment, and met at the house of Caiaphas to consider how the foolish mob could be made to do their malignant will.[1] Heaven

[1] Matt xxvi 3-5.

seemed to bless their conclave. To them came one who had followed the Galilean.[1] Discipleship had become impossible to Judas. The Master who had disappointed him and whom he had deserted, who had become to him so offensive in His friendless and outcast loneliness, must be crushed, ended, that he might be free. While wicked fortune favoured the evil, the Providence that guides the good appeared no less kind. Jesus came from Bethany, entered the city in the twilight, and sat down with His disciples in the humble room where the last supper was prepared. There, while the city was waiting its festival, while the priests were laying the lines that were to close round the Holiest, He and His little band celebrated in celestial calm the supper that was to be for all lands and for all time the memory and mirror of that sacred night. So in our streets, in our homes, in our very lives, heaven and hell meet and touch, while to our coarse eyes every place is common and every time common day.

That supper is an event which profoundly affects the imagination. Its very simplicity increases its significance. The meaning it bears to faith is marvellous on the one hand; the place it has filled, the work it has done in history, as marvellous on the other. If the vision had been granted to Christ of what it was to be and do, would it not, even when His sufferings were deepest, have turned His sorrow into joy? He would have seen His supper surviving for ages, simple in form, transcendent in meaning, a living centre of unity for His scattered disciples, a source of comfort, strength, peace, purity to wearied and sinful men. In upper rooms, in catacombs, where the dust of the dead rested, and the spirits of the living met to speak to each other words of holiest cheer; in desert places and moorlands, where hunted fugitives assembled to listen t_ a voice which, though a man's, seemed God's; in cathe-

[1] Matt. xxvi. 14; Mark xiv. 10; Luke xxii. 3.

drals, where form and space spoke majestically to the eye, and lofty music to the ear; in rude huts in savage or heathen lands; in ornate churches in wealthy, busy, and intellectual cities—men of the most varied types and conditions, saintly and sinful, ignorant and educated, simple and gentle, rich and poor, peer and peasant, sovereign and subject, priest and people, forming a multitude no man can number, have for centuries met together to celebrate this supper, and be by it made wiser, happier, holier. The actual and ideal history of the rite stands in strong contrast to its institution. Of the twelve men who sat and broke bread with Jesus, of the priests who were so anxious to work out their "expedient," of the Scribes who were laboriously interpreting and making tradition, of the Romans who were ruling and guarding Jerusalem—could any one have dreamed what this obscure and humble supper was to be for man, and to do for the world? Yet it is God's way to make the foolish things of the world confound the things that are wise, and His way has ever in the end proved the wisest and best for man.

But it is of special significance to our history to note the thoughts that at the supper possessed the mind of Christ. He is to Himself evidently a sacrifice. The bread that signifies the body broken and eaten has a distinctly sacrificial import.[1] The blood is to be "shed for many for the remission of sins."[2] And it was no mere sacrifice, it was one that symbolized a new relation of God to man, and man to God—His blood was the blood of "the new covenant." The term $\delta\iota\alpha\theta\acute{\eta}\kappa\eta$ is here of peculiar importance. It does not mean either a covenant in the sense of contract or agreement, or a testament in the sense of a will, but it has a meaning which combines ideas distinctive of both. In $\delta\iota\alpha\theta\acute{\eta}\kappa\eta$ there are the conditional elements

---
[1] Matt. xxvi. 26 *Cf* Lev vii 6; Exod xii 8.
[2] Matt. xxvi 28. *Cf.* Exod. xxx. 10.

necessary to a covenant, and the absolute elements necessary to a testament; the first, so far as it denotes conditions, revealed and established by God, which man must accept and obey before he can stand in right relation with Him; the second, so far as it denotes these conditions as the direct and independent and absolute expressions of the Divine will. Covenant is inapplicable, in so far as it signifies that the two parties are in an equal degree concerned in laying down the conditions and enforcing obedience to them; testament, in so far as it implies that the death of the testator is necessary to its validity, or that its terms are as rigid and inflexible as those of a dead man's will. There is a point, indeed, where the two notions almost coalesce. A testament may be a sort of posthumous covenant; a covenant, a sort of pre-mortuary testament. Where a will is conditional, it is because of the wish of a now dead man to act as if he were still alive; where a covenant is absolute, it is because of the wish of a living man to act as if he were dead, a being whose will had received final and irrevocable expression. But even so, we cannot allow either term to be an adequate translation of διαθήκη, but must regard it as containing all the absolute elements of the one with the conditional elements of the other. So understood, we may define the καινὴ διαθήκη as the revelation of a new relation on God's part, with the conditions necessary to the realization of a new and correspondent relation on man's. This revelation, as the expression of an individual will, may be denoted Testament, but as the exhibition of a real relation on God's part, and a possible relation on ours, with the conditions on which its realization depends, it may be termed a Covenant. The καινὴ διαθήκη becomes thus almost equal to the New Religion; it presents God in a character that makes Him a new Being to man, and shows man how to realize a new relation to God. The Hebrew equivalent of διαθήκη, בְּרִית

was used in the same sense, and so applied alike to the legal economy of Moses and the spiritual economy of the prophets.[1] Each was the revelation of God in a new character and relation, with a new correspondent relation made possible on the part of man. And these ideas were, without doubt, present to the mind of Christ when He solemnly used the word. He was instituting a New Religion, revealing a new God to man, making man a new being to God. And this religion He founded in sacrifice, the sacrifice of Himself. The supper was to be the Feast of Commemoration, was to celebrate the hour and act of creation. The founding of the old διαθήκη had been ratified by blood,[2] the founding of the new must be the same. In the sacrifice of Christ the essential Fatherhood of God was to be made manifest, and the spiritual sonship of man made possible.

Now Jesus, full of the great thoughts and emotions that had at once created the supper and been created by it, passed with His disciples out into the cool night air. The city was asleep. All was still, save for here the sigh of a weary pilgrim resting uneasily on his mat, there the quick footfall of a wanderer hastening to his home, or the measured tramp of the sentinel walking his rounds. They issued out of the gate that looked towards Olivet, crossed the Kedron, and were soon hidden in an olive grove. There is an awful silence in a sleeping wood, but never did the silence speak to a heart so still in it agony as the one that was then seeking in Gethsemane a place of seclusion and prayer. That seclusion seems too sacred to be broken. Grief is always holy, and the holier the sufferer the less may we profane his sorrow by our presence. A great painter who painted the Man of Sorrows as an act of highest worship showed at once His genius and His reverence by hiding the marred visage, leaving the less

[1] Exod. xxxiv. 28, Jer xxxi. 34; Isa. liv. 9, 10.
[2] Exod xxiv. 6–8.

noble parts to reveal the agony that had broken His heart. So to us Gethsemane ought ever to be a veiled Holy of holies, to be visited, if at all, only at moments when we can look with purified eyes, and allow the meaning of the Saviour in His passion to steal softly into our minds. We are here on holy ground, and must stand, as it were, with spirit bareheaded and barefooted, reverent while inquiring.

And here it is necessary to note the limits of our inquiry. It is historical, not theological. Few things, indeed, have more profaned the sufferings of Christ than an over-curious speculation. Their nature, their degree and value, have all been discussed and estimated, their quantity and quality most precisely determined. With such questions we have here and now no concern. Our business meanwhile is to attempt to present a great moment in a holy and perfect life, in relation to the person and history of Him who lived it.

Now, looking at it from this point of view, we can say that Gethsemane does not stand alone. It is related alike to Christ's past and future—is an echo of the one and a prophecy of the other—and it is so related because of its essential connection with His person. If Gethsemane is to be understood, it must be understood through the person and character of the Sufferer. The agony of the particular moment came from the essential nature of Him who endured it ; and so to understand the one we must seek to know the other. It is essentially a matter of the spirit. In Christ, sorrow of spirit created physical pain; the physical pain did not create the spiritual sorrow. His cry was, " My *soul* is exceeding sorrowful." The intensity of the sorrow only became manifest when the touch of a Roman spear showed that He had died of a broken heart. But it was the kind and quality of the spirit that made the sorrow ; the pre-eminence of the sufferings was due to the pre-eminence of the Sufferer.

GETHSEMANE.

Given the nature and spirit of Christ, and sorrow, unique, transcendent, was to Him a Divine necessity. There is a sort of adaptation between a sinful man and a sinful earth. The two suit each other. Though it is but a dismal home and he a dismal inhabitant, yet he has never known a better, and, almost unconscious of its wretchedness, he settles down, grimly determined to be as happy as possible. But the sinless Jesus had only the relation of diametric opposition to this sinful world. In it there was nothing correspondent to what was in Him. The feeling of utter homelessness which He must have had while here gives a solemn plaintiveness and depth to His contrast of the homeless Son of man with the foxes of the earth and the birds of the air. A poet tells us—

Heaven lies about us in our infancy.

Now, if this heaven, which is perhaps not so much about as within us in our infancy, were to continue into our manhood, earth would seem to us almost a hell. A child brought up in a lazar-house, to whom green fields and the glory of the summer earth were alike unknown, who had never seen other men than those smitten with "the curse of God," would come to feel as if his strange abode were home-like and natural. But introduce a fresh blooming lad from the hill-side, familiar with the "celestial light" in which earth is apparelled, with the breath of the flowers, the sound of the sea, the glory of the sky, with the faces of noble and healthy men, and him the ghastly lepers, the fœtid atmosphere, the steaming disease would appal and dismay. We are the children of the lazar-house, familiar to insensibility with its misery; Christ the blooming youth, with a soul all open to perceive and feel man's profound wretchedness. He understood it better than even the sufferers themselves, and felt it more. His sympathy had a strange insertive power, causing

Him to feel and bear the man's sorrows much more than even the man himself. And if we think how He knew the hearts of men — the secret griefs, the unuttered regrets, the pining miseries, the blighted hopes, the thwarted wishes, the corroding remorse, that dwelt like ghastly spectres, or burned like devouring flames, in almost every human breast — and how that insertive sympathy would make Him feel all as His own, can we fail to see that there must have been in Him, through the mere fact of His living here, a sorrow such as the collective sufferings of His time gathered into one soul would but poorly express? Life to Him was passion, sympathy, and pain.

Consider again : Jesus alone of those who have lived on earth knew the inner essence and final issues of sin. The holier a man is, the more perfectly does he understand sin ; the more wicked he is, the less. The Prodigal could not see into the depravity and defilement of the "far country" as his father did. The poor victim of seduction who has touched the lowest deep possible to a woman's soul, cannot, even in her hour of remorse, see her sin as her pure celestial-minded sister sees it. And in proportion to a soul's consciousness of what sin is will be its misery at the sight of it. Hell must be more intolerable to an angel's thought than to a devil's experience. A pure spirit in the regions of the lost would, as more conscious of the evil and issues of sin, be more wretched than the lost themselves. Fancy a man suddenly gifted with an intuitive faculty, rendering him as able to read the human heart as the eye is to read the human face. He may feel at first proud of his rare power, at the curious and extensive knowledge it gives. He studies men—deciphers the strange hieroglyphs written on character and memory He makes extraordinary discoveries, reversing most of his former judgments. He sees that a heart, thought sound, is in ruins, though now and then visited by beautiful moonbeams, as if an angel had descended into it, and shed from its wings a soft white light. He sees a head perplexed with doubt while the tongue utters faith. The inner man of the statesman, poet, preacher, furnishes a strange contrast to the outer, and at it our heart-seer now sneers, now laughs, now weeps. But soon other scenes open. Suddenly he confronts a man in whom the brutal passions reign and struggle as did the "hell-hounds" in Milton's Sin. Now he meets a prodigal in the "far country," with "wasted substance," driving out the stranger's "swine," and feeding on their "husks." Then he passes wrapped in the thin torn garments of long-faded finery, a woman

> Mad from life's history,
> Glad to death's mystery,

bearing in her heart an indescribable record of suffering, wrong, ruin, and sin. And as his experience widens and his insight deepens, horror and despair rise within him, until he, the man gifted with unerring intuition, cries, "O God! take back Thy gift, and leave me a short-sighted but happy man!"

Now Jesus alone of men had this intuitive faculty. "He knew what was in man." Man was as "naked and open" to His eye as to God's. And He knew human sin too—what it could and what it would do. The man He loved, the sin He hated; yet day by day He saw the hated sin ruining the loved man. He stood on earth too, yearning in every fibre of His being with the desire to save, bleeding in every pore of His heart with pity for the lost; yet past Him those lost men went, hurrying, trampling each other in their mad haste to be ruined. Sin too, in the very extravagance of insult, turned on Him, plying Him with manifold subtle temptations. He had come to destroy it: it transcended its former self by attempting to destroy Him. Day by day the wickedness He loathed unutterably pressed against His heart, stood in His path, breathed in His face, touched His limbs, rose round Him like a brazen bulwark, which seemed gradually to narrow till it threatened to shut Him in. Ah! there He was, sin everywhere and in every one on earth save Him alone, and it, wrathful at being excluded, storming every avenue, mustering its forces to crush, if it could not capture. Alone He was with an awful loneliness, yet not alone, for the Father was with Him. We can see but a little way into the suffering that was there; but a little way, too, into the strength and joy that came from the hands and face of the Father.

Jesus suffered then—could not but suffer. Significant was that silent lowly advent of His, stepping so quietly across the threshold of the world into the manger of Bethlehem. Not as emperor, not as priest, not as scribe, but as peasant, or rather simple unadorned man, exposed to all the hardships and pains of poverty, had the "Man of Sorrows" to travel through His life. The Father did not annul for the Son the old curse of labour; even this He bore. The moment the Divine Boy realized His Father's business, He realized His own sorrow; bread to earn, yet men to save; a mother to support, yet a world to redeem; around Him the wants and claims of day, away before Him the work He had come to do. And how that work foreseen, therefore forefelt, must have added to His sufferings, pressed its burden upon that heart, which alone knew perfectly how to "take no thought for the morrow," till even He exclaimed, "I have a baptism to be baptized with; and how am I straitened till it be accomplished!" Thou Divine Sufferer, bearer of the world's sorrow, we thank Thee that Thou hast shown its Divine necessity—that he who would in a sinful world be sinless must be that world's outcast and supreme sufferer. Teach us to be like Thee in spirit, though its price be a sorrow like Thine; to have "the fellowship of Thy sufferings," and to be "made conformable to Thy death."

And sorrow had a great function in the life and spirit of Christ. By His sufferings He, "though a Son, learned obedience." There is no implied antithesis to former disobedience. He who was "without sin" had never to unlearn, only to learn. His humanity, while at first equipped with everything that was native to man, had to acquire whatever was acquirable. God creates man innocent, not obedient or disobedient; whether he shall be the one or the other, man himself must determine. Jesus was born as man is born, with human capacities and tendencies in Him, a moral character possible, not actual. His relation to law had been determined by His own will. His obedience began with His first conscious choice; and while perfect as a child's obedience, could only be held as such, not as a man's. As man reaches his perfection in manhood, so manhood can alone render human obedience in its perfection. As it has a phase corresponding to each phase of life, so man has to learn as child, or boy, or youth, or man, an obedience suited to each period. Childhood hands over to boyhood a character which boyhood must develop, amidst its frolic and struggle, towards either evil or good. Youth receives the moral results of boyhood, adds to them its own, and then hands on the work to manhood to complete, to be either made or marred. So the obedience of Jesus progressed through these successive stages, and in each stage He had to "learn" it by "the things which He suffered." Here lay the worth and meaning of His sorrow: it was His great educator. He went into it the one sinless child; He came out of it the one obedient man. He entered its school only innocent; He left it perfectly righteous.

While He could not have suffered as He did apart from His sinlessness, He could not have "learned obedience" apart from His sufferings.

But these general considerations are significant here only as they help us to understand the dark hour in Gethsemane. They show us not only that sorrow was inevitable to Christ, but also the kind and quality of this inevitable sorrow. It was without sin, yet due to sin—the sorrow of the Sinless in presence of the sinful. Holiness is happiness only where all are holy; it is and must be suffering where all beside are evil. The agony for sin will be in proportion to the absence of sin in the sufferer. And this truth received its most awful exemplification in Gethsemane. The sorrow there did not proceed from God. The filial trust of the Saviour was absolute. He entered His agony with the serene consciousness that when His loneliness was deepest His Father would be with Him;[1] He issued from it with a cry of the most perfect and even passionate confidence in His loving presence and helpful will.[2] And midway between those points, in the black centre, where He wrestled with His agony as Jacob had wrestled with God, the name that rose to His lips, as the drops of blood stood out on His brow, was still "Father."[3] And the thing asked and the manner of the asking showed the spirit of the Son: "If it be possible," "if Thou be willing," "let this cup pass." The confidence and the obedience were alike absolute; as if He had said, "Whatsoever Thy will may be, I trust and obey." He had no consciousness of Divine anger, of a face hidden, or love withdrawn; only of a "cup" the spirit was willing but the flesh too weak to drink. What this "cup" was is plain enough. The ideas and language of the

---

[1] John xvi 32. [2] Luke xxiii. 46.
[3] Matt. xxvi 42; Luke xxii 42.

supper were still in His mind. He was thinking of "the cup of the New Testament in My blood." It was His death as a sacrifice, His shedding of His blood "for the many, for the remission of sins."[1] The thought of this death had been for long His daily companion. He had first spoken of it at Cæsarea Philippi,[2] and had never ceased to speak of it since. As it approached Him, it deepened the shadow on His spirit, touched it with a heavier sadness. It was "the cup" He told the sons of Zebedee He must drink, the death He must go to Jerusalem to suffer. And now that the end has come, it seems too awful; as He faces it there is forced from Him the prayer, "Father, if it be possible, let it pass."

Now why should Christ so fear death, a death He had throughout anticipated and foretold? This great horror seems a mysterious thing. Christ had for Himself nothing to fear. Conscience makes a coward only where there is guilt, not where there is holiness. Jesus did not know the remorse that feels the future terrible; only the filial love that yearns for rest in the bosom of the Father. Man had been cruel, God gracious; and by death He could escape from angry man to gentle God. But it was not the issues from death Christ feared; it was the way into it, the *drinking* of the cup. He was in a great terror, not at what was personal, but at what was universal in death — what it involved and signified as to man, not what it involved and signified as to Himself. His death was to be, in a sense, the victory of sin — its victory not over Him, but over His life. The spirit that was willing it could not vanquish, but the flesh that was weak it did. Yet in vanquishing the flesh it was vanquished by the spirit. Christ was obedient unto death, and death, in overcoming the life, did not overcome the will, was rather overcome by it. He sur-

[1] Matt. xxvi 28, Luke xxii 20   [2] Matt xvi 21, Mark viii. 31.

rendered His life, but held fast His obedience; gave Himself up to death, but maintained His holiness, His service of law and love. But in the conflict that ended in these most opposite victories—of sin over His life, of His will over sin—His spirit and sin stood face to face, and knew each other as they had never done before. And the knowledge involved struggle, agony, sorrow unto death. Christ died on the cross, but not by the cross. He died for sin and by sin, His heart broken, but His will strong, inflexible, holy.

How and why this fatal yet victorious conflict with sin should fill Christ with so great and unspeakable horror we must now, though only in the dimmest way, attempt to see. His sufferings might be said to be of two kinds—the necessary and contingent, the general and the special; or those essential to His very nature and mission, and those springing out of His history and historical relations. The necessary were, in a sense, abstract and universal—the sufferings of a holy person obedient, under the limitations essential to a creature, and within the conditions afforded by a sinful world, to the will that made and sent and ruled Him; but the contingent were, in a sense, concrete and particular — the sufferings of a pure and gracious spirit, deserted, hated, betrayed, crucified, by the men He loved and was dying to save. The necessary were, while real and essential sufferings, transformed and glorified by the end, "the joy that was set before Him;" but the contingent were, while concrete and historical, an unrelieved agony, a darkness touched by no ray of light from a higher and diviner world. The former give to Christ's work its peculiar character and worth, and so concern theology; but the latter make Him "the Man of Sorrows," explain at once His attitude in Gethsemane and His bearing on the cross, and so concern history. The necessary sufferings are intelligible only to those who study Christ as Paul and the author of the Epistle to the Hebrews studied Him; but the contingent are intelligible to those who seek to know Him as He is presented in the Gospels, as He lived in history and among men.

Yet it is necessary to note in what sense the word contingent is here used. The sufferings so named were, in a sense, necessary: when holiness like His confronted sin like man's, sorrow that became intensest suffering was, as we have seen, inevitable. But the sufferings so endured did not belong to the essence of His work—were, let us rather say, accessories, almost accidents. His death did not depend for its worth on, was not constituted a sacrifice by, the human crime and passion that gathered round it, and deepened its agony and shame. It had been as precious in the sight of God, as glorious in its issues for man, as it now is, even though the scenes of treachery, malice, hatred, obstinate vacillation, and inflexible revenge that did surround it had never been. Judas and Caiaphas, Herod and Pilate, the rabble rout that did not forbear their shouting even at the cross, were not partakers in the work of Christ, as essential to it as Himself. Though they were not necessary to it, they were sources of sorrow, centres charged with agony, for Him. The vision that in Gethsemane and on the cross stood clear before His soul, we can but dimly imagine. Judas the disciple, a loved, trusted, familiar friend, become an apostate, now urged by passion into treason, now consumed and pursued by the furies of remorse, then a fugitive from conscience, seeking by the flight from time into eternity to escape from himself; Caiaphas the high priest, representative of an ancient people, head of their worship, symbol of their faith, prostituting his sacred office, using noblest opportunities for worst ends; Pilate, upholder of law and order, consenting to do a wrong to please the multitude—administrator of justice, yet, in deep disdain of the clamour and its cause, surrendering innocence to vengeance; the people, suddenly swerving from the enthusiasm of hope to the fanaticism of hate, athirst for blood, renouncing their splendid inheritance, denying their very Messiah, and demanding the death that is to be their dispersion and enduring shame—these and similar forms, with all their dreadful doings and surroundings, pass in a vision more terrible than reality before the eye of Christ. These men, with all their passions and guilt, seemed to encircle Him, to belong to Him, to mix themselves up inextricably with His work, to create and cause the death that was to be His glory and their shame. And He might well feel as if to go forward to His death were to consent to their crime. He had come to be their redemption, but His very act of sacrifice was to be a most calamitous judgment. He had come to save, but His mercy was to be to them in its issues severer than the severest justice. And so it seemed as if into His very cup their crimes had been pressed, as if the very wine He had to drink were dark with their blood. It looked as if He had become the victim of the most dreadful irony that even Providence could indulge; His acts of divinest grace made the condition and occasion of man's most utter and unspeakable sin. And so His soul stood, as it were, clothed in horror before a sacrifice so conditioned, a death so prepared and attended. It was almost more than even His will could do or endure; and the feeling, making Him irresolute in the very moment of His highest resolution, forced from Him the cry, "Father, if it be possible, let this cup pass." Yet the will seemed only to waver that it might settle the more fixedly in its purpose to obey. "Nevertheless, not as I will, but as Thou wilt." The obedience was absolute; the worst of evils could be suffered that the will of God might be done.

And these contingent sufferings were not aimless; they

contributed to the perfection of the Sufferer, to the efficiency and value of His work. They revealed sin to Christ and man, showed the excellence of His righteousness and the misery of our guilt. The death of Christ, with all its evil pomp and circumstance, may be said to have created in humanity the consciousness of sin. After it the seemly and shameless naturalism of Greece, the indulgent and lascivious worships of Syra and Egypt, the unethical beliefs and immoral religious practices of India, became abhorrent to the conscience of the world, lay before the spirit naked, defiled, unclean. Religions that were blind to sin, that trifled with it, were no religions for man. Evil was now a dreadful reality that must be conquered, if He was to remain human, and realize the image of God. And the sufferings that so revealed sin to man were, in the truest sense, redemptive. Sin once seen in its exceeding sinfulness is sin abhorred, renounced. The evil personified in Judas and Caiaphas, in Pilate and Herod, in the priests and the multitude, is evil man no more can love, just as the holy and beautiful righteousness incarnated in Christ is righteousness he no more can hate, but must ever admire and follow after with a Divine enthusiasm. And so the will that required Jesus to drink the awful cup was a beneficent Will—purposed that the One should suffer that the many might be saved. For the suffering that revealed man's sin perfected man's Saviour. "Though He were a Son, yet learned He obedience by the things that He suffered; and having been made perfect, He became the Author of eternal salvation to all them that obey Him." "Inasmuch as He suffered, He Himself having been tempted, He is able to succour them that are tempted."

XV.

THE BETRAYER.

THERE is nothing more remarkable in the history of the Passion than its moral truthfulness, the extraordinary realism with which the varied and most dissimilar characters are painted. The men live and act before us obedient to their respective natures and ends. Each has his own character, and the history but exhibits it in action, articulated in speech and conduct. There is everywhere the finest consistency between the doer and the deed; new events but make us the more conscious of the harmony. And this harmony is exhibited and preserved under the most extraordinary conditions, and in what seems most violent combinations. The central figure is the holiest Person of history, but round Him stand or strive the most opposed and contrasted moral types, every one related to Him and more or less concerned in the tragic action of which He is at once object and victim. The characters and catastrophe are alike beyond and above all the conventional ideals, whether of history or tragedy. The Christ Himself is a wonderful picture. Jesus appears in every moment and circumstance equal to Himself. To paint Him as He lives before us in His final agony was a feat possible only to the sweet simplicity that copies Nature, unconscious of its own high art. It was a work beyond not only the Galilean imagination, but any of the imaginations that had as yet created the ideals of the world. Physical weakness and suffering do not readily lend themselves to the expression of moral dignity and power. The Victim of the scourge and the cross, fated to endure the contemptuous pity of His judge and the merciless mockery of His foes, is hardly the kind of subject imagination would choose as the vehicle or embodiment of a spiritual sublimity so transcendent as to demand our worship and command our awe. Creative art would find it almost, perhaps altogether, impossible to keep the weakness from depraving and so destroying the dignity—the scornful hate that kills the person from casting its shadow over the character. It is only when we compare this simple historical presentation with the highest human art that we see how perfect it is. The splendid imagination of Plato has done its utmost to invest the death of Sokrates with high philosophical meaning, with the deepest ethical and tragic interest. Yet when the closing scenes in the *Phædo* are compared with the closing scenes in the Gospels, how utterly the finest genius of Greece is seen to have failed in his picture of the good man in death. Sokrates is the philosopher, not the man. In his very serenity there is something selfish. His speculations calm and exalt him, but at the expense of his humanity. Affection, passion does not trouble him, and he does not feel how sorely it may trouble other and lower spirits. Death, so far as an evil to himself, he has conquered; but he has not even imagined that his death may be an evil to others, all the greater that he suffers it so unjustly and meets it so serenely. The guilt of Athens in causing his death does not touch so as to awe or overwhelm him; he feels the guilt almost as little as Athens herself. Then the sorrows of Xanthippe do not move him. He remains sublimely discoursing with his friends, while she, face to face with woman's greatest sorrow, is introduced only to be made ridiculous in her grief. Xanthippe indeed has been one of the most ill-used of women. Neglected by her husband in life, she is not comforted by him in death. He has lofty principles and wise speeches for philosophers, but only scornful pity of the woman whose sorrow ought to have touched his spirit and made him feel that death is more terrible to the living than to the dying, and that the sorrows of affection have a greater claim on our comfort and sympathy than the serene souls of philosophers. How infinitely does Christ in His dying passion transcend the most virtuous of the Greeks! Death to Him has no terrors, save those made by the guilt of man. He fears death for the sake of the men that work it; because of their sin it is to Him an agony He cannot bear. The man who followed and betrayed Him, the men who loved and forsook Him, the women who loved and forsook Him not, He pitied, He comforted as far as they would receive the comfort He had to give. The sorrow of Christ in death was diviner than the serenity of Sokrates, and the historians of His sorrow could have made Him so seem only by painting Him as He was. They were without the imagination that could create an ideal so strange yet so beautiful, and only possessed the love that is quick to understand and sure and true of speech. And thus, by their very openness and simplicity of soul, which keeps them remote from invention and near to reality, they so represent Christ in His passion as to make the passion exalt and glorify the Christ. But the transfiguring power is in the person, not in the suffering. It is made sublime through Him; He remains glorious in spite of it. The case is without a parallel. There are no sufferings in the world that awaken the same emotions as Christ's; but the emotions they awaken are due not to them as sufferings, but to the Sufferer. Their transcendent significance only expresses His; and the degree of their significance for the world is the measure of the wonderful unlearned art that had the wisdom to read their meaning and tell their story.

And as Christ remains Himself, true to His ideal character, the other actors in the tragedy no less faithfully and consistently unfold in action and conduct their respective moral natures. While He rises above His sorrow, and commands it, even in the very moment when it works His death, His disciples behave like simple men surprised in the midst of fond illusions, suddenly and fiercely shaken out of them, and too completely bewildered by the shock to know what to think or to do. Judas, perhaps the man of strongest character and will in the band, foresees the catastrophe, contributes to it, but only to be so appalled by the issue as to be hurried to a deed of terrible atonement. And this evolution of moral nature and principle stands in radical relation to the presence and action of the Christ. The men who touch Him in this supreme hour of His history do so only to have their essential characters disclosed. In Him judgment so lived that it acted as by nature and without ceasing. The men who thought to try Him were themselves tried, stood in His presence with their inmost secrets turned out. The stars that look down on us like the radiant eyes of heaven shine out of a darkness their light but deepens. The sunshine makes the plant unfold its leaves, the flower declare its colour, the tree exhibit its fruit. So from Christ there came the light as of a solitary star, deepening the darkness round Him, a heat and radiance that made the characters about Him effloresce and bear fruit, each after its kind. The high priest is made all unconsciously to himself to show himself, not as he thought he was or would like to be thought to be, but as he is before the eye of God and measured by the eternal law of righteousness—crafty, devoted to expediency, using his high office for private ends, turning the forms of justice into the instruments of injustice; scrupulous as to ceremonial purity, but heedless as to moral rectitude; able red-handed but calm-hearted to keep the Passover, feeling in no way disqualified by his part in the trial and crucifixion for celebrating the great religious festival of his people. The Procurator, a Roman, imperious, haughty, scornful of the people he ruled, contemptuous of their religion, impatient of their ceaseless disputes, stands, from his brief connection with Jesus, before all time morally unveiled—a man vacillating, cruel, as a judge in the heart of him unjust, surrendering to a popular clamour he proudly despised the very person he had declared innocent. The priests, fearful of pollution, hating a Gentile as if he were organized sin, are seen, as it were, spiritually unclothed, sacrificing their hitherto greatest to a still greater hate, stimulating in the crowd their thirst for blood, preferring Cæsar to Christ, standing mocking and spiteful before painful yet sacred death. The people, thoughtless, impulsive, are shown, the ready tools of the cunning, demanding the life of a murderer, the death of the righteous; as a multitude, where men, de-individuated, are almost de-humanized, capable of atrocities which each man apart and by himself would abhor himself for thinking either he or any other man could perpetrate. The inner nature in each determines the action, but the contact with Christ shows the quality of the nature, and forces it into appropriate action and speech. As the Passion reveals in Jesus the Christ, its history is but the translation, under the impulse He supplies, into word and deed, of the spirit of the men who surrounded, tried, and crucified Him.

Now this indicates the point of view from which we wish to apprehend the last events in the life of Christ. They are the revelation of very varied moral natures, and they possess a singular unity and significance when studied in relation to the natures they reveal. The standpoint is critical, but psychological rather than historical, the criticism being concerned not so much with the probable order and outer conditions of the events as with their moral source and spiritual sequence. If we can find their subtler inner relations— can, as it were, interpret the drama through the actors, or the plot through the characters, especially in their attitude to Him whose presence gives unity and movement to the whole—it may help us the better not only to understand its truth, but to believe its reality.

The first man who meets us is the man who led the band of captors to Gethsemane. Judas is one of the standing moral problems of the gospel history. What was the character of the man? What motives induced him first to seek and then to forsake the society of Jesus? Why did he turn traitor? Why was he so little penetrated by the Spirit and awed by the authority of Christ as to be able to do as he did? And why, having done it, did he so swiftly and tragically avenge on himself his deliberately planned and executed crime? These questions invest the man with a fascination now of horror and again of pity; of horror at the crime, of pity for the man. If his deed stands alone among the evil deeds of the world, so does his remorse among the acts and atonements of conscience; and the remorse is more expressive of the man than even the deed. Lavater said, "Judas acted like Satan, but like a Satan who had it in him to be an apostle." And it is this evolution of a possible apostle into an actual Satan that is at once so touching and so tragic.

There is an instructive contrast between what we know of the man and how we conceive him. There is, perhaps, no person in history of whom we at once know so little and have so distinct an image. The lines that sketch him are few, but they are lines of living fire. He is too real a person to be, as Strauss argued,[1] a mythical creation, made after Ahithophel, and draped in a history suggested

[1] *Leben Jesu*, § 130 , *Neues Leben*, § 90.

by verses in the very Psalms Peter quoted in his address to his brother Apostles.[1] The man and his part are so interwoven with the history of Christ's last days as to be inseparable from it; the picture of the man is too defined, concrete, characteristic to be a product of the mythical imagination, which, always exaggerative, never works but on a stupendous scale. The objects loom as through the mist—do not look like Judas, clear and sharp-cut as if fresh from the sculptor's chisel. Still less can we allow Volkmar[2] to resolve him into a creation of the Pauline tendency, framed expressly to make a place in the apostolic circle for Paul. His reasons are as violent as his conjecture. Judas is no bestial phenomenon, lying outside the pale of humanity. On the contrary, the human nature of him is terribly real and distinct; and Paul's own reference to the betrayal[3] is, notwithstanding Volkmar's specious exegesis and strained rendering, clear and conclusive. But if the critic is required to spare his historical reality, it is not simply in order to allow the speculative theologian to destroy his humanity. Daub,[4] in one of the

[1] Acts i. 15, ff; Pss cix., lxix.
[2] *Die Religion Jesu u. ihre erste Entwickelung nach dem gegenwartigen Stande der Wissenschaft*, pp. 260, ff.
[3] 1 Cor. xi. 23. Volkmar proposes to translate παρεδίδετο, *uberliefert wurde* (was delivered, given up), instead of *verrathen ward* (was betrayed). But the change does not mend the matter. If He was delivered, some one delivered Him to somebody, which to the Apostles could only appear as a betrayal. This whole theory as to Judas is an example of how a scholar, possessed by an hypothesis, may in its interest do violence to all the probabilities of history and laws of grammar.
[4] *Judas Ischariot, oder Betrachtungen uber das Bose im Verhaltniss zum Guten* (Heidelberg, 1816, 1818). There is no more remarkable figure in modern theology than Daub, and no more gruesome book than his *Judas Ischariot*. He might be said to be the mirror of German Transcendentalism in its successive phases. He began life a Kantian, he ended it an Hegelian, but was throughout distinguished by the most heroic loyalty to the speculative reason, addressing an audience

strangest works of his massive but hardly modern mind, has conceived Judas as the embodied evil who stands in antithesis to Christ as the embodied good. The one was the power of Satan in human form, as the other was the power of God, and without the devilish the Divine agent could not have accomplished His work in the world. Hence Judas was chosen to be a disciple expressly that he might betray the Christ, and so, by enabling Jesus to fulfil His mission, fulfilling his own. But this theory is without historical warrant, its reason is entirely *a priori*, its significance purely speculative. The man is to us simply an historical person, and must be interpreted as one, on principles and by standards applicable to human nature throughout the world.

If Daub is unjust to Judas, sacrificing his historical and moral significance to a speculative theory as to the relation of evil to good, there are two current, yet opposite, interpretations that are, though for different reasons, no less unjust. According to the one of these, Judas is moved by avarice; according to the other, by mistaken enthusiasm, by an exalted notion of Christ's mission and power. There is nothing that can so little explain the act and

always few, though not so constantly fit. When he wrote *Judas* he was under the influence of Schelling's first transcendental theosophy, bent on discovering in God and Nature the dark ground which the eternal Reason had to conquer, and against which it had to establish light and order. To him Jesus and Judas were the universe in miniature— their history veiled the universal truth. "As Jesus Christ had no equal among men, neither had His betrayer. While to the Christian mind the first man was the first sinner, yet among his descendants Judas is the only one in whom sin reached the highest point" (vol 1 p 2). "In him was personified and concentrated all the wickedness of all the enemies of Jesus and evil identified with its instrument, and so for him, as an incarnation of the devil, mercy and blessedness are alike impossible" (vol 1 p 22) With the way in which Daub works out the universal problem given in this moment of the evangelical history, we are not here concerned. It is enough that we see to what extraordinary uses Judas has been turned.

conduct of Judas as greed, the love of money. There is, perhaps, no passion more intense, but there is certainly none so narrow, so selfish, so blind or indifferent to the miseries or misfortunes it may inflict on others. To avarice money is the greatest good, the want of it the greatest evil, and the means that can obtain the good and obviate the evil are ever justified by the end. The miser who can indulge his master passion minds his own miseries too little to care for the miseries it may cause either to persons or States. The remorse of Judas disproves his greed; the man who could feel it had too much latent nobility of soul to be an abject slave of avarice. The "thirty pieces of silver" had no power to comfort him; they were the signs of his guilt, the witnesses of his shame, that in his despair he cast from him in mingled rage and pain. The fact, too, that he was the bearer of the bag [1] proves that he was no lover of money. However his co-disciples may have judged him, Jesus would never have so led him into temptation, fostered avarice in the heart of the avaricious by making him the custodian of the purse. Christ, we may be certain, did not elect him to this office in order that He might cause the offence to come.[2]

And Judas was as little a mistaken enthusiast, a man weary of his master's delay in declaring Himself, seeking by a fond though foolish expedient to force Him to stand forth the confessed and conquering Messiah.[3] This theory has nothing in the history to support it, is indeed, in every respect, violently opposed to the evidence. If he had been an enthusiast, why had his enthusiasm slumbered so

[1] John xii. 6   [2] Matt xviii 7.
[3] Cf. the article "Judas" by Paulus, in Ersch und Gruber's *Encyclopadie*, Whately's *Essays on Dangers to the Christian Faith*, Discourse iii.; and De Quincey's celebrated *Essay on Judas*, which throws the same theory into more literary but also more paradoxical form.

long, and never been expressed till now, and why now in a form so extraordinary and fantastic? And how, if he had so great an idea of Christ's power, had he so mean an idea of Christ's wisdom? If, too, he had meant to compel Jesus to show Himself, would he have chosen the silent night as the time for the capture and still Gethsemane as the place? If, too, while his means were so foolish, his motive had been so good, would Jesus have received and spoken of and to him as He did? The theory is too unreal and violent to deserve grave discussion, and would never have been gravely proposed for belief save as offering a welcome alternative to the commoner and less generous interpretation. There are men who but see in the remorse of Judas the evidence of his sin and condemnation; and there are men who see in it the proof of a sorrow for his act too deep to allow the man to forgive himself. The former are contented to say: " Judas is the one man of whom we know with certainty that he is eternally damned;"[1] but the latter are anxious to find some means of softening the fate of one who died from unspeakable horror at his own crime. Apart from this reason no man would ever have seen in Judas a mistaken enthusiast.

Let us look, then, at the man as he stands before us in history. It is not easy indeed to get face to face with him. His early life lies under the shadow cast by his later; the man is interpreted through his end. And the men who interpret him for us looked at him in a light wonderfully unlike the light in which he had seen and been seen in the flesh. To their eyes, enlightened by Divine events, everything assumed a new meaning. Jesus became another person than He had been—of diviner nature, higher authority, immenser significance. His kingdom ceased to be Israel's and became God's—spiritual, universal, eter-

[1] *Die Evangelische Zeitung*, No. 30, 1863; Hase, *Geschichte Jesu*, p. 549.

nal; His death was changed from a last disaster into a sacrifice "offered once for all," abolishing all need of further sacrifices, and creating a new and living way by which men might draw near to God; the life of humiliation and suffering He had lived to their senses was transfigured and sublimed by the life of exaltation and glory He now lived to their faith. And this change in their notion of Christ changed the proportions and meaning of everything that related to Him or His history. In the presence of the Divine in Christ, acts of the simplest devotion were touched with sublimity, while words of distrust or deeds of disobedience became charged with a darker guilt. And the new light which had risen on their spirits cast a shadow which fell deepest on Judas, stretching along the whole course of his life. The man was to them ever a traitor; in the hour of his discipleship he had still the soul of an alien,[1] and in his last act he was not so much a man as the agent and organ of the devil.[2] But we may be certain that, whatever the man was towards the end, he could not have been bad at the beginning. As Jesus would never have selected a man to be a disciple for the express purpose of making him a traitor, Judas must have had promise in him, possibilities of good, capabilities of apostleship. Christ's act is more significant than the Evangelist's words; and it permits us to infer that in Judas when he was called there was a possible Peter or John, as, perhaps, in these there was a possible Judas. There is no question that he was one of the twelve,[3] nor that he occupied a position of trust.[4] The man Christ so trusted must have seemed to Him a trusty man, not likely to be corrupted by his office or its opportunities. But the

---

[1] Matt. x. 4; Mark iii 19; Luke vi. 16.
[2] John xiii. 2, 27; Luke xxii. 3.
[3] Matt xxvi. 14; Mark xiv. 10; Luke xxii. 3.
[4] John xii. 6, xiii. 29.

THE BETRAYER. 269

unlikely was the realized. He who carried the purse betrayed the Master; and the well trusted became the traitor.

The position, then, from which our constructive interpretation must start in this: Judas the disciple was a possible apostle, chosen to the discipleship that the possible might be realized. It was with him as with the others—they, too, were possibilities; their souls, like his, the battle-ground of evil and good, where the worse often came dangerously near to victory. The struggle was due to the good in Christ and the evil in themselves. The evil was the fruit of ignorance or prejudice or passion, of the Judaism in which they had been nursed, with the false ideas it had created, and the false hopes it had inspired. Their ideas of God, of the Messiah, of the kingdom, of righteousness, of worship, of man, were the very antitheses and contradiction of Christ's. His aim was to lead them from their ideas to His, to expel the Jewish and plant in them the Christian mind. At first they loved Him because they believed He was the one who could realize their ideals; at last they loved Him because they had made His ideals theirs, and had by faith and fellowship been qualified to become agents for their realization throughout the world. But the way between the first and the last was long and hard to traverse, marked here and there by struggles fierce in proportion to the strength of the old convictions and the new love. Where the convictions had the deepest root the struggle was sternest; where the love was most intense victory came earliest and was most complete. But in no case was it easy. Peter, the man forward in speech and action, could rebuke his Master, even after months of closest fellowship.[1] The sons of Zebedee could not trust Him, but must urge that He fulfil their ambitions in their own form and way.[2] They had not learned to trust His wisdom because they had not learned to know His mind;

[1] Matt. xvi. 22, Mark viii 32.   [2] Mark x 35-37.

and His mind was hard to know because it was so utterly unlike their own.

Now of Judas it may certainly be said he was at once the most Jewish and the least attached of the disciples, the man most pronounced in his Judaism and least bound by his affections—the feelings of personal love and social loyalty that could alone have steadied him in the process of violent and distressful change. He was known as Iscariot [1]—the man from Kerioth—the only Judæan in the band. The others were men of Galilee, kindred in blood and akin in faith. Galilee was the circle of the Gentiles; in it the people were more mixed, were freer, more open to new or strange ideas, less fierce and fanatical in their Judaism than the people of Judæa. In the man from Kerioth there lived the hotter temper, the haughtier spirit, the more intolerant faith of the south. The air round his home was full of the oldest traditions of his race; its scenes, consecrated by the wanderings and history of Abraham, by the struggles and early victories of David, may well have coloured the dreams of his youth and the hopes of his manhood. Conscious purity of blood involves austerity of faith, and so his ideals would be national in a degree quite unknown to the Galileans. Learning Christ would be a much harder thing to him than to them, for it implied a more radical revolution. They were alike in this—they followed Jesus at first because they believed His word and mission to be not hostile to Judaism, but completory of it —its vital outcome and fulfilment. But they were unlike in their relation both to Judaism and Jesus. Of all it may be said, that the light as it began to break was not altogether loved, was not always welcome, but even now and then positively hateful. When the new order stood disclosed, it was found so to cross and contradict the inherited prejudices of generations, that only supreme love to Christ's

[1] Matt x. 4, xxvi 14; Luke xxii. 3.

THE BETRAYER.

person could create and maintain loyalty to His aims. And Judas was precisely the man who would feel the contradiction most and the love least. He had no friend or brother in the band; neighbourliness had not drawn him into it, and family affection could not help to hold him there. The solitary Judæan in a Galilean society, he would be, as the least known, the least loved, with fewest personal associations and interests, and least community of thought and feeling. Where friendship, with the confidences it brings, is not spontaneous or natural, the soul is easily forced into the silence that creates misconception and distrust.

Let us imagine, then, the unwritten history of Judas. He is a man of strong convictions, a zealot who has in his south Judæan home brooded over the problems of his race, the splendid spiritual promise of Israel, but its miserable historical failure. He believes in the destiny of his people, dares to confess to himself that, though he pays tribute to Cæsar, the Messiah is his king. Full of these thoughts, he meets Jesus at Jerusalem. The one has come south from Nazareth, the other north from Kerioth. It is in the Holy City that Judas most feels the desolation of Israel; but there, too, he is most conscious of the consolation of hope. In a moment of moody hopefulness he hears Jesus, sees Him drive the money-changers out of the temple [1] and do works that seem to prove Him a teacher come from God.[2] He follows Him, goes with Him into Galilee; but while he believes that Jesus is the Messiah, the Messianic ideal is his own, not Christ's. He is chosen a disciple for what he may be rather than what he is; his spirit is the possibility of an apostle or an apostate. The early ministry in Galilee pleases him. In presence of the miracles, the multitudes, the words of power, his faith lives. One who can so speak and act may well be the Messiah, and pa-

[1] John ii. 15.   [2] John ii 23; iii. 2.

tience is easy when hope is strong. He is zealous in his own way, has a genius for what, in modern phrase, is termed organization, and becomes purser of the little band. He hears and, like the others, dimly understands the Master, but interprets Him through his own desires and expectations. While the bright morning of the ministry endures all rejoice in the fresh sunshine; but as clouds prophetic of storm gathered over its noonday they did not all alike feel the better radiance that came from the serene soul of the Christ. They were like men slowly awaking to a real world, unintelligible because so unlike their ideal—men bewildered by the consciousness that their fondest dreams were illusions destined never to be realized. And now came the conflict in which love to Christ and loyalty to the ancient convictions, which they had hoped to see fulfilled through Him, wrestled for the mastery. They had to believe before they could see, and belief in a moment so trying could only live by love. The alternatives were, assimilation to Him or recoil from Him, and for a while the rival forces, the centripetal and the centrifugal, might be so balanced as only the more to compel the man to continue moving in the path he had chosen. But they could not remain for ever in equilibrium; one or other must prevail. The consequent struggle was felt by all; no man escaped it. Jesus was early conscious of it, knew that there was an evil spirit among the twelve,[1] one who should betray the Son of man into the hands of men.[2] The prophecies of the Passion were a bewilderment to the disciples. Mark, in his picturesque way, shows them walking behind Jesus stunned ($\dot{\epsilon}\theta\alpha\mu\beta o\hat{v}\nu\tau o$), stupefied by wonder, communing among themselves, terrified at His words and the tragedy they foretell.[3] The men were all differently affected. Thomas, faithful in his very despair,

---

[1] John vi 70.   [2] Matt xvii 22.   [3] Mark x. 32.

THE BETRAYER.

was ready to die with Him.[1] Peter, more courageous in speech than action, foretold his own fall by boasting that, while all men might be offended, yet would not he.[2] Judas showed his fiercer and more dissatisfied spirit in open and ungenerous criticism, though the mind that prompted it was shared by all.[3]

In those dark days, then, we see the conflict of the rival forces—the transforming love attracting the one way, the ancient convictions drawing the other. The man from Kerioth could not get near Jesus because of his own ideas as to what the Christ ought to be, and so the love that is the best creator of truthful loyalty could not exercise over him its holy and beneficent influence. The fellowship that does not beget affinity evokes antipathy, the mind that has not learned to love is dangerously near to hate. While Christ's spirit had been growing readier for sacrifice, Judas's had been getting more selfish, waxing bitter over its vanishing ideals. The fuller Christ's speech became of suffering and death the more offensive it grew to Judas—the more like a mockery of his ancient hopes. Such a conflict of mind and thought between Master and disciple could not continue for ever; and it could have but one end. The longer it endured and the more it was repressed, the wider grew the breach and the more bitter the feeling. The moment when Christ's words and acts were most significant of death and sacrifice was also the moment when discipleship became impossible to Judas,

[1] John xi. 16. [2] Matt xxvi 33, 34; Mark xiv 29

[3] John xii 4-6: Matt xxvi 8, 9 These references must be studied together in order to a right appreciation alike of Judas and the other disciples Both evidently refer to the same incident Matthew's narrative shows that the feeling of dissatisfaction was common, and the condemnation of the act common too; but John's seems to show that Judas was the man who fomented or expressed the feeling, who was its cause, or voice, or both In any case Matthew does not here leave Judas in the bad pre-eminence he is made to hold with John.

and apostasy inevitable. While the Master remained to institute the Supper of everlasting remembrance, the disciple went forth to betray Him.

No one hates like an apostate. The cause he deserts is an offence to him. It is the monument of a happier past, of hopes that deluded, of conflicts that have ended in the defeat of conscience and the loss of honour. The more honest the apostate the deeper will be his hate, for his apostasy will imply a more violent distress and disturbance of nature. The man who is not in earnest is incapable of any strong aversion, powerful feelings being everywhere at once the expression and measure of sincerity. And he who forsakes a cause, believing it has deceived and wronged him, feels that he cannot spare it, can only be its remorseless foe. Revenge becomes a passion which must be gratified before the man can be happy. And Judas acts like an apostate to whom revenge is dear. Hate like his is a sure diviner, as quick to recognize hate in all its varying degrees and capabilities as love is to discern love. And so with the unerring instinct of his kind he seeks the chief priests. "And they were glad, and covenanted to give him money;"[1] but the sweet thing was the revenge, not the money. Yet why did they need him? Jesus was defenceless, was in their city, on their streets, teaching openly—what need, then, of a covenant with the traitor? It was not enough to capture, it was necessary to condemn Him, and so condemn Him that the Roman would execute the judgment. Only the most delicate handling could insure the death that had been deemed "expedient."[2] The conditions were dangerous: the millions then gathered in and about Jerusalem formed a most explosive mass. The Jews were a proud and fanatical race, believing themselves the chosen of God, the Jacob He loved, the Israel in whom

[1] Luke xxii. 5 [2] John xi 50.

THE BETRAYER.

His soul delighted. They despised the Roman as a Gentile while hating him as a conqueror. He might be allowed for a little to chastise them for their sins; but once it pleased God to have mercy upon Zion and restore her freedom, the Roman would have to go forth weeping, while they had their mouths filled with laughter and their tongues with singing. And the hope in the return of the Divine favour was just then at its intensest, insensible to discouragement, sensitive to every propitious sign, ready to anticipate or respond to it in deeds of fierce fanaticism. This hope so possessed the people then within and about Jerusalem that it glowed in them like a passion. The sight of the Roman was an insult to their pride and their faith. The millions were conscious of their multitude, of their strength, of ideals of authority and empire that far transcended the Roman. Were the belief to seize them that their Messiah had come, it would raise them into an army of fanatics, inspired by an awful hate to Rome and a sublime enthusiasm for their city and their hopes. The priests knew the possibilities that slumbered in the multitudes, but they knew not the resources of Jesus. The people's action they could forecast, but not Christ's. And with them not to know was to suspect. The bad can never understand the good, fear that their good is only disguised evil, the worse and more mischievous from being so skilfully concealed. And so the priests feared Jesus, believed that He would do what they would have done had they been in His place. They thought that to take Him in public would be to court disaster. The people believed in Him, and to threaten Him might be to force their belief into irrevocable deeds. For to see Him taken captive by the Roman would be to their hot imagination proof of His Messiahship, evidence that Cæsar feared the Christ. So the thing must be done secretly. If there was power in Him, He must not be allowed to exercise it over the people, or the people to see it. If there was faith in Him, it must not be provoked by a public arrest, but be shamed into silence and out of existence by the sight of a broken and humiliated and smitten captive. And so the coming of the traitor was like the descent of wisdom into their counsels; it made the difficult possible and the dark light.

What help the traitor needed he received, and, familiar with the haunts of Jesus, he led forth the band to Gethsemane. There they met the Saviour fresh from His agony and His prayer; and hate, that it might the better gratify itself, tried to use the language and the symbols of love. Over the scene we may not linger, though it is in its tragic contrasts one of the moments the imagination has most loved to picture. There, under the silent stars, in the glare of the red torchlight, two faces that were as heaven and hell meeting, joined in what was at once the holiest and most profane kiss ever given by human lips. But the deed was soon done, and Jesus, in the cold dark midnight, encircled by flaming torches and coarse cruel men, returned to Jerusalem. "Peter followed afar off," and so did another disciple, made bold by a love many waters could not quench. But deep as was their anguish, in another spirit there was a deeper. There is a hate that dies by indulgence—a revenge that, gratified, begets remorse. A mean and miserly nature, incapable of commanding emotions, had been able to sell Jesus and feel only the happier for being free of His presence and possessed of the "thirty pieces of silver," which was His price. But with an earnest and intense nature, whose hate was born of disappointed hope and baffled ambition, it was altogether different. The apostasy of Judas came from the feeling that he had been deceived, but the despair of Judas from the consciousness that he had deceived himself, and so become the author of a stupendous crime. Evil premeditated is evil at its best—attractive, desirable, full of promises which the senses can understand and the passions love; but evil perpetrated is evil at its worst—hideous, hateful, stripped of its illusions, and clothed in its native misery. In his anger at finding Jesus not to be the Christ he had hoped for and desired, Judas deserted and betrayed Him; in the terrible calm that succeeded indulgence he awoke to the realities within and about him, saw how blindly he had lived and hated, how far the Messianic ideal of Jesus transcended his own. There are moments that are big with eternities, when the walls self has built round the spirit fall, and the infinite realities of God stand clear before the soul. Such was the moment after the betrayal to the betrayer. In it he knew at once himself and Jesus, saw his lost opportunity and his awful crime. Above the lurid torch-light gleamed the silent beautiful stars; to the eye of Jesus they were full of pity, but to the eye of Judas they were full of blame. Calm, magnanimous Nature in heaven and on earth made the one peaceful and strong, but the other remorseful and weak. Sorrow subdued into resignation is holy happiness; but revenge glutted is remorse roused.

The suddenly awakened conscience is a terrible power; compared with it justice is gentle and law is mild. The man in whom it lives feels neither inclined nor able to forgive himself, sees only where and in what he is blameworthy. In its burning light whatever can deepen guilt is made to stand out clear, sharp, and distinct; while every apology or extenuating circumstance is consumed. So Judas judges himself with awful severity, and hastens to execute judgment. The moments move swiftly, but with sure consequence. He does not wait for the issue of his act, but anticipates it. He knows the men, watches the trial, hears Jesus condemned, and then abandons himself to his horror and remorse. With the judges, the men whose hireling he had been, he had no part or lot. He was in earnest, they were not; it was a matter of life and death to him, of "expediency" and craft with them. When they had compassed their end, they were satisfied; but he had by the betrayal defeated, as he now understood, his own purpose, given One holy, harmless, and beautiful over into the hands of sinners. Christ before His judges became intelligible to the man with the awakened conscience; His spiritual meaning, aims, Messiahship all stood clear before his eye, while the men that were trying Him, with their hollow and selfish worldliness, turned, as it were, into living transparencies. And so the trial was enough; he could not live to see the end. He would hide himself in the grave; seek the blindness of death. The scene with the chief priests is most characteristic. They calm, cynical, satisfied; he agitated, reproachful, remorseful. He cries, "I have sinned in that I have betrayed innocent blood." They answer, "That is thy own concern. What is it to us?"[1] The "thirty pieces of silver" he cannot keep, each accuses him so. He casts them down in his agony, turns and flees from the temple, a fugitive from conscience, from self, yet only the more pursued by the remorseful self, the reproachful conscience, unable to face life followed by a so awful Nemesis, able only to seek quiet in death and a refuge in the grave.

The end of the traitor became him. It was the way in which he confessed his crime and made atonement for it to his conscience. We ought to think of Judas, if not the better, the more kindly for his end. It proved him not altogether bad—that the actual apostate had been a possible apostle. Imagine how much worse a calmer end had shown him. If he had lived a man without passion or pain; if he had lifted to heaven a serene brow and

[1] Matt. xxvii. 3–5.

looked out on man like a consciously excellent soul; if he had enlarged his phylactery, lengthened his robe, and extended his prayers at the corners of the streets and in the temple; if he had gone daily to the house of his friend, the chief Rabbi, and been often in good fellowship with his honoured and dignified neighbour, the high priest; if he had lived in the exercise of his religion, died in the odour of respectability, and been buried amid the regrets and eulogies of his sect and city—would he not have been a man of lower nature and baser spirit than he seems now as, seeking to escape his sin and his conscience, he flees out of time into eternity? Judas despairful is a better man than Judas respectable had been; and if his remorse has touched the heart of man into pity, who shall say that it found or made severe and pitiless the heart of God?

XVI.

THE CHIEF PRIESTS—THE TRIAL.

It is remarkable that " the chief priests " have at first no place in the evangelical history; they begin to appear only when it begins to be tragic. Their presence is as the shadow of death. While the Pharisees and scribes, like men zealous for the law and careful of the people, anxiously examine every act and criticize every word of Jesus, the priests seem while He is most active to be entirely unconcerned, leave Him untroubled with questions, undisturbed by opposition or argument. The men who are shocked at the good deeds done on the Sabbath,[1] who murmur at the Rabbi that teaches "publicans and sinners," and "eateth with them,"[2] who persistently interrogate Christ and attempt to silence Him with legal maxims and puzzle Him with exegetical difficulties,[3] who even dare to measure His sanctity by their legalism and His truth by their traditions,[4] are the Pharisees and scribes. But while they are the invariable background of the picture, the priests are conspicuous by their absence. They neither resist nor befriend Christ; they simply do not appear. This absence cannot be explained by any gentleness of speech or spirit of conciliation on His part. The Good Samaritan[5] was as severe a satire on the priest as the two men praying in the temple[6]

---

[1] Mark iii 1–6 ; Luke vi. 1–11.
[2] Luke xv 2 ; vii 39; Matt ix 10, 11 ; Mark ii 16.
[3] Matt xix 3, xxii 35–40; Mark x. 2.
[4] Matt. xv. 1, 2, Mark vii. 1–5 , Luke xi. 37, 38.
[5] Luke x. 31, 32.   [6] Luke xviii. 10–14.

was on the Pharisee. But priestly silence did not mean priestly tenderness, as is evident from the first and most significant synoptic reference to "the chief priests." This is made by Christ Himself. He declares, before ever they have appeared on the scene, that He is to suffer many things at their hands, is to be delivered unto them and to be by them condemned to death.[1] If we confine ourselves

[1] Matt. xvi. 21 , xx. 18 ; Mark viii 31 ; x. 33 ; Luke ix 22 It is an extraordinary and instructive fact that no allusions to the "chief priests" in connection with Christ should be made in the Synoptic Gospels till He begins to anticipate His passion and foretell His death. It is a fact of equal critical and historical importance , critical, inasmuch as it shows how the Fourth Gospel can explain otherwise inexplicable references in the Synoptic Gospels (comp with the above texts John vii. 32, 45, 46) ; historical, inasmuch as it brings out the essential character of the great Jewish parties, defines and determines their relation both to Judaism and Christ The mere figures are suggestive and significant. Thus ἀρχιερεῖς occurs (Matt. ii. 4 ; Mark ii. 16 ; and Luke iii 2 having no relevance to the history) first in Matt in xvi. 21, then in xx once, xxi. thrice, xxvi. eleven times, xxvii. seven times, xxviii. once ; first in Mark in viii 31, x once, xi twice, xiv twelve times, xv five times ; first in Luke in ix. 22, xix once, xx twice, xxii six times, xxiii four times, xxiv once ; first in John in vii 32, 45, xi four times, xii once, xvii eleven times, xix thrice. The earlier references, with the exception of those in John vii , are to Christ's predictions of their action: the later describe that action, which belongs entirely to the history of the passion. As to the Pharisees, the order is entirely reversed. The references are, in Matt. iii. once, v. once, vii. once, ix. thrice, xii. four times, xv. twice, xvi four times, xix once (?), xxi. once, xxii. three times, xxiii. (the woes) nine times, xxvii once , in Mark ii four times, iii. once, vii thrice, viii. twice, ix once, xii. once ; in Luke v four times, vi twice, vii five times, xi. seven times, xii once, xiii once, xiv. twice, xv once, xvi. once, xvii. once, xviii. twice, xix once , in John i once iii once, iv. once, vii. five times, viii. twice, ix. four times, xi thrice, xii twice, xviii once. By comparing these references we see that the Pharisaic activity was greatest during the ministry, the priestly during the passion So far as the Synoptics are concerned, the Pharisees may be said to have been as completely absent from the passion as the priests from the ministry. The Fourth Gospel shows them, in the earlier stages of the passion, associated with the priests, but never active as they were, disappearing finally at the capture, taking no part

to the Synoptists, this reference to men who have never either spoken or acted against Him is surprising; but if we turn to the Fourth Gospel it ceases to surprise. There the action and allusions in the synoptic histories are explained. Christ knew the priests to be absolute enemies; His prophecy but expressed His experience. Their antagonism was too deep to condescend to words; deeds alone could declare it. The Pharisees might aim at victory by argument, but the priests did not mean to waste words on one doomed to death. So the moment Jesus came within their reach their fatal activity began. They took offence at His presence and conduct in the temple, demanded the authority by which He acted, and abstained from seizing Him only because "they feared the multitude."[1] Their purpose was one and inflexible; their only point of uncertainty how best and most safely to work His death.[2]

Now, how is this extraordinary difference in attitude and action of the Pharisees and Priests to be explained? Without the former, Christ the Teacher would have been without contradiction and criticism; without the latter, Christ the Sufferer would not have known the mockery of the trial or the shame and agony of the cross. The men who most strenuously argued against Him appear to have shrunk from the national infidelity and crime needed to work His death; while the men who compassed it were the men who had seemed to stand carelessly aloof from Him in the period of His mightiest activity and in-

whatever in the trial and crucifixion. The Synoptists indeed often associate the scribes with the chief priests in the processes that resulted in the death on the cross, but it is evident they did not regard this as equal to the participation of the Pharisees as a party or a body. "Chief priests and scribes" (Luke xxii 2, 66, xxiii 10, Mark xiv. 1) was but a phrase denotive of the Sanhedrin, which, though it contained Pharisees, was essentially priestly in its constitution.

[1] Matt. xxi 15, 23, 46.
[2] Ibid xxvi. 3, 4; Luke xxii. 2; John xi. 50.

fluence. Yet there was no decrease of antagonism on the one hand, or increase of it on the other. The Pharisees did not cease to be opposed to Christ, or the priests then begin their opposition. They had always hated and always been ready to express their hatred, but ever in deadly forms, and only when they promised to be effectual, never in the way of remonstrance or argument. The Pharisees were wishful to controvert that they might convert. We can well believe that the men who would have compassed heaven and earth to make one proselyte, would feel an almost boundless desire to bring to their side the young Rabbi of Nazareth. But the priests had no such desire, had no need or room for Him, had only the conviction that His life was a standing menace to their authority, and His death a politic expedient.

In seeking the reason of these differences we must clearly conceive the historical character and relations of the parties concerned. The Pharisees in their relation to Jesus have already been discussed and described.[1] They were the party of national principle and patriotism, who believed in the absolute kinghood of Jahveh, the continuous and progressive character of His revelation, the supremacy of His law, the obligation of His people to obey Him in all things—the minutest as well as the mightiest. The chief priests, on the other hand, belonged to the Sadducees,[2] the party of expediency and official policy. This association of the chief priests, the highest representatives of Jewish religion, with the Sadducees, the poorest representatives of Jewish faith, may seem curious and almost unreal. But it is as eminently natural as it is undoubtedly historical. In ideal Judaism the priest is as the foremost, also the noblest man. He is the representative of God before men, of man before God, approved

[1] *Supra*, 165, ff.
[2] Acts v. 17; iv. 1. Josephus, *Antt.*, xv. 9. 1.

and trusted of both. With man he is able to sympathize,
with God he is qualified to plead, a mediator the weak
can love and the strong can respect.[1] Into his ear man
can confess his sin, into his hands commit his soul,
certain that he will be gracious to the one and obtain forgiveness for the other. God makes him the vehicle of
His mercy, the interpreter of His authority for men,
certain that he will not weaken the authority or deprave
the mercy. But the ideal priest finds a tragic contrast in
the actual. In Judaism he was as often a mischievous as
a beneficent power. The prophets before the captivity
found sacerdotal worship sensuous, unspiritual, and unethical, strove to repress it by representing Jahveh as
"full of the burnt offerings of rams and the fat of fed
beasts," as One not to be "pleased with thousands of
rams or ten thousand rivers of oil," as not desiring
sacrifice or delighting in burnt offering, but only in the
broken and contrite heart.[2] At and after the captivity
the priests seemed to become a nobler race, possessed of
the prophetic beliefs, the organs of the prophetic ideals,
living to realize in and through Israel the reign of the one
God.[3] Into their worship another spirit had been breathed,
its sensuous forms were ruled by an ethical purpose and
purified by holier and more transcendent ideas. In the
completed Mosaic legislation the theocratic faith was articulated, and every part of the Levitical ritual penetrated
and illumined by the mind which lives and speaks in
Deuteronomy. But the period of exaltation was short
lived, form and routine proved stronger than spirit, and
God and His people were made to exist for the priest
rather than the priest for them.[4] The sacerdotal Judaism

[1] Heb ii 17, 18; v 1-4; vii. 25-28.
[2] Isa. i 11, Micah vi. 7; Psa. li. 17, 18.
[3] Haggai ii. 1-9, Zech iii, iv.; vi. 9-15.
[4] Mal i 5-14, ii 7-10, 17.

and the prophetic Hebraism were distinctly incompatible —a universal monotheism could not be incorporated in a worship that was at once inflexibly sensuous and fanatically national. So there grew up within Judaism a tendency opposed to the priestly, more akin to the spiritual and prophetic. This was embodied in the Sopherim, the wise, the men learned in the law, the written and spoken word of God.[1] These scribes, interpreters of the Scriptures and conservers of tradition, represented the belief in the living God who continued to speak to His people and to act on their behalf. They and the priests were in their fundamental ideas radically opposed. The scribes emphasized the ideas of law and precept, and so believed that man's best service of God was by obedience; but the priests emphasized the idea of worship, and so held that man could best please God by sacrifice and offering. The scribes had a keen sense for the ethical, but the priests for the ritual, elements in Mosaism; the former held the whole of the Hebrew Scriptures sacred, but for the latter sanctity and authority mainly belonged to the books which embodied the Mosaic legislation. The scribes were the interpreters of an ever-living Will, but the priests the ministers and administrators of a constituted system, which invested them with all the rights and authority they possessed. It necessarily followed that these orders, representative of so different ideas, stood in very different relations to the people and their history and hopes. The priests were conservative, the scribes progressive. The priests were zealous for everything that concerned the worship, could allow the intrusion of no alien god or rite, and had proved themselves, as in the case of the Maccabees, capable of the most splendid heroism both in resistance and defence.

[1] Ewald, *Geschichte des Volkes Israel*, iv 162, ff. (2nd ed.) Kuenen, *Godsdienst van Israel*, ii. 237, ff.

The scribes were zealous for everything that concerned the law, *i.e.*, the living revelation of the living God, and were ambitious, not simply that the theocratic worship might be performed, but that the theocratic polity might be realized in society and the State. And so the highest idea of the priest was expressed in the temple, and his best hope for Israel was the maintenance of a clear and well-ordered worship ; but the highest idea of the scribe was a people free to obey the law and entirely obedient to it, and his great hope, the Messiah who was to come, who was to be no priest, but a prince, able victoriously, not to sacrifice, but to deliver Israel from the alien and leave him the willing subject of Jahveh alone.

It ought to be more possible now to understand the relations of the Pharisaic scribes and Sadducean priests to Jesus.[1] The scribes were essentially teachers, and the scene of their activity was the school and the synagogue,[2] but the priests were essentially officiants, performers of a worship mainly ritual, and their proper and peculiar sphere was the temple. These two places, indeed—the synagogue and the temple—represented the two great forces in Judaism, the one didactic and rational, the other sensuous and sacerdotal ; the one diffused and expansive, seeking to instruct and guide the people, the other concentrated and conservative, seeking to maintain its place in the nation and prevent the various disintegrating

---

[1] While in the Synoptic Gospels the scribes and Pharisees are so associated as to be now and then almost identified, yet it is necessary to keep them distinct. All scribes were not Pharisees, nor all Pharisees scribes The Pharisees were a politico-religious party, the scribes a learned corporation. The Sadducees had their scribes as well as the Pharisees , but while the former reposed on the hereditary and family principle, the latter built on Scripture and tradition, and so had much more affinity with the scribes. See Lightfoot's *Horæ Heb. et Talm.*, Works, vol ii. p. 433 (ed. 1684).

[2] Ezra vii. 10.

agencies from breaking up the system it crowned and completed. In the very nature of things the teachers would be the first to be jealous of Jesus. He was a Teacher; His great themes were the very themes the scribes were accustomed to handle. The purpose and end of the Law and the Prophets, their meaning and range, the kind of service God required, the interpretation and value of the different commandments, the nature of prayer, the character of God and His relation to man in general and the Jews in particular, the kingdom of God, what it was, when it was to come, and who were to be its citizens— these, and such-like, were the questions discussed in the Jewish schools and discoursed on by Christ. He was to the scribes one who had invaded their province and defied their authority, who denied the traditons of the fathers, ridiculed and reversed all the interpretations of the schools. And so they resisted Him at every step, opposed Him in every possible way, exhausted the resources of their scholastic subtlety to refute and discredit Him. All this the priests might greatly enjoy. They did not love the scribes, disbelieved their traditions, feared their fundamental ideas, disliked their power with the people. And so they might well be pleased when they heard that a new Teacher had arisen who was confounding their ancient foes. But the matter was entirely changed when He touched their order, threatened their city and system. Once they comprehended His position, saw the action of His ideas and aims, they at once became inimical and vigilant. They did not argue or reason—that was not in their way; they acted. And the reality and design of their action are seen in Christ's anticipations and predictions. To go to Jerusalem is to go into suffering; to fall into their hands is to fall into the jaws of death. In Galilee, where the priests did not reign, He was safe, but He could "not walk in Jewry, because the Jews sought to kill Him."[1] Where He was most active, where He had by His words and acts given deepest and most deadly offence, He was not threatened; but He could not touch Judæa without, as it were, feeling the cold shadow of the cross.

It is here where the Fourth Gospel becomes so significant and, in the highest sense, historical; by showing the attitude of Jerusalem to Jesus it explains His attitude to Jerusalem. The Synoptists, who are mainly concerned with Galilee, have no premonition of the cross till almost, like a bolt out of a blue sky, it breaks on us from the mouth of Jesus; but John, who is mainly concerned with Judæa, shows us Jesus forced on each visit to retire from it in danger of death.[2] The scribes alone would reason, but would not kill; the priests would not reason but would crucify. From the hands of His great antagonists Christ anticipates no evil, but at the hands of the "chief priests and rulers" He knows He is to die.

But the whole case is not yet before us. The "chief priests" of the New Testament can become fully intelligible only when their peculiar historical and political position is comprehended. What may be termed the Sadducean ideal was a hierocracy, while that of their rivals was a theocracy. The very conditions that made the theocracy impossible favoured the growth of the hierocracy. The first could not live in the presence of foreign domination, but the second was easily reconciled to it, and even developed by it. In the high priest the Jewish state culminated; he was its highest authority, its living representative. It knew no native king, but had to bear a foreign rule. During the Persian and Greek dominion the people

---

[1] John vii. 1.
[2] Chaps. iv. 3; v. 16, vii. 1, 19, 25, 30, 32, 44; viii. 59. Jesus significantly escapes from this attempt to stone Him by escaping out of the temple (Chaps. x 31, 39, xi 8, 50–53, 57).

had to appeal to their conquerors through the priest, and through the priest the conquerors had to speak to the people. He was thus, on the one hand, a sort of sacerdotal monarch, and, on the other, a civil ethnarch. This position was at once defined and strengthened by the achievements of the Maccabees. They were in the fullest sense king-priests, possessed both of regal and sacerdotal functions. But the events that ended their dynasty separated these functions. The Idumean Herod might be king, but he could not be priest. The Jew might bear a foreign ruler, but his priest must be of pure blood and belong to the priestly stock. So while Herod usurped the regal, he had to leave untouched the sacerdotal functions. But what he could not take, he did his best to deprave. He made the priest his own creature, instituted and deposed at will. An office that had hitherto been inalienable, he made to depend on his pleasure. And it was his pleasure to offend the tenderest susceptibilities of the Jews. It was not in the Idumean to be gracious to what his people loved; he had joy in being insolent to the office they most revered. He showed his savage insolence both by the kind of men he selected and his modes of displacement. He first appointed Ananel, a Babylonian Jew, of priestly descent, but unimportant family.[1] Him he deposed to make way for Aristobulus, the last of the Maccabees, who was instituted to please the Jews, but drowned to please Herod.[2] He was succeeded by Ananel again, he by Jesus the son of Phabes,[3] who had to make way for Simon, the son of Boethus, an Alexandrian Jew, raised to the high priesthood because Herod wished to marry his daughter, the second Mariamne.[4] From this family of Boethus sprang probably the Baithusin of the Talmud,[5] the de-

---

[1] Jos., *Antt*., xv 2. 4; 3. 1.   [2] Ibid. xv 2. 5–7; 3 1.
[3] Ibid. xv 9. 3   [4] Ibid xv 9 3, xvii 4 2; xviii. 5 1.
[5] Kuenen, *Godsdienst van Israel*, vol ii pp 456, 457

spised enemies of the scribes, and their counterpart in the evangelical history, the Herodians.[1] The custom of Herod was followed both by the Herodian family and the Romans —the ruler for the time being, king or procurator, instituted or deposed for reasons of personal pleasure or political expediency; and so frequent were the changes that in the course of little more than a century, from 37 B.C. to 70 A.D., no fewer than twenty-eight high priests can be reckoned[2] And so it happened that the office which was the holiest and the most significant in Israel, the peak by which the pyramid touched heaven, where man immediately in one point and at one moment met Jahveh,[3] became the tool or plaything of lustful or Gentile tyrants.

Now these changes in the terms and tenure of the office had many disastrous consequences, personal, religious, and historical. The office was depraved in the view of the people; they could not respect the creature of the alien even when invested with the name and dignity of God's high priest. He was an offence to their faith, an insult to their holiest hopes. He did not represent trust in Jahveh, but the power of the Gentile, the last and worst captivity of Zion. So patriotic zeal was not, as in the period of the return, sacerdotal; the national party was strongly opposed to the priesthood. The scribes laboured to make Israel independent of the temple, to substitute for it the synagogue, to develop the elements of individual observance and obedience in the law as distinguished from those collective, hieratic, and hierarchic. Then the men chosen to the office were not of the noblest sort. The motives that determined the choice were not religious, but either personal or political. The man appointed was not he who

---

[1] Matt. xxii. 16, Mark iii. 6; xii 13.
[2] Schurer, *Die ἀρχιερεῖς im Neuen Testamente, Studien u Krit*, 1872. pp. 593, ff. See also his *N. Testamentliche Zeitgeschichte*, pp. 418, ff.
[3] Wellhausen, *Geschichte Israels*, vol. i. p. 154.

THE CHIEF PRIESTS—THE TRIAL.

had, by blood or character, the best claim to the office, but he who had made himself most agreeable to the ruler or could best serve his purpose. The men that most please tyrants and conquerors are not the most pleasant to men; their promotion has no promise of good in it for land or people. The son of Boethus is made priest that he may be ennobled, and Herod enabled with dignity to wed his daughter. Joazar[1] and Eleazar[2] are appointed to the priesthood because brothers-in-law of Herod. Annas,[3] the most fortunate man of his time, sees five sons and a son-in-law raised to the sacred office because he has wealth, and Roman procurators know how to rule provinces so as to enrich themselves. And these were not the only evils. The frequent changes created two classes—one privileged, the men who had held office, another ambitious and time-serving, those who hoped to hold it. A man who had been chief priest did not lose the name with the dignity. He continued to bear it, and with it many of its privileges. He had a seat in the Sanhedrin, with the authority and influence that belong to one who has held the highest place. He could exercise both with a view to his own or family ends. He might hope, like Ananel and Joazar, to be appointed a second time, or he might wish to secure the elevation of a son or brother. "The kindred of the high priest"[4] were potent forces in Jewish politics, constituted the circle to which those ambitious of office belonged. In the period now before us, many as were the chief priests, they were selected from only a few families—three were of the family of Phabi, three of the family of Kamith, six of the family of Boethus, eight of the family

---

[1] Jos., *Antt*, xvii. 6. [2] Ibid xvii 13 1. [3] Ibid. xx. 9. 1. 2
[4] Acts iv. 6. The new Testament in its mode of speaking of "the chief priests" and describing their action is entirely in harmony with Josephus. Cf. *Vita*, 38; *B. J.* ii. 12. 6; 20 4; iv. 3 7, 4 3; 9. 11; 3. 6. 9.

of Annas.[1] These, then, may be said to have been the ruling families, each possessing influence in the council in proportion to the number of past chief priests it could count. As the acting priest was the creature of an arbitrary will, no one could tell how long he might reign. Each family would live watchful of change and anxious to profit by it, yet all united in the common purpose and endeavour not to offend Rome or furnish her with an occasion or excuse for taking away their office or nation.

Let us now see how men like these "chief priests" would act in an emergency such as Christ had created. The family in power was that of Annas. His son-in-law, Joseph Caiaphas, was high priest, the thirteenth in order from Ananel. A crafty man this Caiaphas must have been, for he held office much longer than any other man in this century of change, viz., from 18 to 36 A.D. He and his associates knew at once the rulers and the ruled; knew how easy it was to exasperate Rome and how merciless she was in her exasperation; and knew how turbulent the Jews were, and how susceptible in all things touching their religion. The procurator had proved himself fierce and irascible, was capable alike of utmost contempt for Jewish superstitions and coldest cruelty to Jewish citizens, as the introduction of the imperial eagles into the holy city and the massacre of the Galileans showed.[2] And the priests, as the men who best knew and most feared him, would be sure to dread and seek to repress every sign of discontent or incipient disturbance. They would judge as men whose seats were insecure and whose security depended on the prompt severity of their judgments. And this is one of the

---

[1] The violence and craft of these families is specially lamented in the Talmud. See text in Derenbourg, *Essai sur l'Histoire et la Géographie de la Palestine*, pp 232, 233. See also Geiger, *Urschrift und Uebersetzungen der Bibel*, p 110

[2] Jos., *Antt*, xviii 3 1, *B. J* ii. 9. 2. 3; Luke xiii. 1.

THE CHIEF PRIESTS—THE TRIAL.

features of their sect Josephus specially emphasizes: the Sadducees were much severer as Judges than the Pharisees. And this is no less apparent in the New Testament. It is a man of the Pharisees who speaks in the council in defence of Jesus, and on these grounds: "Doth our law judge any man before it hear him?"[1] It is a man of the same sect who pleads that it is better to leave the Apostles alone, and to the judgment of God.[2] It is to the Pharisees that Paul appeals as against the Sadducees, and not in vain.[3] If the Pharisees could not persuade they would not persecute: it is the priests and Sadducees alone that harass and distress the Church in Jerusalem. And the reason is obvious; the sincerity of the Pharisees made them mild, the policy of the priests made them severe. The former could not invoke Cæsar without denying their faith; the latter must please Cæsar or lose office and influence. The man faithful to principle is never cruel; the victim of expediency always is.

These men, then, find themselves suddenly confronted by Christ, forced to judge as to His claims, and decide how to act in relation to Him. The situation is complex and critical. He has entered the city amid exulting and expectant enthusiasm. He speaks and acts like one having authority, not now simply against the hated Pharisees, but also against the priests. He invades the temple, deals sharply with their vested interests, declares Himself the foe of the old and the founder of a new order. His ideas of worship contradict theirs, and threaten to abolish sacrifice, priesthood, and temple. And He does not belong to their class, is of no priestly stock, is without hierarchic notion or reverence, has lived without respect to their ritual and their sacerdotal laws. They have found it

---
[1] John vii. 51. And to the same sect the one dissentient in the Sanhedrin that condemned Jesus (Luke xxiii. 51).
[2] Acts v. 34-40.   [3] Ibid. xxiii 6, 7.

impossible to vanquish Him by ominous speech, or dark looks, or open and violent reproofs. The people believe on Him, wait on His every word, watch His every act. Miracles have made Him marvellous, and to excited hope He is the Messiah, the Redeemer who is to deliver them from their later and most hateful captivity. And the multitude is immense. Jerusalem alone might be managed, but Jerusalem is not alone. Israel is there, men out of all Judæa and Galilee, Jews from the uttermost parts of the earth. The strangers are stirred by the strange news, expectancy and wonder are abroad, and men feel their spirits thrilled by the presence of hopes that had seemed too glorious to be realized. And in the heart of the city the abomination of desolation stands; over it there floats the ensign of Rome. Always a bitter sight, it was made far more bitter by being in Jerusalem and at the feast, when Israel came to confess his faith and realize his unity and mission. But to the men who found by the coming of Jesus their Messianic hopes kindled into burning passion and desire, it must have seemed an affront hardly to be borne, an hourly provocation to revolt. And Pilate, suspicious, cruel, unscrupulous, was in his palace watching all, ready to let loose his legions and begin the work Rome but too well knew how to do when dealing with a subject people that would rebel. All this the priests divined and understood; but what was to be done? Rebellion simply meant destruction; it yet seemed inevitable if Jesus were spared. "If we let Him thus alone, all men will believe on Him; and the Romans shall come and take away both our place and nation."[1] They had no concern with His claims, only with their own safety. They knew Him as at once the enemy of their order, temple, and worship, and the cause of all those dangerous and explosive hopes. The case was one

[1] John xi. 48.

where Caiaphas' craft was sure to seem wisdom. He went right to what they thought the heart of the matter when he said to the council, "Ye know nothing at all, nor consider that it is expedient for us, that one man die for the people, and that the whole nation perish not."[1] There was no need to name the "one man." The men who ruled by pleasure of the Roman would sacrifice the greatest Person of their race that the Roman might be pleased and they allowed to live.

To decide was to act; promptitude was necessary to success: the people must be surprised into connivance. and Rome into judicial approval and action. The priests proceed with wonderful courage and tact. The first thing is to get Christ into their power. Captivity will break the spell that binds the people to Him, and may even change them into enemies. By the grace of Judas the first step is taken. In the still night Jesus is seized and carried bound to the palace of the high priest. There all was wakefulness; and, though yet in the night, a council was summoned. While it was being got together, Annas, the head of the reigning house, saw and examined Him. This is one of the finely significant details we owe to John, the more historical and vivid that it is so unexpected. Yet, once the situation is comprehended, nothing is more probable. Annas was in all likelihood the oldest past chief priest. Appointed in the year 6 after Christ, his family had ever since, with a break of only two years, held office. The old man was subtle; his was the serpent's brood, theirs, as the Talmud says, the serpent's hiss.[2] Where the family had managed so excellently, its founder was sure to come by his honour. In the inner circle he could not but remain the high priest, though to the city and people the son-in-law filled the office. So John, with most conscious verbal incon-

[1] John xi. 50.   [2] Derenbourg, *ut supra*, p. 292.

sistency, but most significant accuracy, names now Annas and now Caiaphas high priest.[1] And the private process before this patriarch—reckoned happiest of men because the man with most sons in the priesthood—was most characteristic. The subtle old man used his opportunity dexterously. He "asked Jesus of His disciples and of His doctrine." These were the very points on which a little knowledge, privately gained, was sure to be most helpful at the trial and after it. For what purpose had He organized a school, what sort of men formed it, how many were they, and what, without their head, would they be likely to attempt or do? In what principles had He instructed them? What did He think, how had He spoken, of the scribes, the priests, Rome? But Jesus declined to satisfy his astute curiosity. He had formed no secret society; what He had spoken to His disciples He had spoken "openly to the world." He had no secret doctrine; had taught in the most public places, in synagogues, in the temple. Let those who heard be asked; they knew what had been said. The answer was offensive because so mild, yet true, and the reply to it was a blow from one of the attendants. The master is known by his servants, the priest by his ministers.

But now the hastily summoned council is ready, and the captive is led bound into its presence. The judges sit in a semicircle, Caiaphas in the midst, before them the accused, at either end of the crescent the clerks or secretaries. A judicial process was necessary, and the priests were masters enough of legal forms to use them for illegal ends. Christ is there alone; no friend beside Him, no advocate to speak for Him, no opportunity granted to call witnesses in His defence. But what need of defence? No charge is as yet formulated; He is being tried for a

John xviii. 13, 19.

crime that has yet to be discovered. He is an accused without an accuser, or rather, with only accusers and no judge. In their hour of need why did they not call the traitor? He had known Christ, had heard His most confidential words and doctrines, and so might have helped them to frame a charge. But he had done his work, and it was now doing a most unexpected work in him. It was not ill to find witnesses, but it was not easy to make their testimonies agree, or agreeable to the purposes of the prosecuting judges.[1] But at last two witnesses came who said, "He said, 'I am able to destroy the temple of God, and to build it in three days.'" This seemed enough for the council; it could be made to prove Him a plotter against the existing order, an enemy to the worship and law of his people. The witnesses had, indeed, changed His saying. He said, " Destroy "—the destruction was to be their work, not His—" and I will build it up in three days." It was a parable, too; a speech which showed in symbol the destructive work they were daily doing, and the restorative work He was victoriously to achieve. But as they took it, it was, remarkably enough, the gravest charge they could formulate. Out of all the words He had spoken and works He had done they could find no graver. They could not charge Him with violation of the Sabbath law without approving the interpretations of their old enemies, the Pharisees. They could not charge Him with violent conduct in purifying the temple, for it was precisely conduct all the Pharisees and zealots would approve. They could not prove that the triumphal entry had had any political origin or purpose, for He had not used it or made to it any public reference. His denunciations of the Pharisees they could not condemn; nor in His discourses in the city could they find matter to their mind. The utmost they could do was to build on this poor per-

[1] Mark xiv. 55-59; Matt. xxvi. 59-61.

verted misinterpreted saying, "I am able to destroy the temple of God and build it in three days."

The priest must be careful of the temple; so it was with the air of one whose very heart was touched that Caiaphas demanded, "Answerest thou nothing? What is it which these witness against thee?"[1] But Jesus, with serene dignity, "held His peace." Before expediency, imitating justice that it might the better work its unjust will, He could not condescend to plead; speech had only dealt with the semblance as if it were reality. In His silence there was a majesty that awed the council, and though now was the moment for the high priest to gather and declare its mind, Caiaphas was too crafty to do so. He could not condemn and he would not acquit, and so, with the cunning of his house, he resolved to change his method. He would enlist on their side the honour, the conscious kinghood, of the Victim they had doomed to death. So in the name of the Holiest he appealed to Jesus to declare who and what He was—"I adjure thee by the living God that thou tell us whether thou be the Christ, the Son of God." Silence was not now possible to Jesus. He could not be unfaithful to Himself, or to the Name which had been invoked. "I am," He said. The consciousness of His Messiahship was never serener and stronger than now. In His hour of deepest humiliation He was most consciously the King; in the moment of utmost loneliness and desertion He knew Himself the Son of God, and feared not, even before the priestly council, to complete His confession. "Ye shall see the Son of man sitting on the right hand of power and coming in the clouds of heaven."

The high priest well knew what the words meant. Into the one phrase—"the Christ, the Son of God"—the hopes of a Psalm,[2] dear to Judaism for the victory and dominion it promised, were expressed; into the other the high

---

[1] Mark xiv. 60, 61; Matt xxvi 62 63.   [2] Psa. ii. 7-12.

THE CHIEF PRIESTS—THE TRIAL. 299

apocalyptic dreams of Daniel were condensed.[1] In His soul He had little regard to either. They belonged to the things in which the Pharisees gloried, on which the zealots lived. He had seen many enthusiasts live and die, had often seen the fanaticism created by the ancient Messianic hopes break into useless rebellion and perish in blood. The man of expediency regards enthusiasm with cold and cynical scorn, while the child of enthusiasm regards expediency with blind and passionate hate. But in the hate there is more intelligence than in the scorn. Caiaphas could not distinguish between a Jesus of Nazareth and a Judas of Gamala, did not dream that the confession he had heard was to be the symbol of a New Religion, wherein man was to become consciously the Son of God, and God to be loved as the Father of man. All he knew was that his subtlety had succeeded. In claiming to be the Son of God, Jesus could be charged with blasphemy under the law of Moses; in claiming to be the Messiah, He could be represented as denying the authority of Cæsar and setting up as the Jewish king. So, happy in his exultant horror, the priest rose, rent his clothes, and cried, "What further need have we of witnesses? Lo, ye have heard the blasphemy! What think ye?" And the response came, clear and unanimous, "He is worthy of death!"[2]

Over the scene that followed it is well to draw the veil. Leaving the men who had the heart so to spit and buffet One so meek and guileless, let us watch a scene proceeding in the court below. There a fire was burning, and its lurid light fell upon a circle of faces pressing round to share its warmth. Into the court love had drawn two disciples. Peter was one, and, chilled by his sleep in Gethsemane, he stood forward to warm himself. The flame fell on his face, and a serving-maid, recognizing the strongly marked features, said in the hearing of the coarse and truculent

[1] Dan. vii. 13, 14, 22.   [2] Mark xiv. 63, 64; Matt. xxvi. 64, 65.

band, doubtless discussing, in the brutal manner of their class, the terror in which "all had forsook Him and fled," "Thou also wast with Jesus of Nazareth." The sudden charge was too much for Peter's ebbing courage, and he denied that he knew the Man. Withdrawing into the shade to escape further notice, he only stumbled upon another recognition and into another denial. Wretched, out of heart and hope, yet held by his very misery to the spot, he was not equal to a third recognition, and denied with cursing. But just at that moment a calm eye met his, and the passion changed into penitence, the cursing into tears. That night the silent heaven looked down on two men, the one driven by a tearless remorse and the burning stain of innocent blood on his conscience to seek the awful consolation of death; the other led by the tenderness of denied yet Divine love to tearful penitence and a nobler life. Without Peter the penitent we might never have had Peter the apostle. The love that impelled him to follow Christ was mightier than the shame that surprised him into the denial. He rose by falling. The event that showed him his own weakness also revealed the secret of stability and strength.

In the morning, "as soon as it was day,"[1] the full Sanhedrin met. The proceedings of the council that had sat over-night had to be revised and ratified. Without this these could have no validity. Judaism was at least merciful, and provided that the criminal should be tried by day and condemned by day; but, that temper might not control judgment, he was not to be condemned on the day on which his trial began. But the scruples of the scribes did not trouble the Sadducees, especially when commanded by expediency. The process begun by night was ended in morning. The session was short, the witnesses were not called, the confession was not repeated, there was no dis-

[1] Mark xv 1, Luke xxii 66.

cussion as to the guilt or innocence of Jesus. The only question was, What shall be done with Him? The priests were too adroit to hesitate. The sooner He was in the hands of the Procurator the safer they would be. While they held Him, there was no saying what the people might do; once He was in the power of Rome disbelief would be universal—no one would believe in a Messiah who could not resist the Gentile. The Pharisees might dislike asking Rome to punish an offender against their own law, but the Sadducees were not so nice of conscience, knew that Rome, and not they, had the power of life and death. So the council resolved to deliver Jesus to the Governor.

In Pilate there appears the character that was needed to make the tragedy complete. In him Heathenism as it then was lived, and now, side by side with Judaism, confronted Christ, each asking the other what was to be done with Him, each helping the other by deepening His present shame to heighten His ultimate glory. Three religions here stood face to face, two of the past and one of the future. The religions of the past were exhausted, hollow, and unreal, but the religion of the future a thing of infinite promise and potency. Pride and strength seemed to belong to the old, humiliation and weakness to the new; but within the old the merciless forces of decay and disintegration were at work, while within the new germinative and organizing energies were generously active. The persons that act in this drama but veil great principles, and help us to see how the evil, even where most victorious over the good, may be only the more working its own defeat, and fulfilling the Divine purpose.

Pilate was, so far as he stands revealed in Christian and Jewish history, a true child of the Roman Empire in its period of insolence and victorious aggression. His was precisely the kind of character sure to be formed under the combined influences of its conquests and cosmopolitanism. Few races can bear conquest undepraved; the subject often suffers less than the subjecting people. The man who rules the men his kinsmen have vanquished is prone to regard them as a lower race, made of poorer and feebler stuff than his own. And where the ruler so regards the ruled, justice is impossible; his administration will be too thoroughly penetrated by his own spirit to be, where most regular or legal, altogether just. And this radical evil vitiated the Roman rule. What was wise and generous in it was perverted and poisoned by the men it employed; and they by the false attitude they occupied. The only remedy for the evil was the complete incorporation of the provinces with the empire; but this was less possible in its earlier than in its golden period, the days of Hadrian and the Antonines. Rome was tolerant of national institutions, but national instincts and institutions were not always tolerant of Rome. And where they were recalcitrant she was severe; and where the subject was an insubordinate race, too weak to rebel, too proud to be submissive, too tenacious of its own will and customs to love Rome, there her ruler would find his task the heaviest—exercise and apology for qualities imperial rather than regal or legal. Then while conquest depraved, cosmopolitanism enervated, weakened the faith that had created the moral and political ideals of Rome. As the Roman came to know many peoples he came to know as many religions; each believed within its own circle, unknown or disbelieved beyond it. To his rigorous practical intelligence the main matter in each was its political significance. All could not be true, none had a universal truth, and each served a local purpose and had a particular use. A religion had only to be national to be recognized at Rome; she tolerated all that she might the better rule all peoples. The inevitable consequence was the one so well stated by Gibbon—while all religions were to the people equally true, they were to the philosopher equally false, to the magistrate equally useful.

And Pilate was in these respects a true Roman magistrate. His attitude to the Jews is expressed in the history of his government, his careless sacrifice of life, his insolent affronts to their deepest and dearest convictions. His attitude to religion is expressed in the question, asked in cynical impatience, "What is truth?"[1] meaning, "What is your truth to me? Fools may reason about it, statesmen cannot rule by it; he but wastes his time who seeks it." To such a man the Jews were an insoluble problem, and their religious discussions and differences an irritating trouble. He had come from Cæsarea to Jerusalem because of the feast. The multitudes were dangerous and discontented, and he had to be there at once to overawe the people and administer justice. His memories of the city were unpleasant. He had been truculent, but they fanatical, and his truculence had been defied and mastered by their fanaticism. And he finds them again agitated and fierce over these religious differences of theirs. And, what is worse, they evidently mean to draw him into their disputes, and use his authority for their sectarian ends. The priests had got soldiers the night before to capture a Man who was no political offender, and now here in the early morning they are bringing Him to the Prætorium.[2] Their conduct is irritating, a succession of small yet exasperating offences to a hard, vain man like Pilate. They send their Victim into the Prætorium, but they themselves will not enter. They are but Jewish priests, yet would feel defiled by contact with the majesty of Rome. They wish him to work their will, but he has to go out to speak with them: they, for reasons he must as a governor respect, and as a man despise, refuse to plead in the hall of judgment. His feeling of impatient and fretful contempt is expressed

[1] John xviii. 38.   [2] Ibid. xviii. 28–32.

in the question, "What accusation bring ye against this man?" They attempt, by standing on their dignity, to carry their point at once: "We deliver Him to thee; that is proof enough of His guilt." He, determined not to be their tool or any friend to their factions, stands on his authority and legal rights. "If I do not try Him, I will not execute Him. Judge Him according to your law." They, forced to feel that as they have no power to inflict they have no right to award the last penalty, have to submit their whole case to Pilate. But the new is not the old indictment; it is skilfully modified and enlarged into what seems a capital offence, whether measured by the law of Judæa or Rome. The charges are three—He has corrupted the nation, has forbidden to give tribute to Cæsar, and has claimed to be King Messiah.[1] Pilate, having heard their charge, returns to examine Christ. He asks, seizing the cardinal point for him, "Art Thou the King of the Jews?"[2] But the question is not so easily answered; it may admit of either a yes or a no. So Jesus wishes to know whose it is—Pilate's or the Jews'? Pilate declares ignorance; he knows but what he has been told; he would never have imagined that the Person before him could claim to be a king. Then Jesus breaks into a wonderful exposition of His kinghood and kingdom—"My kingdom is not of this world. If My kingdom were of this world, then would My servants have fought that I should not be delivered to the Jews; but now is My kingdom not from hence." And Pilate, anxious to reach what was for him the root of the matter, asks, "Art Thou a king, then?" Jesus answered, "Thou sayest that I am a king. To this end was I born, and for this cause came I into the world, that I should bear witness unto the truth. Every one that is of the truth heareth My voice."

These words are so remarkable, and form so striking a

[1] Luke xxiii. 2.   [2] John xvii. 33-38.

contrast to the sayings and conduct of Christ, as given in the Synoptics, that their authenticity has been amply doubted. But comparison with the synoptic narratives confirms rather than invalidates their truth. It is evident from all the Gospels that Pilate condemned Jesus most reluctantly, or rather, refused to condemn Him, and allowed Him to be crucified only to please the Jews. He could not be made to believe in His guilt, believed instead that He was the victim of factious and unjust hate, struggled hard to save Him, and yielded simply to avoid a tumult. Now how had Pilate been so deeply impressed in favour of Jesus? Why so strongly convinced that the Jewish clamour was utterly unreasonable? Simple pity cannot explain it. He had seen too much to be easily touched, and was too much of a Roman to be ruled by sentiment. And where political claims and fiscal agitation were concerned he could be as pitiless as any of his class. But grant this interview, and all is plain. These words would make on Pilate the impression of innocence unsurpassed. They would seem to him like the speech of a child, a simple and unworldly idealist, too remote from the politics and concerns of life to be a trouble in the State. He knew the Jews, right well understood the kind of men that disguised policy in religion. But this was not one of them. His speech was without worldliness, a sweet and limpid idealism, no sour and impracticable fanaticism, and must be offensive to the Jews for reasons that concerned their superstition and in no way concerned Rome, which they did not love. And so the governor tried to save the Christ. He first pronounced Him innocent, but only to hear the chief priests the more fiercely charge Him with corrupting the people from Galilee to Jerusalem.[1] Then, anxious to be rid of the matter, he sent Him to Herod. But Herod, with the cruel and self-indulgent spirit of his race, only made

[1] Luke xxiii. 5-11.

sport out of the Sufferer, and sent Him back derisively arrayed to Pilate. With Jesus once more on his hands, the governor was forced to assume the responsibilities involved in judgment. He did not wish to sacrifice Jesus, but still less did he wish to risk a tumult. So he tried to avoid both by a mean expedient. Should he—addressing the excited multitude now gathered before his palace, and skilfully fomented into vindictiveness against Him who had deceived them into the thought that He was Messiah —should he, as they were accustomed to an act of grace at the feast, release unto them the king of the Jews? But "the chief priests moved the people" to cry, "Not this man, but Bar-Abbas."[1] By this appeal to the crowd the control of events passed from the hands of Pilate. Passion now reigned; the only question was, how long he would hold out, and how best it could compel him to yield. He ordered Jesus to be scourged, clad in the symbols of mock royalty, and then showed Him, bleeding and humiliated, a spectacle calculated to awaken pity and satisfy revenge. But the only response was the cry, "Crucify Him, crucify Him!"[2] If they would have it, then they must know the guilt was theirs. He would not condemn Him; He would remain "innocent of the blood of this just person." But the guilt they were ready to assume: "His blood be on us and on our children."[3] "Shall I," then said he, now willing to execute any sentence they might determine, "crucify your king?" And they, sealing their national crime by national infidelity, shouted, "Crucify Him! we have no king but Cæsar."[4]

And so the conflict of the three religions ended; the Christ who held the future was to be crucified by the passion of sacerdotal Judaism and the weakness of cosmopolitan Heathenism. The tragic story is a parable in action.

[1] Mark xv. 11. [2] John xix 4–6. [3] Matt. xxvii. 24, 25.
[4] John xix. 15.

The religion of Israel falsified by priests, perverted from a service of the living God into a sensuous worship, where the symbol superseded the reality, the temple overshadowed the God, and the hierarch supplanted His law, could find no love in its heart, no reverence in its will, for the holiest Person of the race: met Him not as the fruition of its hopes and the end of its being, but as the last calamity of its life, a being that must perish that it might live. The religion of the Gentile, penetrated and transformed by the thought of Greece and the political ideal of Rome, stood between Judaism and Christ, saw its want of the holy and hate of the good; saw, too, His innocence, the beauty that made His marred visage winsome, and His ideal of manhood sweetly reasonable; but it had not heart enough to love the Christ, had not even conscience enough to compel the Jew to forego his hate and love his King. And between these there is the religion of Christ, which is the religion of man and his future, made the victim of their vices, sacrificed, as it might seem, to their blended hate and impotence. But His death is its life. Christ is like a holy and beautiful being bruised and broken by the collision of two brutal forces that cannot understand the sanctity and loveliness of Him they have destroyed, but they bruised Him only that there might escape from Him a fragrance that has sweetened the air of the world, made it for all time and for all men balmier and more healthful, like a diffused celestial presence, the very breath of God passing over the earth and abiding on it. His kingdom was not of this world, and in its unworldliness has lived its permanence and power. While the empires of Augustus and Constantine, of Charlemagne and Barbarossa, of the Frank and the Teuton, have flourished and perished, the kingdom of Christ has widened with the ages, strengthened with the truth, and now lives in the heart of humanity, the one presence of infinite promise and hopefulness and love.

XVII.

THE CRUCIFIXION.

THE cross of Christ, as if it were the glittering eye of God, has in a most wondrous way held man spell-bound, and made him listen to its strange story " like a three years' child " who " cannot choose but hear." Were not the fact so familiar, men would call it miraculous. Had its action and history been capable of *a priori* statement, it would have seemed, even to the most credulous age, the maddest of mad and unsubstantial dreams. For it is not only that in the immense history of human experience it stands alone, a fact without a fellow, the most potent factor of human good, yet with what seems the least inherent fitness for it, but it even appears to contradict the most certain and common principles man has deduced from his experience. We do not wonder at the cross having been a stumbling-block to the Jew and foolishness to the Greek. We should have wondered much more had it been anything else. In the cross by itself there was nothing to dignify, and everything to deprave. Men would at first interpret it rather by its old associations than its new meaning. It had by its positive achievements to prove its peculiar significance and merit before it could make out an indefeasible claim on man's rational regard. But the extraordinary thing was how, with its ancient obloquy and intrinsic unsuitableness to its destined end, it could ever accomplish any positive good. There would indeed have been little to marvel at in the posthumous fame and power of Christ. His was a name and personality that could hardly but be made beautiful by death. One who had been so loved and lovely could not fail to be idealized when He lived only to the memory too fond to forget, and the imagination too deeply touched to be prosaic. The dead are always holier and more perfect to us than the living. To lose is only to love more deeply, to become forgetful of faults that pained, mindful only of virtues that ennobled and graces that adorned. Could we love and think of our living as we love and think of our dead, the loftiest dreams and most hopeful prophecies as to human happiness would be more than fulfilled. But Christ's death was in all that strikes the senses not one the memory could love to recall, or the imagination so dwell on as to idealize and glorify. It was the worst the men that hated Him could think of. Even they were satisfied with its horror and shame. It made Him, in the eye of their law and people, accursed.[1] We can hardly imagine what the cross then was—so different has it now become. It stood almost below hatred, was the instrument of death to the guiltiest and most servile. Rome in her nobler and simpler days had not known it, had only, when depraved by conquest and brutalized by magnificence, borrowed it from the baser and crueller East. But she had used it with proud discrimination, too much respecting herself in her meanest citizen to crucify him; crucifying, as a rule, only the conquered, the alien, and the enslaved. To be doomed to the cross was to be doomed not simply to death, but to dishonour, to be made a name hateful, infamous, whose chief good was oblivion. The death was horrible enough, so cruel as to be abhorrent to the merciful spirit that animated the Hebrew legislation. But the very horror that surrounded the death now commended it to "the chief priests and elders." He who had claimed to be above their law was

[1] Deut xxi 23, Gal iii 13.

to die a death it hated. The very act that ended His life was to outlaw Him, was to prove Him a disowned Child of Abraham, a Son Moses had repudiated. The name that had so gone down in infamy could never be honoured, bore a curse from which it could be saved only by oblivion. The voice that had first cried, "Crucify Him!" seemed to have formulated a new and final argument against all high Divine claims—disproof by odium, refutation of the claim to the Messiahship by the abhorred symbol of shame and crime.

But Providence, by an irony infinitely subtler and more terrible than the priests', was to prove their genius but idiocy. Their elaborate attempt at refutation by odium became only the most splendid opportunity possible for the exercise of Christ's transforming might. The cross did not eclipse His name, His name transfigured the cross, making it luminous, radiant, a light for the ages, the sign of the gentleness of God. What is so extraordinary is the suddenness and completeness of the change. It was accomplished, as it were, at once and for ever. Suddenly, by the very fact of Christ's dying on it, it ceased to be to the imagination the old loathed implement of death, and became the symbol of life. Time was not allowed to soften its horrors; it was not left to distance to weave its enchantments round it; in the very generation when, and the very city where, He died the cross was glorified. This is one of the strangest yet most certain historical facts. There is nothing more primitive in Christianity than the pre-eminence of the cross, and apparently there is nothing more permanent. Peter, in his earliest discourses, emphasized the fact of the crucifixion.[1] The one object Paul gloried in was the cross,[2] and the one thing he determined to know and make known in the cities he visited was

---

[1] Acts ii. 22-24; iii 13-15; iv 10.   [2] Gal. vi 14.

Christ and Him crucified.[1] The death and its symbol constituted the very heart of His theology, what gave to it being, vitality, and significance. In the very age when the cross was most hated, when its bad associations were intensest and most vivid, Christ crucified was preached as the power and the wisdom of God.[2] And as extraordinary as the preaching was its success: "the word of God grew mightily and prevailed." Suddenly, as it exchanged infamy for imperishable fame, it became the organ of Divine re-creative energies, stood up like a living being, breathing the breath of life into our dead humanity. And its might has not been short-lived; its energies seem inexhaustible. For centuries it has been the sign of the grace that reigns through righteousness, the pledge of God's peace with man and man's with God, the comfort of the penitent, the inspiration of the philanthropist, the symbol on fields of slaughter of Divine charity working through kindly human hearts and gentle human hands, the banner which, as a New Shechinah, has witnessed to the Divine Presence in the van of every battle good has waged with ill. If we think what the cross had been to the centuries before Christ, then what it has been to the centuries since Christ, we may find it in some degree a measure of the exaltation of Him who could so exalt it. His enemies meant it to make an utter end of Him and His cause, but He made it the emblem of the eternal reconciliation worked through Him of God and man. Their worst against Him became their very best for Him. The setting of crime and passion which they gave to His death only makes it look the Diviner, surrounds it with a glory more wonderful than any the radiance of heaven has ever woven out of the darkness of earth. The shadow of the cross is like the shadow of the sun, the light and life of the world.

[1] 1 Cor. ii. 2. [2] Ibid. i. 24.

Now, how was it that Christ was able to work this most extraordinary, as it were, posthumous miracle? For miracle in a real sense it undoubtedly was. The achievement of His death was a more violent contradiction to the probabilities or uniform sequences which men call laws of nature or of history than any achievement of His life. No death has had for man the same significance as His; no instrument of death has ever exercised so mysterious a power or subsumed and symbolized so many transcendental truths as the cross. And why? Why out of the innumerable millions of deaths that have happened in history has His alone had so extraordinary a meaning, and been a spiritual force so immense and permanent, capable of working the mightiest changes while itself incapable of change? The reasons are not apparent to the senses. A sensuous description of Christ's death may fill us with horror, or touch us with pity, but cannot subdue us to reverence or win us to love. There have been thousands of deaths more tragic and terrible, more ostensibly heroic, with more immediate and evident and calculable results. Nor can the dogmatic meaning attributed to His death explain its unique pre-eminence in place and power. The very point is, why it only, of all the deaths man has suffered, came to have this dogmatic meaning, to be so construed and interpreted? Dogma did not create its pre-eminence; its pre-eminence created dogma. Christian doctrine is but a witness to the infinite peculiarity which belongs to Christ's death. Centuries before Augustine and Anselm speculated the cross had proved itself to be the power and the wisdom of God; and their speculations were but attempts to find a theory that would explain the fact. Nor can the reason be found in the nation and descent of the Crucified. The Jews had, indeed, an ancient sacerdotal worship, a system of sacrifices extensive and minute; but the thing after idolatry they most abhorred

THE CRUCIFIXION. 313

was the association of the sacrificial idea with any human death. Into the heart of Judaism, pure and simple, the notions, so familar to the apostles, which represented Christ as the Lamb of God bearing the sin of the world, a propitiation for sin, dying for our sins, could never have entered. Then, too, as we have so distinctly seen, the affinities of Jesus were not with Jewish sacerdotalism. It crucified Him; He stood in absolute antagonism to it. The pre-eminence of the death is due to no secondary or accidental cause, but to the pre-eminence of the Person who died. It is only as the death is interpreted in its relation to Him and His history that its wonderful significance and charm for the world can be understood.

But is the significance attached to His death really due to Jesus? Was it not rather created by Paul and other and later Christian teachers?

We touch here one of the most interesting problems in the history of New Testament thought. How was it that the apostles came to give such prominence to the death of Christ, to assign to it a place so cardinal, and to attribute to it so constitutive a significance? The Tubingen school used to argue: The primitive Christian creed was simply this, Jesus of Nazareth is the Messiah. In making this confession the first Christians did not renounce Judaism. They remained good Jews, distinguished from their brethren—all of whom held Messianic beliefs, many of whom believed particular persons to be the Messiah—only by their special faith, Jesus is our Christ. But this speciously conceals a radical difference. The predicative term may be in each case the same, but what it expresses is an absolute antithesis. Jesus is *not* the Jewish Messiah —is in character, mission, fate the exact opposite. He is no prince, no victor in the sense known to Judaism, no militant incorporation of its most violent antipathies. He is meek and lowly in heart, gentle to the alien, tender to the sinner, friendly to the publican, a patient sufferer who, disbelieved by the Pharisees and priests, is crucified by the Gentiles, and pitied for His pains and weakness by the Gentile who crucifies Him. Now there were no notions so radically incompatible with the Messiah of Judaism, and the development and interpretation they at once received made them more incompatible still. What has to be determined, then, is how this set of new and alien notions came to be associated with the idea of the Christ in order that Christhood might be attributed to Jesus? Pfleiderer[1] has ingeniously attempted to explain this by tracing the psychological genesis of the Pauline theology. Paul comes to believe in the resurrection of Jesus; that changes his whole mental attitude and outlook. One who has risen from the dead and now lives and reigns must be the Messiah. It was a more wonderful thing to die and to rise than never to die at all. The death, as the condition of the resurrection, was glorified by it, became, with all its passion and pain, necessary to it, and therefore to the full and perfect Messiahship. The moment this position was reached Old Testament prophecy came to help out the Apostle's thought. He recalled the idea of the Suffering Servant of God, despised and forsaken of the people, bearing their sins, carrying their sorrows, for their sakes stricken, smitten, and afflicted, yet by His very patience and self-sacrifice redeeming Israel, and working out for him a nobler and holier being. The attributes and achievements of this servant Paul transferred to Jesus, and so gave a new significance to His passion and death, and planted Him in a relation to Old Testament prophecy that made Him at once its fulfilment and Messiah.

Now, all this is clever, ingenious, subtle; indeed, exceedingly so; but — is it historical? Grant that it explains the genesis of the Pauline theology, what then?

[1] *Paulinismus*, pp. 1, ff.

Greater things are left unexplained, and things that are necessary to explain it. There is the power of this ingeniously analyzed and derived doctrine over the hearts and minds of men, Gentiles as well as Jews. It did not strike them as a dogma strongly marked by the idiosyncrasies of an intensely Hebraistic nature, working with scholastic tools and combining old convictions with a new belief; but it came to them as a revelation of God. It was not the theology of Paul that converted men and created Churches, but the doctrine of the cross common to him and the other Christian preachers. The speech to Peter at Antioch,[1] the confession in the crucial passage in the First Epistle to Corinthians,[2] that by Apollos as well as by himself men had been persuaded to believe, proves that Paul on this point recognized their essential agreement. Then Pfleiderer's evolutional theory might show how well adapted Paul's theology was to conciliate the Jew; but it fails to show how, with all its adaptation to the Jew, it was so deeply offensive to him, and how, in spite of its twofold root of rabbinical scholasticism and prophetic idealism, it was so splendidly real and potent to the Greek. This ingenious theory but helps to throw us the more strongly back on the reality. The passion and death of Christ do not owe their significance to Paul, but to Christ. The Apostle sought to explain a belief he found in possession, but the belief was created by the Person in whom he believed. The ideas as to the death of Christ current in the primitive Church were Christ's ideas. He is here the creative Presence; His Person dignifies the death; His words interpret it.

It is necessary, then, to reach Christ's own idea of His death and what it was to be, and then see how He realized it. He early anticipated His death, knew that without it He could not be faithful to Himself and His mission. Its

---

[1] Gal. ii. 14, ff.   [2] Chap. iii. 5.

scene was to be Jerusalem, its agents "the chief priests."[1] Its place and meaning in His history were typified to the imagination of the Evangelists by the Transfiguration.[2] Just about the time when He began to speak of it openly, Moses and Elias, the founder and reformer of Israel, the representatives of the Law and the Prophets, appeared to Him. "The decease which He should accomplish at Jerusalem" they approved; their approval was ratified by Heaven and symbolized by the glory which changed "the fashion of His countenance" and made His raiment "white and glistering." The idea so expressed is evident: the death is to perfect His work and make it the fulfilment alike of Law and Prophecy in Israel; though it may seem to shame, yet it is to exalt and transfigure Him; though it may be worked by human hate, yet it pleases and glorifies God. And these ideas penetrate all Christ's references to it. He is the gift of God, sent into the world that the world through Him might be saved.[3] He is the good Shepherd who giveth His life for His sheep.[4] His death is to be so rich in Divine meaning and power as to draw all men unto Him. And these thoughts possess Him the more the nearer He comes to death. They receive fullest expression in the words that institute the Supper, in the Supper He institutes. Its symbols perpetuate the mind of One who believed that He died for man, shed His "blood for many for the remission of sins."[5]

But, now, we must see how Christ realized His own idea of what His death was to be. In order to this we must study Him in the article of death. And, happily, in it He stands, as it were, clear in the sunlight. It is not here as in the trial, where the shadow cast of man almost hides Him from our view, save when by the

[1] Matt xvi 21.
[2] Ibid xvii. 1-13; Mark ix 2-7; Luke ix 28-35.
[3] John iii 16, 17. [4] Ibid. xi. 11.
[5] See *Supra*, pp 243, ff.

graphic hand of John He is drawn forth from the shade and set living and articulate before our eyes. But now in death and on the cross He fills the eye and prospect of the soul, the shadow of man only helping the better to show Him clothed with a light which makes the very place of His feet glorious. In those last hours how dignified His silence, how Divine His speech, how complete His self-sufficiency! Round Him there is fretful noise, in Him there is majestic calm; about Him violence, within peace. In His last extremity, when man's faith in Him has perished, He knows Himself, and dies, while He seems to men the vanquished, the conscious Victor of the world.

In every moment of the Passion Jesus stands before us as the calm self-conscious Christ. He knows Himself, and no event can unsettle His knowledge or disturb His spirit. The hour of greatest prostration is the hour of supreme solitude; where He was most alone there He felt most awed by the magnitude of His mission and the issues it involved. But man's action, however fierce and fatal, failed to touch the quietness and the assurance which possessed His soul. The priests and the people, Herod and Pilate, were all depraved by the trial; no one of them was after it as good as he had been before. Successful crime, disguised in legal or patriotic and pious forms, is more injurious to the moral nature than crime ineffectual and confessed. Judas was happier in his death than Caiaphas or Pilate in his life. The priest would henceforth be more a man of subtlety and craft, the readier to use his sacred office for selfish and immoral ends. The governor would be a man less upright before his own conscience, fallen deeply in his own regard, less careful of justice, more respectful to astute strength, more fearful of the intrigue that could create a tumult, and might work him grief. But the trial had not broken Christ's spirit or lowered His judgment of Himself, had only made Him the more clearly and consciously the Messiah. The mockery, the scourging, the presentation to the people, did not make Him in His own eyes any the less the Christ. We feel the almost infinite impertinence in Pilate daring to pity and patronize and, in his obstinately vacillating way, seek to save Jesus; but He was too lofty to feel the impertinence, was too surely the King to feel as if anything could deny or destroy His kinghood.

And this serene consciousness of His Divine dignity and mission He carries with Him to the cross. He does not go to it as one condemned, or as one who feels evil mightier than good. He is not despondent and reproachful like conscious virtue driven vanquished before victorious vice. Luke enables us to see Him as He emerges from the trial on His way with the cross to the crucifixion.[1] The men around Him are brutal enough, but the women leave Him not unpitied. The once loved but now forsaken, round whose name so many hopes had gathered, of whose deeds so many praises had been spoken, they cannot now dislike or despise. The contrast of His present misery with His past fame only the more appeals to their imaginative sympathies, and, womanlike, it is the mother they pity even more than the Son. But an object of pity He cannot allow Himself to become. His lot is not one to be bewailed or lamented—theirs is who are working His death. There is nothing pitiful in His sufferings as He bears them, though much to pity in those by whom they have been inflicted. The standpoint is not subjective or egoistic, but objective and universal. He does not need compassion, but is able to give it Suffering can be to Him no ultimate evil, is rather the condition of perfect obedience and perfect power. But to the men that

[1] Luke xxxiii 26-31.

work it it must bring ill. The last calamity to the doer of a wrong is complete success in doing it, for then it becomes a challenge the Righteousness that rules the world cannot allow to go unaccepted. And retribution cannot always touch the guilty and spare the innocent. The guilty so contain the innocent, so act and speak for them, that they become, as it were, incorporated, participators in the crime and in its fruits. All this is most apparent to the mind of Christ. There has been a national sin, which must have national consequences, and the calamities which come of criminal folly show no mercy to those who have been neither criminal nor foolish. And the heart of Christ is touched not at the thought of Himself, His wrongs, and His sufferings, but at the thought of the innocent who are to suffer with and through the guilty. "Daughters of Jerusalem," He says, "weep not for Me, but weep for yourselves, and for your children." And then, in language which recalls His later and prophetic discourses, He tells what the end is to be. Two pictures stand before His soul, one grimly real, the other finely ideal. He sees a besieged city, gaunt famine and hungry pestilence in its homes, fierce and fanatical factions in its councils, impotence in its hands and on its ramparts; while despair has turned the mother's love to misery, and made the barren seem blessed, and the warrior's courage to the despondency that covets death to escape defeat. This is the picture of what is to be; the answer to the cry, "His blood be on us and our children."[1] Then beyond it He sees another vision—two trees, one of ancient growth, immense, many-branched, umbrageous, but utterly dry and decayed, its vitality spent, its glory almost gone; the other, green, young, sapful, a tree that has sprung from the roots and grown under the shadow of the older and vaster. Wisdom had said, " Spare the green; let the

[1] Matt. xxvii. 25.

withered perish that the vigorous may live." But craft and passion struck down the green that it might underprop the dry; yet all in vain. Trees live not by being propped or girded, but by their own vital and inherent energies. The fate of the green tree will only make the fall of the dry more utter and inevitable. Here is the ideal picture. Christ is the green tree, Judaism is the dry. He must be sacrificed that it may be saved. But Nature laughs at the cunning of man; in her realm there is only room for the living; and he who seeks by destroying the living to preserve the dead will find that Nature disdains his sacrifice, and, in her own beneficently inflexible way, preserves what ought to live, removes what must die.

Jesus, then, even while He bears the cross, knows Himself to be a source, not an object of pity; able to compassionate, not fit to be compassionated. The evil that was being worked in selfish fear was an evil to its workers, not to Him. In the bosom of their future there was lying the most calamitous retribution; in His the most enduring glory and power. The dry tree which was to be burned with fire unquenchable needed pity; the green tree, which no flames of their kindling could consume, needed it not. And this consciousness waxed rather than waned under the experience of the cross. It was a kindly Jewish custom, unknown to the harsher Romans, to mitigate the agonies of crucifixion by giving a stupefying drink to the condemned. But when, in conformity with the custom, drink was offered to Jesus, He refused it.[1] His death was of too universal significance to be suffered in stupor. He must know both dying and death; conquer not by drowned senses, but by victorious spirit. And the spirit stands before us incorporated, as it were, in its own words. Jesus uttered seven sayings on the cross—three in the earlier stages, while the tide of life was still strong; four in the later,

[1] Matt xxvii 34, Mark xv. 23.

THE CRUCIFIXION. 321

while life was painfully ebbing away. The first concern His relations to the men and the world He is leaving, the second concern His relations to God and the world He was entering. Together they show us how Christ in this supreme moment was related to God and man.

The three sayings of the earlier period form a beautiful unity, showing Christ, first, in His universal, next, in His particular relations to the guilty, and then in His personal relation to the true and saintly. The first saying is like the tender echo or Amen to the reply to the weeping women, is the perfect expression of compassion for the guilty and pity for the innocent who were to suffer after and for them. In His supreme hour self, in a sense, ceased to be, and Christ was sublimed into universal love. He had no tear for His own sorrows, no lament for Himself as forsaken, crucified, dying. His grief was for those wicked enough to crucify the Sinless, to sin against the light. Before Him lay the city, white, beautiful, vocal with religious songs, busy with festive rites and preparations for solemn sacrifice, but its heart defiled with blood, a bond of invisible darkness lying across its radiant sunlight. Round Him were the priests and scribes and people, untouched by pity, spiteful while their noble enemy was in the very article of death, crying at Him in mockery, "He saved others, Himself He cannot save." "If He be the King of Israel, let Him now come down from the cross, and we will believe Him."[1] And their blindness, their guilt, their insensibility even to sensuous pity, filled His soul with a compassion that could only struggle to His lips in the cry, "Father, forgive them, for they know not what they do."[2] The flight from man to God, the sense of the Divine paternal presence amid the desertion of man, is most beautiful. The prayer, "forgive them," is the finest blossom of His own teaching, what makes forgiveness of enemies a

[1] Matt xxvii. 42   [2] Luke xxiii 34.

reality to all time and a possibility for every man. It was the creation of a new thing in the world—love deeply wronged daring to love, unashamed, in the face of the enormity that wronged it; and the new was to be a creative thing, making the apothesis of revenge for ever impossible. But the miracle of tenderness is the reason—"they know not what they do." Passion is blind, hate sees only the way to gratification, not whither it tends or what it means. Christ does not extenuate the ignorance, but He allows the ignorance to lighten the sin. It does not cease to be a sin because done in ignorance—the very ignorance is sin— but Christ wishes, as it were, that everything personal to Himself should perish from the Divine view of their act. The prayer may be said to embody the feeling of God as He looks down upon man, sinning in fancied strength, heedless that Omnipotence lives, Omniscience watches, and Righteousness rules, just as in the crowd about the cross we see man, untouched by the wondrous Divine pity, going on his mocking way, vengeful to the bitter end.

The saying that expresses His particular relation to the guilty is also peculiar to Luke.[1] The priests, no doubt, thought it a happy stroke of policy to place Jesus between the two thieves. Association in death was the nearest thing they could get to association in guilt. It made it impossible to deny that He had died the death of the guilty with the guilty. The men who had loved Him could not recall His life without also recalling His death; but the one was so steeped in horror that they would be willing, in order to escape it, to forget the other. The death on the cross and between the thieves was sure to break the beautiful image of His life, and make it a thing too hideous to be loved, too horrible for memory. But Mephistopheles is most foolish when most cunning; his subtlest are his

[1] Luke xxiii 32, 33, 39-43.

THE CRUCIFIXION. 323

least successful deeds. The transfiguring force in Christ compelled their wicked design to speak His praise. Their fine combination became an acted parable, a living symbol of Christ's action in time. The inmost nature of the men beside Him blossomed at His touch. The one thief was possessed by the spirit of the multitude, the other was penetrated by the spirit of Christ. The first mocked with the mockers, felt no sanctity in death, no awe in its presence, no evil in sin, dared, though stained with many a crime, to associate himself with the Stainless, and demand with cool profanity, " Save Thyself and us." The second, like one who sits in the shadow of eternity and gropes that he may touch the hand of God, feels that men who are "in the same condemnation" ought to be sacred to each other, knows himself to be justly, while Jesus is unjustly, condemned, believes that One who is condemned for His very goodness, and is so good as to be gracious to the men who condemn Him, must be indeed the Christ, the very gentleness of God come to live and suffer in soft strength among men. And so he prays Jesus to remember him when He comes in His kingdom, recognizing the Messiah in the very article of death. The answer is extraordinary—" To-day thou shalt be with Me in paradise." Christ is serenely conscious of His dignity. The cross has not shamed Him into silence as to His claims. He knows Himself to be the Son of God, that He has paradise before Him, that He has the right and the might to save. Perhaps in no other saying does Jesus so strongly witness to Himself as the Christ. In beautiful silence He hears the railer, leaving him to be reproved by the echo of his own words; in beautiful speech He answers the prayer of the penitent, and promises more than is asked. Was the promise but an empty word? The heart of the ages has confessed, if Jesus was ever real it was now. He who after such a life could so speak in the face of death to the dying must hold the keys of paradise; and if He could open it then, what must He be able to do now?

But more than the guilty demanded His care. At the foot of the cross stood a group of women, in its heart the mother of the Crucified, by her side the disciple Jesus loved. The tearful face of the mother touched her Son, and called up perhaps visions of childhood, memories of the happy home at Nazareth, where care dwelt not, and love brooded, and the shadow of the cross was too distant to dash the sunlight that streamed over all. But the visions of the past died before the sight of the present. Before His mother's agony He forgot His own. The look of desolate and ravished love, of the despair that had quenched her once splendid hopes, of horror at the loneliness that was creeping into and poisoning her very life, pierced Him to the heart. He seemed to feel what it was to a mother so to lose such a Son; and so with richest tenderness He gave her one she could love for His sake, who himself would be comforted in loving the mother of the Master he loved. "Woman, behold thy son!" was His word to Mary; "Son, behold thy mother!" His charge to John. The world has loved Him the more for His filial love, and feels maternity the holier for His dutiful and beautiful Sonship.

But now we must consider the four sayings of the later period of the agony, when the tide of life was painfully ebbing. They fall into two pairs. Of the first pair, the one expresses His physical distress, the other His spiritual desolation. The cry of physical distress is, "I thirst;"[1] the cry of spiritual is, "My God, my God, why hast Thou forsaken Me?" The first is significant of the coming end, and stands fitly enough in the Fourth Gospel, where the very history is an allegory and each event the symbol

[1] John ix. 28

of a sacred truth. To the mind of John, Christ is the Paschal Lamb; at His cry the men about Him who have prepared Him for the sacrifice now make ready for the feast. Their acts are a mockery of the real, a perversion of the true. He thirsts for the consummation, and in derision they prepare Him for the end. But the cry of spiritual desolation is of immenser meaning, and must be understood if Christ in His death is to be known. Does it mean that at this tremendous moment the Father hid His face from the Son, turning away in wrath from Him as the bearer of human sin? Does it mean that Jesus was in His darkest hour absolutely forsaken of the Father, left, when His need was sorest, without the light and help of the Divine Presence? Looked at from the standpoint of system, these positions may be affirmed; looked at from the standpoint of spirit, there is perhaps no position more deeply offensive to the moral sense. It introduces the profoundest unreality into the relations of the Father and the Son, and empties the most tragic event of time of all its tragic significance. Here there can have been no seeming, and the cry must be interpreted in the light of principles valid and universal. Here, then, two points must be noted:

1. The relation of the Father to the mission of the Son. He sent the Son to be the Saviour of the world. The Son came to do the Father's will, made obedience to it His delight. He did ever the things that pleased God, and God was ever pleased in Him. But if the death was necessary to the work, if the very obedience culminated in the cross, how could it be that the Father would then desert the Son, or turn from Him as from an object of wrath? The hour of death was the moment of supreme obedience; how, then, could the Love obeyed forsake the Love obedient? If there was reality in the relations of Father and Son, if the work the one did the other approved,

then it was simply impossible that He who is faithful to His love and His promise could have forsaken the One who most trusted Him in life and trusted Him most of all in death.

2. The person of the Son in relation to the Father. Jesus Christ was a being in whom man could find no sin and God only holiness. His joy in God was perfect. In Him the union of the Divine and human was absolutely realized. He was in the Father, and the Father in Him. He had a will, but the will was not His own. His words and works were not His, but His Father's who had sent Him. The union of His being and will, heart and conscience, with God's was so complete as to become almost identity. He lived and He died to finish the work the Father had given Him to do.

Now the cry of desertion must be interpreted in the light of these two principles. It cannot stand in conflict with either. It is the solitary cry with despair in it that ever proceeded from the lips of Christ; but the despair was the child of human weakness, not of Divine conduct. He went into His sorrow deserted of man, yet upheld of God, certain that He was not alone, strong in the strength of the Unseen Hand.[1] He went out of His suffering into the silence and peace of the Eternal, certain that the Father waited to receive His forsaken and crucified Son.[2] And the cry that stands between these filial confessions describes no act of God, but a real and sad human experience, which only the more showed Jesus to be the Brother of man while the Son of God.

But we must now seek to understand the experience which prompted the cry. Here, then, it is necessary to note that Christ, while a supernatural person, accomplished His work under natural conditions. His power existed and was used, not for Himself, but for others, not for per-

---

[1] John xvi. 32. [2] Luke xxiii. 46.

THE CRUCIFIXION.

sonal, but for universal ends. His Divine might helped man, did not help His own weakness or relieve His own hunger. The paralyzed under His touch stood up strong and supple, but He Himself had to rest by a wayside well and ask water to quench His thirst. The sick unto death came back at His bidding, but though He had power over His own life, He never used it to escape the doom that compels every child of Adam to go down into the silence and darkness of the grave. He is the splendid and solitary example of One who was by nature and for others more than man, but by choice and for Himself man only. And being man in all things, born into our common lot, unaided in His work, in His conflict with evil and against sin, by any supernatural energies or diviner agencies than are common to man, He tasted in the exceeding weakness of man the exceeding terror and gloom and strength of death. And yet He could not feel in the jaws of death like one of its common victims; He was more to it, it was more to Him. His consciousness was vaster than ours, His relations with man as with God infinitely closer and more complex. He came to death as incarnate humanity, our race personified, the second Head, the type and germ of a new and spiritual mankind. And so the issues in His dying, as in His living, were immenser than in man's. The father is a man, but also a father, bears in him the happiness, well-being, comfort of a loved home, and death to him is painful not for what it is, but for what it brings to them who love and are about to lose. The general is a man, but also a general; and if he falls wounded in the battle, he fears death less for his own sake than his army's, the men who in losing him may lose everything. So Jesus dies as the Man and as the Christ; and the cry of desertion comes from Him as the Man, but the Man dying as the Christ.

In order to understand why it was so, two points must

be considered; first, the universal experience in death, and next, the particular circumstances of Christ. As to the first, He was experiencing at this moment what man in all his multitudinous generations had experienced, or was to experience, in the hour and article of death. What death is to man, to human nature as such, it then was to Christ. He tasted it to the uttermost—its darkness, its loss to the living, its dread to the dying, its mockery of hope, its cruelty to love, its fateful defeat of promise, the stern and merciless foot with which it walks over and tramples down the fondest dreams and affections of the heart. It is hardly in human nature to love God in death, for death seems the negation of God. In dying, time is lost, eternity is not yet won, the known is fading, the unknown has still to show its unfamiliar face, so as to let it be seen, all old experiences are perishing, no new experiences are formed. And so the supports of faith have fallen utterly from the spirit, and it feels for the moment absolutely alone. It is a moment when neither time nor eternity is to the spirit, and God has ceased to be. And this moment, inevitable to human nature, Christ realized as Man—as, in a sense, collective Humanity—and out of its absolute loneliness, out of its dense gloom, came the despairing cry, "My God, My God, why hast Thou forsaken Me?" The experience so expressed completed, as it were, His identification with man. Our nature's last and utmost misery was tasted, and the Captain of our salvation died perfected through suffering.

As to the particular circumstances of Christ's death, it is to be noted how they intensify the common human experience as realized in Him. These were creative of the sorrow that was realest suffering. The wooden cross of Calvary was not the cross of Christ, but what it symbolized, the contradiction of sinners, the bitterness and evil of sin. In physical suffering as such there is no intrinsic good, but much actual evil. It does not by itself tend to elevate and sanctify the mind, but rather to harden and deprave. In plague-stricken cities the worst passions are often developed. Men grow indifferent to life, indifferent to death, coarse, even brutish, in thought and feeling, speech and action. If a distinguished sufferer is also a distinguished saint, it is not because of the suffering, but because of a Holy Presence in the soul transmuting the base metal of earth into the pure gold of heaven. Now the grand thing about Christ is not His physical pain, but His spiritual sorrow. And this sorrow is due to sin. The guilty may feel its legal penalties, but the guiltless are touched and pierced by its moral results. The devil's sin is a greater sorrow to God than to the devil, and the crime of the crucifiers is a pain to Christ infinitely beyond what retribution can ever make it to them. He had loved, still loved, them, yet their only response is the cross, with all its mockery and hate. And His sorrow for their sin is mightiest as He goes down into death. For the moment His experience is double; coincident with His sense of being forsaken is His sense of the power of sin. Loss of God is a transcendent evil; loss of being were better. A saintly spirit would prefer annihilation to exclusion from the vision of the Divine face. But to feel as if the soul had lost hold of God just as the life was being quenched by victorious sin, may well indeed seem the last and worst agony. And this was Christ's—a moment long perhaps, yet intense as eternity, expressed in the cry that has so long thrilled with awe the pulses of the world, " My God, my God, why hast Thou forsaken Me? "

But the darkness soon passed. The Father heard and answered. Into the consciousness of the Saviour a Presence came that changed His consciousness of desertion and loss into one of victory and peace. And this consciousness lives in the sayings that are His last. One breathes the serenest resignation, the most holy and beautiful trust, like the smile that comes across the face of the dying in response to greetings not of this world—" Father, into Thy hands I commend My spirit." The other welcomes the end, celebrates the triumph, proclaims that the death accomplished is the work done—" It is finished." In the first, He confesses that God has not forsaken Him, that the eternal hands are round His spirit and the eternal face brooding over His uplifted soul; in the second, He declares that sin is not victorious, that He is, that its evil has but helped the completion of His work. And fitly, with the double testimony, " He bows His head and gives up the ghost." He dies on the cross, but not by it. Men marvel that His struggle is so soon over; pierce His side, and show to the reverence and love of all ages that—He died of a broken heart. And they love Him, and are constrained by His love to live not unto themselves, but unto " Him who died for them and rose again."

XVIII.

THE RESURRECTION.

THE Resurrection of Christ is in the Christian system a cardinal fact, one of the great hinges on which it turns. Certain miracles have only an accidental, while others possess an essential value. The first are but incidents in the gospel history; the second belong to its essence, constitute, as it were, its substance. The accidental miracles are those Christ did, but the essential are those constituted by His person or realized in it. The former enrich and adorn the evangelical narratives; while their loss would impoverish the setting of the evangelical facts, it need not abolish their reality. But the latter make the very matter believed—are the gospel. Then, too, the essential may involve the accidental, but the accidental do not necessarily involve the essential. So long as Jesus remains the risen Christ, the Child of Mary, but the Son of God, He is by His very nature so supernatural that His normal action can hardly be ordinary; the miraculous to us must be the natural to Him. But were the essential miracles denied and the accidental affirmed, it would be as if the trees were cut down to get at the fruit, or the main figures of a picture erased to let the background be seen—the creative source would perish, the end which required and determined the others' existence would cease.

The essential miracles may be said to be three—the Birth, the Person, and the Resurrection. These all stand indissolubly together; partition is impossible. A supernatural person cannot be the result of natural processes, or be the victim of a natural destiny. He is, by the very terms of his being, above what the forces of nature can produce, and above what they can destroy. Whatever, therefore, tends to prove the Person of Christ miraculous tends to make alike the supernatural Birth and the Resurrection more credible. On the other hand, whatever tends to vindicate the reality of the supernatural in these events tends to make the miraculous Person at once more conceivable and more real. We have already seen how the conception of the Person justifies the belief in miracles; we have now to see how a miracle may justify and confirm the idea of the Person.

Of the two supernatural events just specified, the Resurrection alone is capable of distinct historical proof or disproof. The other, which culminated in the birth, is not. There we must believe, we cannot know. Where and when and to whom the Child came can be known, but into what lies behind sight cannot go, faith alone can. But the Resurrection, however extraordinary, can be dealt with as an historical fact. All the forces creating its opportunity can be traced, the witnesses for it examined, its evidence sifted, compared, weighed. By what we may term a Divine instinct its pre-eminent importance was understood at the very first. It was the fact which the oldest Christian testimony placed ever in the forefront; it was everywhere confessed as the reality on which the Church was built, and which it could not afford to forget. The apostles were its witnesses, existed to preach it. Had it not happened they would have had no mission, would never have been what they were. The Resurrection created the Church, the risen Christ made Christianity; and even now the Christian faith stands or falls with Him. The Resurrection is a *resumé* of historical yet supernatural Christianity. If Christ be not risen our faith is vain. If it

THE RESURRECTION

be proved that no living Christ ever issued from the tomb of Joseph, then that tomb becomes the grave not of a man but of a religion, with all the hopes built on it and all the splendid enthusiasms it has inspired.

The story of the Resurrection is one of exquisite pathos and beauty. The crucifixion had created despair, had smitten the shepherd and scattered the sheep. The cry had gone forth, "Leave Him alone; every man to his own." In loving secresy and weeping silence the faithful few had removed the body from the cross and laid it in the new tomb of Joseph. The great feast came, and while Jerusalem held holyday the disciples had to bear as best they might their bitter shame and ruined hopes. But the women could not forget the marred visage, now rigid in death, but once so expressive of holy and beautiful life, and, with characteristic devotion, waited to seize the earliest moment to look on it once more, before the effacing fingers of decay had swept the lines of its lingering beauty, and in the little, yet to the living great and helpful, ministries of tender, regretful affection, at once express and relieve the sorrow that burdened their hearts. So in the dim dawn of the morning after the sabbath they stole to the tomb, but only to find in it no buried Lord. They never thought of a Resurrection; thought only, "the grave has been rifled;" and one fled in an anguished woman's way, blind to everything but her awful loss, crying, "They have taken away my Lord." But the angels within the tomb and the Lord without made the tear-blinded woman and the sense-bound men slowly awake to the strange glad fact, "He is risen, as He said." "God has not allowed His Holy One to see corruption." In that tomb, the gloomiest earth had known, because the grave of the Holiest known to earth, a torch had been lighted that made sable death luminous, and forced from him his dread secret, translating it into Resurrection and Life. And so there was set under the weak but wishful feet of hope, no instinct of the human heart, or inference of the human reason, but the strong rock of historical yet eternal fact— the Person of the risen Christ.

Before attempting to discuss the historical and critical questions involved, it may be as well to glance at the beautiful and exalted ideal truths which find in the Resurrection their fittest expression. For it is not an arbitrary and violent fact, standing in sharp contradiction to the spiritual, which are the true regnant, forces of the universe; nor is it an irrational unconnected event, whose only right to be believed is that it happened. It is the sublime symbol, perhaps rather prophetic realization, of truths which the colder intellect of the world has doubted and criticised, fearing they were too good to be true, but which its warmer heart has everywhere victoriously striven to believe. Man is not born to die, and death, though universal, has not quenched his belief in his own immortal being. There is no fact of human experience so remarkable, so significant of the power of the reason to command, to conquer, and to defy the senses. The intelligible world is created from within, not from without; what man believes he believes in obedience to the laws of mind, often in rigorous opposition to the alien and inhuman forces of matter. And this is nowhere so vividly seen as when he stands throughout all the centuries of his history daring, in the very face of death, to believe in his own continued being. An experience as old and as universal as the race has not been able to compel the reason to regard the grave as its end, or physical dissolution as meaning annihilation of spirit. Death man can better explain as the result of his own wrong than as the rightful and ultimate lord of life, allowed to reign only that it may by chastising the more completely reform him, by dissolving the body the more perfectly liberate the soul. And so he has ever tended to believe that where man's sin is not, death's reign must cease, where his wrong has no place, its dominion can have no force. And thus when One is born into our common lot, not as a simple link to bind the generations each to each, but to become a Sinless Personality, to be the only holy Person of the race, then it would be but according to the nature which God animates, according to the spiritual ends for which all material things exist, that He achieve the victory over death. He must achieve it if the moral is to remain the supreme power, if brute force is not to become mightier than spirit and reason. By achieving it He becomes the symbol of what God is aiming at—the prophecy of what God will do. If death come to Him by wicked hands, what they do God must undo, that righteousness may not perish or human hope die wearied with the greatness of its way. Over the reason that remains Divine even while incarnate, death cannot be victor; may be allowed to seem to triumph, but only that it may be the more utterly broken and defeated. The vitality of God can never fall before the breath of mortality. And so Jesus, while He dies upon the cross, dies only to issue from the grave, on the one side, a response to the prayers of mortals, conscious that they ought to be immortal, on the other, the victorious proof for all time that He who made our spirits will, when our spirits are what He made them to be, draw them out of cold and desolate death back into the light of His countenance, to their eternal home in His bosom.

The Resurrection of Christ raises many questions, philosophical, historical, literary, and critical. The philosophical question is general, refers to the possibility and credibility of miracles; but the others are particular, concern the reality and proof of this special fact, the authenticity, truth, consistency, credibility of the narratives, the veracity, qualifications, trustworthiness of the witnesses, the nature, validity, sufficiency, or insufficiency of the evidences. The philosophical question it is not necessary to discuss; it would carry us too far into simple and assumed first principles. Miracles are supernatural, and indeed impossible to a nature without God, but possible and indeed natural to a nature with Him. To Theism nature exists for God, God does not exist for nature. It is the arena on which He is working out His purpose, and the arena must be subordinated to the purpose, not the purpose to the arena. Nature and history must be interpreted through our idea of God, rather than our idea of God through scientific and empirical ideas of nature and history. Denial of the possibility of miracles is possible, then, only where there is denial of the being and personality of God, or, what is equivalent, where nature is made His God, and its laws the bars of the prison within which He is confined. But with this theistic problem we are not now concerned, and allude to it mainly to protest that, measured by our idea of God, the Resurrection of Christ is neither miraculous nor supernatural, but normal and natural, an event in finest harmony with His character and the attributes that determine His ends. Our immediate concern is with the particular questions, and we must endeavour so to conduct the discussion as to cover as nearly as possible the whole field.

The question may be discussed either from the subjective or the objective side. The men either did or did not believe that Christ rose from the dead. If they did not, the whole thing was a fabrication, the story an invention from beginning to end. There must have been falsehood of the most daring and deliberate kind, aided by the most credulous folly. The men who had the audacity to concoct the story would be audacious enough to steal and conceal the body, and so to tell their tale as to win the faith of the simple-minded people who are always only too willing to be

THE RESURRECTION.

deceived. This is the sort of theory against which Paley's argument of the twelve honest men is absolutely conclusive. Happily, it is not one that need now be argued against. If any hold it, it can only be the utterly illiterate. The man capable of believing it is a man incapable of being reasoned with, too passionful of nature to be either rational or just. A sane and honourable and informed spirit could never either conceive or believe such a theory. That a company of men could be confederate in evil for purposes of good; that they could be throughout life a society of organized hypocrites without ever smiling to each other, or letting the mask fall; that they could preach virtue or live virtuously with a damning lie on their consciences; that they could nurse their souls, most of all in the very face of death, in the hope of being with Christ for ever in blessedness, while aware that He was rotting in an unknown grave—are positions that involve so many psychological impossibilities that any grave discussion of the matter would simply be absurd. Criticism must postulate the honesty of the witnesses; without it the history is not one any reason can handle, or out of which any good can come.

The witnesses, then, did believe that Christ rose from the dead. In this belief they were absolutely honest, were as certain that Christ had risen as that they themselves lived and preached in His name. But honesty of belief is no proof of the reality of the thing believed. The possibilities of mistake are almost infinite, and the honest belief of fictions is as common as the honest belief of facts. The honesty saves the character of the believer, but not of the thing believed. Modern criticism unreservedly accepts the truth and reality of the apostolic belief. That its historical sense is too sure and too keen to question or doubt for a moment. Baur's position was this:[1] the Church is inex-

[1] *Kirchengeschichte der drei ersten Jahrhunderte*, pp. 39, 40. English Trans pp. 42, 43.

plicable without the belief in the Resurrection; it supplied Christianity with a firm basis for its development. But what history requires is not so much the reality of the Resurrection as the belief that it was real. How the belief became real, whether by an objective miracle or a subjective psychological process, is of minor importance; the grand thing is that the Resurrection became a fact to the apostolic consciousness, and had to it all the reality of an historical event.

But this position is unscientific and inconclusive. It can as little satisfy the claims of historical science as of Christian faith; both must equally strive after the truth of the matter and be contented only when face to face with it. Science can never be sure that it knows either Christ or Christianity till it has ascertained whether He rose or did not rise; and if He did not, by what psychological process so many honest men came to believe that He did, and so to believe it as to persuade the civilized world to be of their mind. Faith can never be satisfied with a theory that leaves it uncertain whether its most transcendent fact was an objective reality or the creation of a psychological process, which is but an euphonius paraphrase for the dream or delusion of a too credulous and visionary mind. It must ask, What is it that I believe, a reality or an imagination? The subjective thus necessarily falls over into an objective inquiry, each, indeed, when it becomes fundamental, involving the other. The question, then, in its objective, which will also be found to raise all the issues of the subjective, form, is this: Did the Resurrection of Christ happen or did it not? Is it or is it not an historical fact? To the question so stated there are three possible answers. Either—

1. Christ did not die on the cross, only swooned, and afterwards reviving in the grave, issued from it and appeared to His disciples in His proper physical form; or—

THE RESURRECTION.

2. He died and did not rise; or—
3. He died and rose.

These questions we will now discuss in succession.

1. Jesus did not die on the cross, only swooned; and reviving in the grave, issued from it, appeared to His disciples, and was by them regarded as having risen from death. Astonishing as it may seem, this theory has had its advocates, and may have its advocates still. It existed in two forms, a more and a less gross. The one made Jesus feign death for the express purpose of making His reappearance seem a resurrection, another made the swoon real, the result of exhaustion and agony, from which He was restored by the cool atmosphere of the tomb and the stimulating fragrance of the spices. But no conjecture could be more gratuitous, absurd, impossible. The mere physical difficulties are insuperable. That a person exhausted, wounded, half-dead, in need of delicate nursing, of quiet and rest, of choice and strengthening food, with bleeding feet and a pierced side and a body shaken and out of joint, should be able to steal out of the sepulchre, escape the vigilance and merciless malice of His enemies, represent Himself to His disheartened and scattered friends as the victor over death and the grave, is conceivable only as a series of cumulative absurdities that would be merrily ridiculous were they not so terribly profane. Such an appearance had appalled the men that witnessed it, frightened out of them the little faith and hope that remained. And as on to this supposition the half-dead Jesus did soon die, was dying all the while He was appearing to the men He had known, the only conviction He could have left must have been of a broken and vanquished life lingering into hideous death. It is impossible to believe that from any such miserable source the faith in the Resurrection could have been derived.

2. Christ died and did not rise. This theory seems to have the merit of simplicity and definiteness, and may be

said to be built on two positions; first, that history can recognize no miracle, and must regard the events it seeks to explain and describe as natural, happening according to known or discoverable laws; and, secondly, that the evidences in this case are entirely inadequate, the narratives inconsistent, the testimonies perplexed, confused, often contradictory. Now, for reasons already stated, the first position need not be discussed here. It is a question of first principles; it entirely depends on the philosophy of the historian whether miracles are or are not to him impossible. The best history is the history without dogmatic assumptions, that does not determine beforehand what must or must not be, but simply examines what has been or is. As to the second position, it will be discussed later on, and meanwhile we simply note that on one point there is perfect agreement, the reality and the sincerity of the belief in the Resurrection of Christ. No modern critic questions it, or doubts that without it the history of the Church had been impossible. But now, how is the origin of the belief to be explained? by what mental or psychological process was it created? The problem is very complex, and as delicate as complex. There is the question as to the first inception of the belief—how a notion so extraordinary as that Christ had risen or could rise first came to be entertained. Then, why was it that it did not remain singular, but became general—the faith not of one excited and credulous person, but of many sane and doubtful men? And how was it that it exercised over the men an influence at once so sober and rationalizing, and so inspiring and determinative? Why, too, was the belief so primitive and, as it were, aboriginal, flourishing at the centre, on the very spot and in the very city where Christ had died? These and many similar points are so hard to resolve, and start so many difficulties, that Baur was content to leave the matter in a, for him, curiously nebulous state, certain only that the faith was real, entirely uncertain how it became so.[1] But later inquirers could not rest where he did. An event that happens by an unexplained or inexplicable process is to history little better than a miracle; and so the criticism that denies miracles could not feel satisfied of having achieved anything scientific until it had discovered and described the psychological process by which a real belief in an unreal event was possible and became actual. Clearly this is the cardinal problem—granted the honesty of the witnesses and the reality of their belief, how, on the supposition that Christ died and did not rise, did they come by their belief? and how did it come to wield such a tremendous power over them, and through them over the Church and over mankind? This problem has been attempted to be solved by two dissimilar yet related theories, which we may name respectively the phantasmal and the visional. Let us see with what success.

I. THE PHANTASMAL.—The theory so named we owe to the brilliant and fertile imagination of M. Renan. It is one no other modern scholar and critic is capable of conceiving, and unfolding in grave and graceful sentences. It is so strongly marked by his peculiar idiosyncrasies that it is fully as interesting for the light it sheds on M. Renan, as for its significance as a serious attempt to explain the

[1] For this indecision Strauss, in one of his fiercer moments, rather truculently assailed Baur. It was, perhaps, in his old pupil's eyes the cardinal sin he committed while using the historical interest as a defence against fanaticism, like the legal fiction which sacrifices the Ministry to save the Crown. But, curiously enough, Baur owed the idea to Strauss, who had many years before, in the apologies for his first *Leben Jesu*, expressly and earnestly maintained that the great point was more the reality of the faith than the reality of the fact (*Streitschriften*, Part I. pp. 33-48; Part III. p. 41). But Strauss changed with the changing times. Baur never ceased to labour on his own lines constructively at primitive Christianity; but Strauss became ever more dogmatic in his negations, and less patient of historical methods, with the uncertainties and anxieties they necessarily involve.

origin of our belief. It starts from this position—the creative power of enthusiasm and love. They play with the impossible, and, rather than abandon hope, will do violence to all reality.[1] Heroes do not die, and God could not allow His Son to see death.[2] The immortality of the soul was a Greek idea, not clear to the Jews; their notion was the kingdom of God, which consisted in the renovation of the world and the annihilation of death. The disciples could not believe that He who had come to institute the kingdom could be the vanquished of the grave; and so they had no choice between despair and an heroic affirmation [3]—which is a very fine phrase for not so fine a thing. The heroic affirmation was chosen; the little Christian society worked the veritable miracle, raised Jesus from the dead in its heart by the intense love which it bore to Him. The creative spirit was Mary of Magdala; she made the faith of the future.[4] She was an imaginative creature — had once been possessed of seven devils.[5] When she came to the tomb, the stone was rolled away, the body gone; surprise and grief seized her, crossed, perhaps, by a gleam of hope. Without losing a moment she ran for Peter and John. They examine the tomb, and depart; she remains before it weeping, possessed by the thought, Where have they laid Him? Suddenly she hears a light noise behind her, and thinks, "'Tis a man, the gardener," and cries, "Where have ye taken my Lord?" For answer she hears the old familiar voice say, "Mary!" "O my Master!" she cries, and turns to touch Him; He forbids, and His shade gradually disappears. "But the miracle of love is accomplished. What Peter was unequal to, Mary has done."[6] "Peter saw only the empty tomb; Mary alone so loved as to surpass nature, raise and vivify the phantom of the gentle and beautiful Master."

[1] *Les Apôtres*, p. 2.
[2] Ibid. pp. 3, 4.
[3] Ibid. p. 5.
[4] Ibid. p. 7.
[5] Ibid. p. 11.
[6] Ibid. p. 11.

THE RESURRECTION. 343

In such marvellous crises, to see after another is nothing; who sees first has all the merit.[1] And so the glory of the Resurrection belongs to Mary; after Jesus, she did the most for the foundation of Christianity, and has, as became the queen and patroness of idealists, imposed on all the sainted the vision of her impassioned soul.[2] Ecstasy is contagious. What she has seen the others see. The society is conquered in detail. Each section, women and men alike, has its own separate vision, tells its separate tale, and swells the general excitement. As they are gathered together with imaginations made vivid by these weird tales, the wind breathed in their faces, and lo! it became His voice murmuring " peace." " In these decisive moments a current of air, a window which creaked, a chance murmur, fixed for ages the belief of the peoples." [3] And thus was crowned and completed the achievement of the Magdalene.

Such is the theory stated, in all sobriety of spirit, with all his wonted brilliance of style, by M. Renan. But we have here to do with it simply as a professedly scientific and veracious account of how the faith in the Resurrection came into being. Can we regard it as what it professes to be? Well, then, its first and cardinal defect is evident— it does not save the honesty of the men. It reduces them to a society of fools, whose folly was all the deeper that it was so knavish. They behave like a circle of hysterical women, no one having sanity enough to ask whether their alarms or their joys were real. The men believed because they wished to believe, and by an utter suppression of reason and rational inquiry. Then, the body of Jesus was gone—whither? and by what means? It must have been removed; more than one must have been concerned in its removal—why were they silent? If foes had removed it, how they could have crushed the nascent belief! if

[1] *Les Apôtres*, p. 12.   [2] Ibid. p. 13.   [3] Ibid. p. 22.

friends, they could be silent in its presence only by conscious and wicked conspiracy. The enemies were too thoroughly bent on suppression to allow so dangerous a belief to take root while they had irresistible evidence of its utter falsity; the circle of friends was too limited to permit any single member to remain ignorant of the new belief and untouched by the new enthusiasm. In either case, therefore, knowledge of what had become of the body could not fail to reach the disciples, and only their silence could allow the fiction to be believed as fact. But connivance in a deception so enormous was at such a moment morally impossible. Enthusiasm was necessary to the life of the belief; but conscious deceivers, while they may imitate an old ideal, cannot create a new enthusiasm or form a new religious faith. Men, too, who are smitten to the heart, pierced through and through with a great sorrow, are too earnest to be insincere, to speak a cruel falsehood to their own and other consciences. This, indeed, is one of the many cases where the critic proves himself strangely destitute of moral sense and spiritual insight; and so but little able to read the transcendent moments of the history he has so long and so deeply studied.

But further: M. Renan's first principle is false, quite opposed to the evidence. Enthusiasm and love are creative, but what of the love without the enthusiasm, with only the numbness and the dumbness of new and desolating loss? Enthusiasm is creative when living, impersonated, victorious; but how could it live in the face of the cross, the symbol of utter defeat, and of the tomb, the symbol of corruption and decay? Were the belief created it must have been early, while the sense of loss was deepest; but the sense of loss means simply the inability to create the belief. The further they got from the death, the less would they feel the need of the living Christ; the nearer they stood to the cross, the less able were they to imagine

THE RESURRECTION.

the Resurrection. And we gather as much from the narratives. They prove, if they prove anything, that the state of expectancy M. Renan's theory requires did not exist. Death had conquered, and before his iron hand and silent lips hope, now as always, ceased to live. The men who had lived through the agony of the last two days, who had seen the Roman spear do its work, and the grave receive its dead, must have been in no mood to be carried away by the tale of a possessed and frenzied woman, who had seen a ghost. Expectant minds may be prone to faith; minds doubtful from despair, despondent from loss, are the most deeply incredulous.

But again: the theory leaves unexplained the most characteristic thing in the belief—its remarkable and altogether unique form. The conception stands absolutely alone; there is nothing like it in the history of thought and belief. Many societies of men have been situated as the disciples were, and have created curious myths, but all the myths have had a generic character, embody ideas radically unlike those embodied in the Resurrection of Christ. The Jews believed that Enoch and Elijah had not died, but been translated, vanished from earth into heaven. Omar might rush, sabre in hand, from the tent where the body of Mohammed lay, declaring that he would strike off the head of the man who should say, " The prophet is dead." The Roman world might live in the fear that the terrible Nero was yet to return to vex and disturb it. Mediæval Germany might believe that Barbarossa was asleep in his mountain cave, and would yet awake and come forth to restore the glories of the empire and the house of Hohenstaufen. Our own legends might tell how Arthur had sailed away to his island home of Avilion, whence, when happier days dawned, he would come to elect his table round, and open his chaste and chivalrous court. But all these rest on similar ideas, speak of the mythical imagination, as they speak to it. Death is in each case denied; the men can return because they have escaped death, and are only absent or asleep. But here it is altogether different. Christ dies—His death is real, absolute; He is buried, going down into the very grave. And His return is not an expected thing. He has escaped from the very hands of death, come out of the very grave, and has done so before the eyes of the men that knew Him best. In the other cases the contradiction of our universal experience is apparent rather than real, but here it is direct and absolute. In these, death is eluded, in this, it is endured; there, hope is because life is; here, the belief rises, as it were, sheer out of the tomb. Now, how are these characteristics to be explained? M. Renan never sees them, never feels their meaning, yet till he does so he has not even grasped the problem he has set himself to solve. Where the problem has been so misconceived its handling may have an æsthetic or personal worth, but can have no rational significance.

2. THE VISIONAL.—This is a much more scientific and rational theory than M. Renan's. Its first and ablest exponent was Holsten. It found a genial interpreter in the late Heinrich Lang, was adopted by Strauss in the *Neues Leben*, and has been accepted by the author of *Supernatural Religion*. Its starting-point is this—Paul does not make any distinction as regards nature or kind between Christ's appearance to himself and His appearance to the first and earliest witnesses.[1] In each case the same term ($\overset{"}{\omega}\phi\theta\eta$) is used; in each the same reality, the same evidential and historical value is attributed to the appearance. And of what kind was the appearance to Paul? It was a vision, *i.e.*, a state or process of his own mind, investing with reality what was not real. While he maintains that he has seen the Lord,[2] yet in the history of his conversion he

[1] 1 Cor. xv. 5–8. [2] Ibid. ix. 1; xv. 1.

speaks only of an internal revelation.[1] His was a nature prone to ecstasy, and so visions were frequent and familiar to him.[2] In immediate connection with these visions he speaks of his "thorn in the flesh,"[3] just as if they stood in some relation to each other. Now, by an ingenious interpretation, this "thorn" is made out to be "epilepsy," or some form of nervous disease, which made him peculiarly liable to visions and hallucinations. To this physical tendency he owed his sight of Christ, which to him had all the effects of reality while purely ideal. And from his language the other appearances were no more real, all belong to the same category, are subjective, not objective phenomena, were creations and visions of the mind.

Now this is a much more scientific and rational theory than M. Renan's. It deals with the matter gravely, is exegetical, psychological, careful in its analysis, and minute in its criticism—but is it historical? Well, then, the first dubious point is its interpretation of Paul. He was no diseased visionary, but a man of sane strong nature. His admittedly authentic epistles are full of the most radiant sanity. In things intellectual his reason reigns, in things emotional his judgment. No man was ever less governed by impulse, more by firmly grasped principles. When he speculates, there is no cloud on his intellect; when he reasons, his dialectic is dexterous, his logic sharp and swift. The ethical are, perhaps, the most remarkable parts of his epistles, they are so wise, so practical, and practicable, yet they are so really magnanimous, so explicative of ideal relations between man and man. In his conduct to the men from whom he differs he is the very antipodes of a visionary. Nervous dislikes, hatreds without reason, behaviour governed by petulance or passion or states of physical disease, are unknown to him. His difference with Peter at Antioch, his view of the Corinthian parties and

[1] Gal i. 13-17. [2] 2 Cor xii 1-5. [3] Ibid v. 7.

mode of dealing with them, his most complex and perplexing, yet admirably maintained relations to the Churches, his power of work, his physical vigour and extraordinary recuperative energies — all imply qualities, bodily and mental, utterly incompatible with the notion that he was an imaginative epileptic. The Pauline epistles are wonderful examples of unconscious autobiography; but they are, perhaps, least significant of the man where he is most consciously autobiographical. There is a proud reserve in him which makes him dislike speech about himself, and he reveals himself least where he writes most under conscious restraint. The Paul of the visional theory is not the Paul of the epistles, but of a few texts forced into novel relations and ingeniously interpreted. The one is too sane to be a visionary, but the other is a vision indeed.

But the theory is open to other and graver objections. It fails to distinguish sufficiently between the mental attitude of Paul and that of the earlier witnesses. His was one of anticipation, theirs was not. He knew of the belief before he saw the Christ; it was in his mind, even though only to be contradicted and denied. But the first witnesses did not find the belief; it found and made them. Hence their belief cannot be explained through Paul's; his must be explained through theirs. We are, therefore, thrown back on the prior question, How did they come by the belief? And it cannot be answered without a discussion of the evangelical histories. And on this ground the visional theory lies open to the criticism directed against M. Renan's. Once it comes to handle the facts, the explanation built on its Pauline psychology ceases to be applicable. Visions come only where there is distance, expectancy, and creative enthusiasm; they come not to minds face to face with hard, sensuous facts, minds desolate, despondent, irresolute, divided. The very reasons that render the theory applicable to the mind, once the belief has come into possession, render it inapplicable before the belief has come to be. The laws or factors that operate in periods of ecstasy and exaltation do not exist in periods of desolation and dismay. Where there is an exultant belief in the Resurrection, visional appearances are not only possible but inevitable; but where there is no such belief, how are they to be explained? Where the creative conditions are absent, how can the creation arise?

We reach, then, the conclusion that, on the terms fixed and defined by modern criticism, there is, on the supposition that Christ did not rise from the dead, no sufficient explanation of the origin of our belief. It is impossible to account for it and yet save the honesty and rationality of the men. We must, then, seek the explanation along another line, and this brings us to our next position —

3. CHRIST DIED AND DID RISE. — Let us see, then, whether there be evidence to sustain this position; in other words, whether the belief necessarily leads back to this as its only and sufficient cause. Here, indeed, a plea may be entered in bar of argument or further proof. The witnesses do not always agree; their testimonies are often inconsistent and discrepant. But to what extent do they disagree? Of what nature is their discrepancies? Do they extend to cardinal or essential matters? or do they concern simply points of detail? On details they are discrepant; on the cardinal matter there is absolute and emphatic agreement. Independent testimonies are, where thoroughly independent, made more not less credible by differences in detail. They prove conspiracy or concoction impossible; each new witness is a distinct and independent voice, not a mere echo of his neighbour's. Standpoints differ, and where the same thing has been seen from many and dissimilar standpoints, their con-

current testimonies are strengthened by the varieties in their respective narratives. Instead, therefore, of seeking to minimize the discrepancies, let us acknowledge their existence to the full, and proceed at once to examine the evidences for the historical origin of the belief.

Let us start, then, from this point :—The Resurrection of Christ is the most prominent, the most distinctly emphasized, fact in the New Testament; one, too, as regards which there is, amid almost every possible variety of detail, on all hands the most absolute agreement. No one denies it; nor is there in the oldest literature any hint that at Jerusalem or among the Jews there was any attempt at denial, or inquiry, with a view to disproof, into the facts of the case. The Christian writers are unanimous in setting it forth as the one fact which gives Christians the right to be and to be believed. This agreement is the more remarkable that it exists amid the most pronounced differences. Parties existed, opposed schools and tendencies, each zealous for its own men and doctrines. But though they differed in their views as to the person of Christ, His work, His relation to the old economy, His authority and place in the kingdom of God, they all affirmed most absolutely His Resurrection from the dead. The Petrine and the Pauline tendencies, the Hebraistic and the Hellenistic parties, the men who held that Jesus had respected and observed the law, and the men who held that He had utterly abolished it, were at one in the belief that He had risen, that without His Resurrection faith in Him were vain. And what does the unanimity so remarkably emphasized signify? That every Christian writer and every community they represented believed that the Resurrection was their grand creative fact, the event to which they owed their existence, what entitled them to live and claim man's faith. This fact lies behind their doctrines, is their common source, was

THE RESURRECTION. 351

before their differences, and exists amid them as their one bond of union. Their faith is a witness to the action of the event, testifies that before it they were not, after it they were, and without it they had entirely ceased to be. And this testimony history corroborates in a wonderful way. Christianity, as the oldest documents prove, was not a secret but a public faith, singularly outspoken and aggressive. Its career began in the very city where its founder had been crucified; and there, where the hate to Him was deepest, where the memory of His fate must have been most vivid, the faith in His Resurrection lived a fearless and victorious life, challenging an exposure which never came, invincible before the combined interests and passions of priests and rulers. Grant the Acts of the Apostles a late and untrustworthy book, yet here is a fact no criticism can touch:—Ten years after the crucifixion a fierce persecution was raging at and around Jerusalem;[1] one that implied that the Christians had utterly broken with Judaism, and were working within and against it with extraordinary daring, activity, and success. Not only was no charge of deception or imposition attempted in that persecution, but its most distinguished leader became a Christian convert. And the ground of his conversion was the belief that Christ had risen from the dead.

Now, the testimony of Paul is of singular force and value. It is twofold, verbal and historical, consists of what he says and what he becomes and does. The verbal is mainly valuable for the light it sheds on the historical and personal. Let us put the case:—A new religion has risen in the heart of Judaism, denying its authority, renouncing its most honoured customs, depriving the Jew of his most exclusive privileges, and looking kindly on the Gentiles. Its warrant is the

[1] Gal. i. 13, 22, 23.

Resurrection and exaltation of the Christ the priests had crucified. Now, there is no hate like religious hate, and religious hate is deepest where the kinship is most near and the division most recent. But though the new religion is hated, the old cannot suppress it. The priests had the will but not the power, and the most eminent of the Pharisees is significantly hesitating in his attitude,[1] does not assail the Christians as his party had assailed Christ, but leaves them alone, as if half convinced, even against his will, that God was on their side. In this man's school there is a strong, resolute spirit, a young man fresh from Tarsus, full of glowing enthusiasm for the city and faith of his fathers. Apostasy is to him a hateful thing, and the Christians seem apostates, daring, even within the very holy city, to deny Moses and be unfaithful to God. He sees them through the prejudices of the school, and holds that they ought to be dealt with as if the law were no dead letter, but a living power. The law commanded that the man who denied Moses should be stoned, and Saul, with the courage of his convictions, was prepared to obey Moses. The first that fell was Stephen, but the success in this case only made Saul the more anxious to do more. He "made havoc of the Church," haling men and women to prison, and, Pharisee though he was, asking help of the chief priest. But now a curious thing happened—actual contact with the persecuted worked a change in the persecutor. Once he confronted them in the flesh, came to know their actual belief and behaviour, he was so moved as to be shaken out of his old faith and made ready to receive the new. Now, what was it that so worked on him? There can be no doubt that it was the Christian belief in the Resurrection. It was this belief that predisposed him to the heavenly vision. This belief became the centre

[1] Acts v. 34, ff.

THE RESURRECTION. 353

of his system; round it his ideas all crystallized. It revolutionized his notion of Jesus, of His mission, death, cross, His relation to the law; his notion, too, of God, of His purposes and relations to the Jews and to mankind. There never was a completer conversion, a more radical and penetrating change. And he was not a man to whom change was easy. His was not a flexible nature, must have resisted long, yielded reluctantly and with a tremendous shock. And his words show that he had not believed without anxious searching and sifting. He had evidently questioned Peter, as evidently inquired of the five hundred. He speaks like a man who knew the survivors, who had known those fallen asleep, watching them as a man will watch those to whom he owes his highest spiritual good. Here, then, is the point: can this man who stood so near the event, who was certainly the keenest-eyed and loftiest-souled of all the men who did stand near it, who hated it with passion, who came to it with the most rooted prejudices, yet was, by the sheer strength of evidence, compelled to believe in it, to the entire change of his spirit, his objects of faith, his purposes and aims in life, to the absolute renunciation of his dearest ambitions, his kin, his fame, his home—can this man, I say, with all the splendid reason and reality that were in him, and the work he achieved, be explained as the child of delusion, the dupe of illiterate enthusiasts, who were themselves the dupes of their own excited fancies and morbid nerves? Were he so, he were a greater miracle in the region of the spirit than the Resurrection in the region of nature.

But now, turning from Paul, let us look at the other apostles. They share his certainty, his, indeed, being the creature of theirs; but it is not their words, but themselves we wish to cite as witnesses, their testimony being strongest where it is unconscious and indirect.

We know what they are in the Gospels, fishermen, like their class, ignorant, superstitious, weak, impulsive. Their ideas are Jewish; not as refined in the schools, but as vulgarized and conceived in the village. The only kingdom they expect is the ancient commonwealth restored. Their notions of the future world are the shadowiest; what is not realized here and in the old political forms they cannot understand. They hardly know that there is a great world beyond Judæa and Galilee, or know it only to hate the foreigner who has conquered, or despise the Gentile because he is no Jew. But now these men experience a twofold change: (1) they believe what before they had shown no capacity even to conceive, that their crucified Master had risen from the dead; and (2) they become, because of this belief, the apostles of a new religion, the agents of the most splendid change that was ever worked in the faith and conduct of man. It was an altogether wonderful thing—the change, the exaltation of spirit was simply miraculous. We know what the fishermen on our own coasts are capable of; we know what these Galilean fishermen have achieved. In their original state the latter had a narrower range of ideas, more limited ambitions, grosser notions of religion, of God and man, than even the former; yet these Galileans were so transformed and inspired as to conceive and proceed to realize a scheme of conquest far sublimer than had ever dawned on the mind of Alexander or Cæsar. And what caused the change? If they themselves are to be believed, the Resurrection and the ideas it worked in them. If they had created the faith, they had remained unchanged; if it created them, the change is explicable, and finds an adequate cause. Without it they remain the greatest riddles in history; with it they and their achievements become alike natural. The Resurrection is a sufficient

THE RESURRECTION. 355

reason for the men; but without it the men are no sufficient reason for Christianity.

But there is another line of indirect evidence quite as significant as the last; the attitude of the Jews to the belief is quite as remarkable as the change worked by the belief in the apostles. The Jews hated Christianity even more than they had hated Christ, and scrupled at no means that promised its suppression. They were then, as now, an ubiquitous race, living in all lands, trading in all cities, a separate community, touching the Gentiles everywhere, mingling with them nowhere, yet remaining in their dispersion Jews still, bound to Jerusalem by subtlest affinities, familiar with her story, with all that concerned her present and her past. They had then, as now, a wonderful faculty for searching out profitable secrets, knew how to make their way into the heart of social mysteries, and how to use them for what they esteemed the best. Much of the dislike they then awakened was due to this special gift of theirs, and their skill in working it so as to accomplish their own ends, without too much delicacy as to the means. Now it was to the Jews the apostles first went, and from the Jews their troubles came. They raised riots, fomented the ignorant passions of the Gentiles, persecuted the Christian preachers from city to city, poisoned the atmosphere around them with insidious slanders, and even dragged them before magistrates who cared nothing for the subtle points of Jewish law. But one thing, so far as can be discovered from the oldest literature, they never did—they never denied the reality of the Resurrection, or even questioned it.[1] If they could

[1] This may seem a very strong statement in face of the narrative, Matthew xxviii. 11-15, and what we know from other sources as to Jewish statements. The *Toledoth Jeschu* distinctly repeats the story as to the theft of the body (Eisenmenger, *Neuentdeckt. Judenthum*, I. pp 190, ff). Justin Martyr represents the Jews as proclaiming throughout the world that the disciples stole Jesus by night from the

have proved that Christ had not risen from the dead His religion would have died before the proof. And if such proof was possible to any one, it was possible to them. The scene of the Resurrection had been their own capital; its rulers had been the authors of the death, and were certain to be most suspicious and watchful of the disciples in the days that followed their loss. The children of the Dispersion lived everywhere in communication with Jerusalem, and every feast would bring fanatics to the city, determined to put down this new and spreading apostasy, each eagerly demanding of the chief priests how it was to be done. But here is the extraordinary matter—this adroitest, most dispersed, yet most concentrated of peoples, urged by the strongest of human hates, willing to gratify it by means party passion can always justify, daintily leave untouched and unquestioned the creative and cardinal fact of the religion they abhor. How can this be explained? The fact was not concealed; the men who declared themselves its witnesses testified everywhere concerning it, offered themselves for examination, asked that their narrative be compared with the events it professed to describe. Yet the men who heard their testimony, and were most interested in discrediting it, never attempted to do so, but allowed it to go throughout the world unchallenged and

tomb (*Dialogue with Trypho*, c. cviii.). Celsus makes his Jew insinuate the same thing, and subtly suggests as alternative explanations the fanatical phantasy of the woman who first persuaded herself that she had seen Jesus, or the temperaments of the disciples predisposed to believe in it, or their wish which was father to their thought (Origen, *Contra Cels*, ii 55, 63, 68, 79). There were thus widely circulated stories and theories which negatived the Resurrection, the most prominent being the one which we find in Matthew But all this in no way touches the statement of the text Our oldest and our most certainly authentic literature—the great Pauline epistles—show no trace of such stories, nor do they seem ever to have so met him as to have demanded either serious or incidental notice. And this is the significant point, late rumours are but myths, expressive of the action of mind, not of the transactions of history.

THE RESURRECTION. 357

undenied. Why? In the attitude of Gamaliel there is a suspicion that the apostles may be right, that God may, after all, be on their side. Put his suspicion alongside the avoidance by the Jews everywhere of the main issue, an issue they had every opportunity and inducement to meet openly and directly, and does not the conclusion seem inevitable that the Resurrection was left unquestioned because it could not be disproved, and because discreet silence was at least better than a dangerous inquiry? So interpreted, the silence of the Jews is as significant as the speech of the Christians.

But, now, there is another point that must here be emphasized: the speech that was unchallenged by the Jews was most offensive to the Gentiles. For a resurrection from the dead was not a credible thing to the then world, did not harmonize with its prejudices and superstitions. Such a harmony has turned many a happy fancy into a trusted fact; but though the contrary has often been assumed, it did not exist here. To preach the Resurrection was not to make faith easier, but rather more difficult. Experience seemed to give it emphatic contradiction; no man had any associations that could explain or suggest it. The unheard-of event was contrary to experience, was twin-sister to the impossible. And so at first it was a burden weighing down the gospel rather than a wing favouring its flight. The attitude of the Sadducee was typical; the very mention of the Resurrection raised his anger or his scorn. The Pharisees, indeed, believed in it, but it was under conditions and with limitations that would make them only the mere utterly incredulous as to Christ's. His was solitary, unattended by a renovated earth and a restored Israel; an event altogether too spiritual in its nature and results to find a place among their gross ideas. When Paul named it to the Athenians, they greeted it with a mockery that brought his speech to a sudden and undesigned end.[1] Festus, when he heard of it, thought Paul mad.[2] The greatest intellectual difficulties of the primitive churches were connected with the belief, and what it involved. Indeed, so insuperable were these that Paul had to invoke the evidence and authority of the other apostles in its behalf. It is the one case in which he does so, and his doing so in this case alone shows the strength of the prejudices against which he had to contend. Now what does this signify? That only the absolute certainty as to the reality of the Resurrection can explain the persistence of the belief; that without the reality of the event the apostles could have been under no temptation either to imagine or stand by the belief. Take a parallel case— the crucifixion. It rests on no ampler evidence than the Resurrection; the one is no whit better authenticated than the other. Yet no man has ever questioned it. And why? Because it is so unlike what any one would consciously or unconsciously invent as the kind of death suffered by a person he loved as a Saviour, and believed in as the Son of God. Yet it is hardly too much to say, the idea of the Resurrection was as alien to the then reason of the world as the idea of the crucifixion was abhorrent; and so the tenacity with which the apostles held by their belief was due not to the favour with which it was received, but to the strength of their own convictions— the invincible consciousness that the Christ had risen, and had, as risen, spoken to them and been with them.

These still remain but a fragment of our evidences. The power of the belief is made manifest by the place it occupied, the system that crystallized around it. All Christianity confesses the belief, runs back into it, and what is most ancient is here most strong. On this point institutions, customs, doctrines, hopes, and fears are alike

[1] Acts xvii 31, 32.   [2] Ibid xxvi. 24

unanimous and emphatic. Remove the Resurrection from primitive Christian theology and its speech, and they would cease to be coherent or intelligible. There is nothing older in Christianity than the Lord's day, nothing more universal than the Supper and Baptism; yet without the Resurrection, its ideas and associations, these are utterly inexplicable — without any historical source or significance. On it, too, hope lived—all the conceptions and reflections of what was to be grew out of it and stood clustered round it. Approach the question from any side, and it only the more appears that without the risen Christ the Church is without a source or a cause. If historical evidence is sufficient anywhere, it is here; for the written testimony of the evangelists is our weakest testimony, almost perishes before the mightier witnessing of those splendid facts that marked the birth of the new religion, the building of the City of God. If men object to it as a stupendous miracle, too immense a departure from the ways of Nature to be believed by men who observe Nature and mark the operation of her uniform and inflexible laws, let us say to them, "Look above Nature; there is a higher and diviner order. Nature is not an end, is only a means: she expresses her Maker's mind and exists for her Maker's ends. What is necessary to His ends is according to His nature, though it may seem opposed to man's. Interpret the universe through the idea of God, place God and man in living relations to each other, let the conditions necessary to the realization of these relations be fairly conceived, and there will be the consciousness of an order sublimer than any Nature reveals; an order which not only has room for the Resurrection, but demands it, to the end that eternal grace may reign through righteousness unto the glory of the Eternal."

(1)

www.ingramcontent.com/pod-product-compliance
Lightning Source LLC
Chambersburg PA
CBHW071226230426
43668CB00011B/1329